THINKING ABOUT PUBLIC POLICY
A PROBLEM-SOLVING APPROACH

THINKING ABOUT PUBLIC POLICY
A PROBLEM-SOLVING APPROACH

MELVIN J. DUBNICK
University of Kansas

BARBARA A. BARDES
Loyola University of Chicago

JOHN WILEY & SONS
New York • Chichester • Brisbane • Toronto • Singapore

Figure 3.1 reprinted from *A Framework for Political Analysis* by David Easton with permission of the University of Chicago Press. Copyright 1965 by Prentice-Hall, Inc.

Figure 3.3 adapted from and reprinted from *The Limits to Growth: A Report for the Club of Rome's Project on the Predicament of Mankind*, by Donella H. Meadows, Dennis L. Meadows, Jørgen Randers, William W. Behrens III, with permission of Universe Books. Copyright 1972. A Potomac Associates Book published by Universe Books, New York. Graphics by Potomac Associates.

Figure 4.1 reprinted from *The Dynamics of Public Policy*, edited by Richard Rose with permission of the author. Copyright 1976 by Sage Sage Ltd.

Tables 5.6 and 5.7 reprinted from *Public Policies Toward Business*, Sixth Edition, by William G. Shepherd and Clair Wilcox, by permission of Richard D. Irwin, Inc. Copyright 1979 by Richard D. Irwin, Inc.

Figure 6.1 reprinted with permission of Macmillan Publishing Co., Inc. from *Foreign Policy Decision-Making: An Approach To The Study Of International Politics*, edited by Richard C. Synder, H.W. Bruck, and Burton Sapin. Copyright 1962 by The Free Press, a Division of Macmillan Publishing Co., Inc.

Table 9.2 reprinted from Progress Against Poverty: A Review of the 1964–1974 Decade, by Robert D. Plotnick and Felicity Skidmore, with permission of the authors and Academic Press, a subsidiary of Harcourt Brace Jovanovich, Publishers. Copyright 1975.

Copyright © 1983, by John Wiley & Sons, Inc.

All rights reserved. Published simultaneously in Canada.

Reproduction or translation of any part of
this work beyond that permitted by Sections
107 and 108 of the 1976 United States Copyright
Act without the permission of the copyright
owner is unlawful. Requests for permission
or further information should be addressed to
the Permissions Department, John Wiley & Sons.

Library of Congress Cataloging in Publication Data:

Dubnick, Melvin J.
    Thinking about public policy, a problem-solving approach.
    Includes index.
    1. Policy sciences.   2. Problem solving.   I. Bardes, Barbara A.   II. Title.
H97.D8 1983   361.6'1   82-21782
ISBN 0-471-86464-1

Printed in the United States of America

10 9 8 7 6 5 4 3 2 1

TO DALE AND CARA
RANDI, HEATHER, AND P.D.

PREFACE

This book was written with a seemingly simple purpose in mind: to enhance the reader's ability to think about public policies. As simple as that objective may seem, the challenges it poses are formidable. In an era of major technological advancements in communications and information processing, the average citizen is increasingly aware of the complex problems facing modern society. But awareness is not enough; he or she must be able to clearly understand and effectively deal with that complex world. This book is intended to make the task of understanding public policies easier and more interesting for students, and in that way to improve their capacities for developing effective means for contending with government activities.

With that purpose in mind, it is useful to see the challenge of thinking about public policies in terms of problem solving. Public policies—what governments do and say—are more than mere historical events recorded by the media and scrutinized by professional policy analysts. They are, in fact, potential solutions to public problems. Even more significant is that we must contend with public policies, in whatever form they take (e.g., taxes, student loans, health services), directly or indirectly on a day-to-day basis. In that sense, public policies are personal problems as well as public sector solutions. We can effectively deal with public policies as problems only if we understand them. Understanding calls for the application of analytic tools that help us articulate and gain insight into the problem and its various dimensions. Analysis, in other words, lets us solve the problem of understanding public policies.

The theme of problem solving is the single thread running throughout this book. It provides a useful handle for students to grasp as they open the mind's door to the study of public policies. In accomplishing that task, this book does not merely provide information on substantive policy areas. There are a number of fine books that survey what government has done or is doing in the areas of energy, the environment, education, the economy, defense, and so on. Nor does this book concentrate on the sophisticated methods and quantitative techniques used by policy scientists and other expert analysts who earn their livings providing policymakers with professional advice. Here too, there are many useful textbooks that offer such material.

What *Thinking About Public Policy* does is bridge the gulf between books that *inform* undergraduate students and those that *train* professional analysts. In emphasizing understanding and a systematic problem-solving approach, it complements both endeavors. On the one hand, by introducing the fundamentals of analytic thinking it provides students new to the field with the means for going beyond simple awareness of government activities. On the other hand, it lays the conceptual and intellectual foundation for those who are about to enter the world of scientific and professional policy studies.

The book is organized in three parts. Part one contains three chapters that introduce the problem-solving perspective. Chapter 1 stresses the pervasiveness and problematic nature of public policy while Chapter 2 provides an in-depth discussion of public policy thinking and the problem solving approach. The methodology of the problem-solving approach is detailed in Chapter 3 where special emphasis is given to analytic models and their usefulness in public policy thinking.

Part two contains six chapters that explore the use of the problem-solving approach in describing, explaining, and evaluating public policies. Chapter 4 examines the nature of policy description and surveys various types of descriptive models available to policy analysts. In Chapter 5 the reader is provided with examples of analytic descriptions from economic policy studies. Chapter 6 focuses on policy explanation while Chapter 7 offers examples from the study of foreign policy. The assessment of policy consequences is outlined in Chapter 8, and this is followed by a discussion of how evaluative methods are applied to social welfare policies (Chapter 9).

The single chapter in part three (Chapter 10) serves as both a conclusion to and an introduction to the field of public policy analysis. There are various types of policy thinking ranging from the truth-seeking of the scientist to the mundane day-to-day contending with government that faces all citizens. Each form of policy thinking demands different assumptions, training, and methods of the policy analyst. These are surveyed in the final chapter as the reader is provided with an overview of public policy studies and the options offered to all students of government.

There are a number of colleagues and friends whose ideas, support, and work helped convert a few fundamental ideas into a full-blown book. Those ideas were first developed between 1974 and 1976 when one of the authors had the great fortune to meet and work with Elinor Ostrom, Moshe Rubinstein, and William Coplin. John Stout was responsible for converting the ideas into a contractual commitment in 1977, and the final product owes

PREFACE

a great deal to Mark Mochary, Connie Rende, and Wayne Anderson at John Wiley. Besides the authors, only those who went through the drudgery of typing and assembling the manuscript as it developed over a four year period really know what was involved in writing this book. For that reason we owe a great deal to Margaret Kranzfelder of Loyola University of Chicago who typed the initial drafts and June Ward of Kansas University who transferred that draft and subsequent changes onto the word processor.

The final manuscript was reviewed by several readers. Their comments and suggestions, along with the valuable copy editing of Pamela Goett, were extremely useful in developing the final version of the manuscript that went to press. Their impact on the book is noticeable to the authors, and we hope they find the results pleasing. In the end, of course, we assume all the burden of criticism.

Melvin J. Dubnick
Barbara A. Bardes

CONTENTS

CHAPTER 1   PUBLIC POLICIES: PERVASIVE AND PROBLEMATIC   1

    The Pervasiveness of Public Policy   1
    The Problematic Nature of Public Policies   5
    Endnotes   9
    Key Terms   10

CHAPTER 2   ANALYZING PUBLIC POLICIES   11

    A General Definition   11
    Public Policy Analysis is Applied   12
    The Use of Problem-Solving Techniques   14
    The Questions of Public Policy Analysis   16
    Dealing with Expressions of Government Intentions   19
    Analyzing Government Actions   22
    Policy Thinking and Policy Analysis   24
    Endnotes   24
    Key Terms   26

CHAPTER 3   THE PROBLEM-SOLVING APPROACH: A PRIMER   27

    What We Know About Problem Solving   28
    On the Nature and Usefulness of Models   35
    Model-Building   43
    Sources of Models   48
    Choosing a Model   50
    Endnotes   53
    Key Terms   55

CHAPTER 4   POLICY DESCRIPTION   57

The Nature of Description   57
Typologies and Policy Description   59
What to Describe: The Attributes of Public Policy   63
Evaluating Descriptive Typologies   73
The U.S. Budget as a "Concrete" Policy Description   78
Types of Policy Descriptions   80
Endnotes   85
Key Terms   87

CHAPTER 5   DESCRIBING ECONOMIC POLICIES   89

Understanding the "Perspective"   89
Strategic Economic Policy Descriptions   98
Descriptions Based on "Purpose"   112
"Level of Activity" Descriptions   116
The "Tools" Approach   118
Describing Specific Activities   120
An Historical Alternative   137
Endnotes   138
Key Terms   144

CHAPTER 6   POLICY EXPLANATIONS   146

What is an Explanation   146
Explanatory Models I: The Policy Sources   154
Explanatory Models II: The Dynamics
   and Process Factors   166
Conclusion   173
Endnotes   174
Key Terms   176

CHAPTER 7   EXPLAINING FOREIGN POLICY   178

Foreign Policy as Public Policy   178
Perspectives on Foreign Policy   181
Models Explaining Foreign Policy   185
Endnotes   201
Key Terms   202

CONTENTS   xiii

CHAPTER 8   EVALUATING PUBLIC POLICY   203

               Studying Policy Consequences   203
               The Analytic Purpose   204
               What is Being Studied   206
               Models and Scales   213
               Conclusion   221
               Endnotes   222
               Key Terms   223

CHAPTER 9   EVALUATING SOCIAL WELFARE POLICIES   225

               A Definition and an Overview   225
               The Politics of Evaluating Welfare Policy   227
               Models for Evaluating Social Welfare Policies   230
               Conclusion   251
               Endnotes   252
               Key Terms   253

CHAPTER 10 POLICY THINKING AND POLICY ANALYSIS   254

               Where to Go From Here   254
               The Roots of Modern Public Policy Analysis   255
               Motives, Methods and Training   256
               Personal Policy Analysis   261
               The Problematic Foundations   262
               Endnotes   265
               Key Terms   267

FURTHER READING   268

INDEX   273

CHAPTER 1

Public Policies: Pervasive and Problematic

THE PERVASIVENESS OF PUBLIC POLICY

Every day of our lives we come into contact with government. It is constantly present from before the hour of our birth to many months after the moment of our death. Typically the contact is made through statements and actions called *public policies*. These policies affect the care we receive as infants in hospital maternity wards, the manner in which we are raised and educated, the occupations we undertake during our "productive years" (the length of which is itself determined through public policies), how we spend our years of retirement, who will bury us when we die, and what will happen to our worldly possessions once we've departed. In addition, public policies influence how much money we earn at work, what of that amount we take home, what we are able to purchase with that money, and even how we consume what we buy.

If all this seems an exaggeration, consider the pervasiveness of public policies in your own life. You're probably reading this book as part of an assignment for a course at an institution of higher education in the United States. That institution is either public (operated and financed by state or local authorities) or private. If it is public, it is likely that your attendance at school is being subsidized, for in most cases public institution tuition and fees do not cover the full cost of the education students receive. If your school is private, there is still a good chance that it is receiving government grants for research or capital expenditures (e.g., that new chemistry building on campus); at the least, it probably receives a special status on public tax rolls and is exempt from property and other taxes. Consider your personal situation. Are you attending classes on a state scholarship? On a government guaranteed loan? Or are you working your way through college using the "work study" program financed with federal funds?

And how will you get to class today? Will you take public transportation? Or will you come by a car registered in your state of legal residence which meets federal and state pollution and safety standards, using a driver's license issued by the state, traveling on public roads and highways built and maintained through local, state, and federal government cooperation? Or perhaps you live on campus and simply walk to class from a dormitory which is under the jurisdiction of local law enforcement and fire safety authorities.

Of course, it is not enough to merely show that public policies touch upon our daily lives. What governments do to us makes a difference! Besides directly and indirectly affecting us in a surprising number of ways, public policies constantly add to or subtract from the quality of our lives.

They can add to our lives by making us feel more secure or by providing us with amenities we might otherwise do without. The provision of educational facilities and opportunities from pre-elementary to post-doctoral training is one significant example. By providing for your education the government not only expands your knowledge and awareness of the world, but also enhances your socioeconomic position in the community and thereby increases your economic security in life.

Consider the impact of public education on our mean annual incomes (see Figure 1.1). Although there are major disparities between the influence of education on the incomes of males and females due to occupational segregation and different career patterns, the overall positive relationships between the two factors is clear: higher educational achievement is associated with higher average incomes in later life. For example, in the year ending March 1976, full-time employed men 25 and over with 12 years of schooling made an average of $14,251 while their counterparts with 7 years or less of schooling averaged $9,225.

Figure 1.2 illustrates the extent to which *public* authorities in the United States have been responsible for a great deal of that educational advantage. As that graph indicates, public institutions have played the major role of education provider over the years—a role that has meant a great deal more income for many individuals. Since 1929, more than 80 percent of the total population between the ages of 5 and 17 have been enrolled in educational facilities supplied by the public sector. Some observers have argued that in addition to helping improve individual income levels, public education has also been a means for socializing immigrant populations and improving upward mobility for the nation's poorest groups.[1]

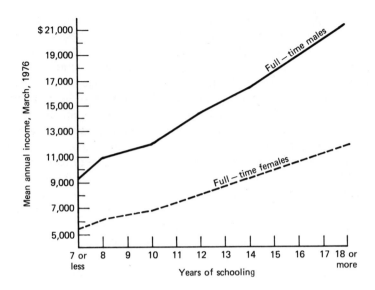

Figure 1.1. Education and income.

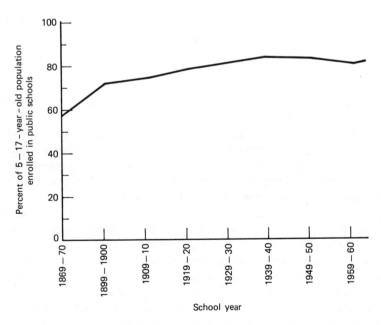

Figure 1.2. Public school enrollment. (Source: National Center for Education Statistics, Department of Health, Education and Welfare.)

But while public policies may add to our lives, they can also impose costs—both financial and nonfinancial. Education, for instance, is no longer a simple matter of choice. With the exception of Mississippi, every state has a mandatory attendance law requiring that children attend an approved educational institution from about age 5 to around age 16. Among other things, these laws have effectively precluded the option of home instruction for most Americans. If a child attends public schools choices are further restricted, for state and local policies generally control district boundaries, transfer practices, the curriculum followed and textbooks used, and they dictate health immunizations and sometimes even student dress and appearance. In addition, the availability and quality of private education facilities is also influenced by public policies. While no federal, state, or local laws prohibit the operation of public schools, government requirements and tax policies have historically determined their number and size. The very existence and survival of private institutions often depends on meeting certification standards and requirements imposed on physical facilities used to house school operations. In addition, tax exemptions and the availability of direct and indirect subsidies can make the difference between a viable or nonexistent private school option.[2]

As it is in education, so it is in all areas of public policy: while policies add to our lives, they also subtract from them; where there are benefits, there are also costs. Consider the issuance of a driver's license. By passing an examination you earn the privilege of doing something that would otherwise be illegal—driving a motor vehicle on public streets and highways. However, to obtain that privilege and the benefits that go with it, you must subject yourself to the rules and regulations of state authorities regarding behavior along those thoroughfares: driving within the specified speed limits, using a vehicle which is in "safe" condition, signaling your intentions when appropriate, and so forth.

In short, public policies are not just pervasive. They are also *meaningful* in the sense that they constantly affect the quality of our lives. For that reason alone we ought to become aware of what governments do and develop an understanding of current and proposed public policies. In this day and age we all must think about public policies.

This is a book about understanding public policies. More specifically, it is a book about how we should think about public policies. In the chapters that follow, you are asked to adopt a logic and method for thinking that may at times seem too simple and at other times seem very challenging. We believe you will find the results of your efforts well worth the work and concentration it demands. The ability to think about public policies will enhance your capacity to deal with them. In a world in which governments constantly touch our lives this is no minor talent.

THE PROBLEMATIC NATURE OF PUBLIC POLICIES

The foundation of our approach to thinking about public policies is set in the assumption that they are, by their very nature, problematic. In order to better understand public policies we should recognize them as *responses to and sources of problems*. What makes them unique as subjects for our consideration can be traced to the kinds of problems they are intended to resolve as well as the types of problems they tend to create.

On the one hand, public policies are problem-facing; that is, they are one of the many ways we deal with the dilemmas and issues confronting us both individually and collectively. For example, we often depend on public policies as potential solutions to perceived social ills, as when we provide *public* financial support for the poor, *public* health care for the sick, or *public* relief for those victimized by some natural or social disaster. At other times the problems are of a different and more positive nature, as when we develop policy "solutions" that send astronauts into space and deliver electrical power to rural areas. And even when our intentions have been neither so grand nor altruistic, policies have been made to deal with our problems: e.g., the "bailout" of the Chrysler Corporation, the "protection" of the domestic shoe and clothing manufacturing industries through import quotas or high tariffs, or other policies that meet the needs and demands of so-called special interests.

But public policies are problematic in a second sense as well; that is, they are problem-generating. After our brief discussion of the pervasiveness of public policies, it should come as no surprise that what governments choose to do (or not do) affects us all. Whether we are directly affected as the target of those actions or indirectly affected as taxpayers, there can be little doubt that public policies influence our lives. In fact, the impact of public policies is so pervasive that we frequently deal with them unknowingly. Everything from the food we eat to the cars we drive to the interest we pay on loans and the prices we pay for telephone calls are to some degree reflections of policy actions. We do more than just live with those actions—we also contend with them through the laws we obey, the prices we pay, and the steps we take to either adhere to or avoid the rules and costs involved. Public policies, in other words, generate many of the problems we deal with from day-to-day, month-to-month and year-to-year.

The problematic nature of public policies is so fundamental to our approach that we can define "public policy" in problem-based terms.[3] Problems take a variety of forms. They are usually defined as human needs, dissatisfactions, deprivations, or injuries for which some relief or redress is sought.[4] Of course, public policies are not solutions to just any kind of problems. They are responses to public problems. Therefore, to understand public policies we must first understand what makes a problem "public."

We do this by noting that any problem can take one of three basic forms: private, social, and public. Which form a problem takes will depend on the resources mobilized to solve it and who is involved in the problematic situation.[5] A problem is private when it can be solved with essentially private resources and involves either a small group of people or a larger group whose difficulties do not arouse public attention. Most family disputes are private problems under this definition; under normal circumstances they can be handled without using social or public resources and typically do not call for the involvement of more than a few people who are close to it.

Social problems arise when at least one of those basic conditions changes. For example, when a family dispute escalates it may demand the use of resources outside the family unit. Neighbors and friends might provide help, or the disputants could call upon the services of a professional family counselor. On the other hand, the dispute may be minor but involve a large number of families or one family that is so important that their problems become a matter of social concern because of their importance to the community.

Finally, a problem becomes public when it calls for the use of government resources or involves groups so large in number or politically significant that government policymakers cannot ignore them. Government involvement is not unusual when the family dispute becomes violent or focused on legal questions dealing with property rights and child custody. Nor can policymakers ignore a dispute where the participants have an impact on a large number of voters or important interest groups. It is in this sense that public policies are established as possible solutions to problems—*public problems.*

BOX 1.1

Although the distinction between private, social, and public problems may seem straightforward, it is in fact quite complex. Economist Lester C. Thurow provided an example of how an essentially private problem can take on the status of a social or public problem given certain economic conditions. At any point in time there are a great many changes taking place in the economy. "Many people are suffering real income losses and many people are making real income gains," notes Thurow. In an economy without inflation, those who are suffering losses have only themselves, their individual "bad luck," or some particular circumstances to blame; "but," states Thurow, "they cannot blame the whole system, since the system is not allocating income reductions to everyone."

However, in a period of inflation those *same* income losses can be attributed to general conditions in the economy *even if they were not the result of inflation.* In other words, what was a private problem under "normal" conditions can be turned into a social problem under "abnormal" conditions despite the fact that those changed circumstances had no real impact on the individual's situation. Taking the lessons of Thurow's example one step further, if people suffering income reductions perceive inflation as a problem that the government has either caused or can solve, then personal money losses move from being a social problem to the level of a public problem.

See Lester C. Thurow, *The Zero-Sum Society: Distribution and the Possibilities for Economic Change* (New York: Basic Books, 1980.)

One other characteristic of public problems must be stressed in order to help us understand the concept of public policies. Public problems are neither inherently or immediately controversial. An infinite variety of problems facing us as individuals and members of groups might be resolved by using the resources of government, and a great many "politically significant" people who are having difficulties can attract the attention of policymakers. Yet, relatively few of these problems achieve public status. To become a subject of government activity, these public problems must become part of a *public policy agenda.* That is, the question of what governments should say or do about a given public problem must be under active consideration. Where there is some debate over alternative solutions to an agenda item, then we say that this is a *policy issue.*[6] At that point, government actions—what governments say and what governments do about an issue—constitutes what we define as a *public policy.*

BOX 1.2

Public policies deal with problems ranging from what is necessary for survival (e.g., the provision of food, clothing, and shelter for impoverished families) to demands for some of the amenities of life that only an affluent society can afford (e.g., public swimming pools, public museums). What is especially fascinating (and somewhat frustrating) about public policies is that the "public-ness" of a problem does not depend on where it falls along that range. Some critical problems remain private or social, while some of the most unimportant ones get a "public" status.

For example, in the United States some matters of life and death have essentially been regarded as private or social problems rather than public ones. Before the passage of the 1906 Pure Food and Drugs Act, the adulteration of food and the marketing of potentially dangerous pharmaceuticals was a social concern rather than a public problem. Until the 1960s and early 1970s, occupational ailments such as the black lung disease which afflicts coal miners and worker safety were outside the range of public policy concerns. Until very recently the safety of children riding in privately owned vehicles was a private matter, but now several states have declared this to be a public problem and have mandated that child restraints be used for children under a certain age.

At the same time, some rather trivial matters have received government attention in spite of their minor or private nature. A prime example was an issue that developed out of the National Football League's policy of imposing a television blackout in areas immediately surrounding the site of professional football games. Done with the obvious intent of increasing attendance at local games, this private policy drew the ire of many fans throughout the country, especially politically significant ones living in the Washington, D.C. area. Thus, it was not surprising that what was in essence a private problem susceptible to private solutions (e.g., the fan could have spent his or her resources to either purchase tickets to the game or travel to a viewing location outside the blackout area) became a social problem (e.g., generating a great deal of comment in the media) and eventually a public problem (e.g., stimulating action by some politically important fans—the members of Congress). The result was a public policy—a federal statute—which mandates that if a local game is sold out by the Thursday before the Sunday kickoff, then the blackout must be lifted.

Faced with public problems, governments respond with statements and actions. For our purposes, those government statements and actions are at the heart of public policies. The statements express the intentions of government actors, while the actions reflect the steps taken to fulfill those intentions.[7] Putting all these ingredients together we arrive at a problem-based definition which sees public policies as *the expressed intentions of government actors relative to a public problem and the activities related to those intentions.*

Having established this problem-based view of public policy, we are now ready to turn our attention to the primary purpose of this book: improving our abilities to think about public policies. Our objectives are rather modest, for developing a better understanding of what governments say and do about public problems will take a great deal less time and energy than learing how to make better public policies. There are individuals who think about public policies on a full-time basis or who concentrate on developing new or better solutions to public problems. As a group, these individuals call themselves *public policy analysts*. We will discuss them and their work in the final chapter of this book. What we will be learning, however, is closely related to their work, for all thinking about public policy has a common foundation in analyzing what policies are, how they are derived, and what their consequences are or might be. In Chapter 2 we will explore that common foundation by discussing just what public policy analysis involves.

ENDNOTES

1. This "mainstream" view of how public education has contributed to the economic well being and social lives of Americans has been challenged by analysts who point out how (1) the socialization of immigrants has in fact deprived certain ethnic populations of their identities, and (2) the U.S. educational system has worked against upward mobility among the most deprived sectors of our society. On the socialization of immigrants, see G. David Garson, *Power and Politics in the United States: A Political Economy Approach* (Lexington, MA: D.C. Heath and Co., 1977), pp. 212–225; on the relationship between education and economic mobility, see Samuel Bowles and Herbert Gintis, *Schooling in Capitalist America* (New York: Basic Books, 1976).
2. Most policies related to education since the turn of the century have limited the development of private alternatives to public schools. A number of policy proposals that might promote rather than restrict the "private education" option have gained considerable support in recent years. The most common and simple proposal involves offering a tax deduction for tuition. A more sophisticated proposal is the "voucher system" program which is described in Milton Friedman, *Capitalism and Freedom* (Chicago: The University of Chicago Press, 1962), Chapter VI.
3. "Public policy" has been defined in a variety of ways. Some stress the "policy" factor; for example, Harold D. Lasswell and Abraham Kaplan defined public policy as a "course of action" taken in relation to others or some situation. Thus, they view public policy as "a projected program of goal values and practices." See *Power and Society: A Framework for Political Inquiry* (New Haven, CT: Yale University Press, 1950), p. 71. In contrast, Robert Eyestone puts the emphasis on the "public" when he defines the terms as "the relationship of a government unit to its environment." See his *The Threads of Public Policy: A Study in Political*

Leadership (Indianapolis: The Bobbs-Merrill Co., Inc., 1971), p. 18. For definitions that bridge the two extremes, see James E. Anderson, *Public Policy-Making*, 2nd edition (New York: Holt, Rinehart and Winston, 1979), p. 3; Richard I. Hofferbert, *The Study of Public Policy* (Indianapolis: Bobbs-Merrill, Co., Inc., 1974), p. 5; and Robert L. Lineberry, *American Public Policy: What Government Does and What Difference It Makes* (New York: Harper and Row, Publishers, 1977), pp. 43–44.

4. See Charles O. Jones, *An Introduction to the Study of Public Policy*, 2nd edition (North Scituate, MA: Duxbury Press, Inc., 1977), Chapter 2. Also Anderson, *Public Policy-Making*, Chapter 1; and Robert Eyestone, *From Social Issues to Public Policy* (New York: John Wiley & Sons, 1978), Chapter 1.

5. Cf. Eyestone, *From Social Issues to Public Policy*, Chapter 1.

6. See ibid; also Roger W. Cobb and Charles D. Elder, *Participation in American Politics: The Dynamics of Agenda-Building* (Baltimore: The Johns Hopkins University Press, 1972); and Matthew A. Crenson, *The Un-Politics of Air Pollution: A Study of Non-Decisionmaking in the Cities* (Baltimore: The Johns Hopkins University Press, 1971).

7. The distinction between statements and actions is discussed in Thomas R. Dye, *Policy Analysis: What Governments Do, Why They Do It, and What Difference It Makes* (University, AL: University of Alabama Press, 1976), pp. 19–21. It is a distinction rooted in David Easton's division of political system actions into statements and performances; see his *A Systems Analysis of Political Life* (New York: John Wiley & Sons, Inc., 1965), Chapter 22.

KEY TERMS
Policy Issue
Private Problems
Public Policies
Public Policy Agenda
Public Problems
Social Problems

CHAPTER 2

Analyzing Public Policies

A GENERAL DEFINITION

The term "public policy analysis" is thrown about rather loosely these days. It is applied to work underway in journalism and economics, in political science and sociology, in both policymaking and policy implementing agencies—and in the United States and abroad. As we noted in Chapter 1, our goal is to improve the way we think about public policies. In that sense, we are concerned with learning the basics of public policy analysis—at least enough to give us an informed understanding of what governments say and do. We might say that we will be learning to be citizen policy analysts. As a first step in that direction, let us consider what the task of public policy analysis entails in the broadest sense of its use.

In very general terms, *public policy analysis is the application of problem-solving techniques to questions concerning (1) the expressed intentions of government relative to a public problem and (2) those actions government officials take (or avoid) in attaining those objectives.* The purpose of any definition, of course, is to delineate, specify, and narrow the applicability of a given term. Put in a more positive way, definitions set forth certain key characteristics, or defining characteristics, that make the defined term useful.[1] Regarding our definition of public policy analysis, there are five such definining characteristics to take note of:

1. public policy analysis is applied;
2. public policy analysis uses problem-solving techniques;
3. public policy analysis deals with specific questions;
4. public policy analysis focuses on expressed government intentions; and
5. public policy analysis examines actions taken or avoided in the fulfillment of those intentions.

These five characteristics represent inseparable qualitites of public policy analysis. So, for instance, public policy analysis is an *applied* enterprise, but what are applied are *problem solving techniques*. Similarly, what these techniques are applied to—*questions*—are also inherent to the analytical effort, as are the topical focal points for the questions: *expressed government intentions* (i.e., statements) and *related actions*. In the rest of this chapter we discuss each of those characteristics.

PUBLIC POLICY ANALYSIS IS APPLIED

The task of the public policy analyst goes beyond merely "knowing the facts" about a government statement or action. One can have an extensive knowledge of a public policy and still not understand it. We can know, for example, that between 1961 and 1973 over 8¾ million Americans served in Vietnam and that more than a quarter of a million U.S. casualities were reported during that period, including 46,000 battle-related deaths. But having that information does not help us understand why those forces were there or what factors contributed to the relatively high casuality figures of that conflict. Nor do those facts help us comprehend the impact the Vietnam conflict had on American society. Comprehension comes not from a simple knowledge of facts; it derives from a self-conscious *application* of appropriate tools, techniques, and conceptualizations to those facts. Understanding, in short, involves the processing of known facts. In this sense, public policy analysis is applied.

Consider the difference between knowing about stagflation and understanding it. Stagflation describes an economy characterized by inflated prices and stagnant economic growth. The term was first used to describe the state of the U.S. economy between 1973 and 1975. During that period the consumer price index (CPI) rose from 133.1 to 174.9 (in both cases, the CPI for 1967 = 100), while the number of unemployed in the civilian labor force increased from 4,304,000 to 7,830,000—an unemployment rate jump from 4.9 percent to 8.5 percent. Inflation combined with stagnant economic growth was a new phenomenon and called for a new word—stagflation—to give it meaning.[2] In a similar fashion, all public policies must be given meaning, made understandable. This, in turn, implies that someone, usually an analyst, must take steps to convert the knowledge of basic facts into understandable information.

The distinction stressed here is an important one, especially in the study of public policy where many writers tend to ignore the implications of the word analysis and its role in changing what is known into what is understood.[3] Analysis is a process by which "transformation processes" (i.e., problem-solving techniques) are applied to information "so as to make transparent the obscure or hidden."[4] Economists know about unemployment, but they understand it through the application of macroeconomic analysis techniques. Sociologists know about discrimination, but they comprehend its consequences through the application of analytic methods used throughout the social sciences. Political scientists know that voters are predisposed to identify with the political party of their parents, but they are able to explain such behavior only through the application of various theories adapted from psychology and sociology. So it is with public policy analysts who undertake the *application* of certain information processing techniques in order to *understand* policies, *comprehend* their consequences, or *explain* their existence.

BOX 2.1

The distinction between "knowing" and "understanding" is not easily grasped in the abstract, but it is more easily described through examples. Fortunately, major newspapers throughout the U.S. utilize the distinction on a daily basis. For example, in most cases the main news sections of *The New York Times, The Washington Post, The Chicago Tribune,* and your local daily newspaper are filled with column after column of factual information about "who, what, where, when, and why." In these articles we find the basic information, e.g., that there is turmoil in the Middle East, that Congress passed a tax bill, that the city commission voted to rezone two blocks in your neighborhood to permit the construction of multiple family dwellings. Fine. You now have the "facts" at your disposal.

But, what does it all mean? How do problems in the Middle East affect us? What was the rationale for the federal tax bill? How will the commission's rezoning effect your life? The straight news stories are unlikely to give you answers to such questions, although they might report how others respond to those questions. Thus, they may ask the U.S. Secretary of State to comment on the situation in the Middle East; or an aide to a prominant member of Congress to explain the tax measure; or a local real estate broker to describe the implications of the rezoning. In each case the news story is reporting on the analysis of a policy situation by these individuals—that is, their application of "understanding" to known facts.

Sometimes those same pages contain articles which provide readers with the views of the reporters on the job. Usually these are clearly marked "News Analysis," and at other times they are located on editorial pages or in special columns. In these columns the reporters try to provide readers with some idea of what a given series of events means and what the future might hold in store. This is analysis, and it reflects the fact that application is a key characteristic of the analytic process.

THE USE OF PROBLEM-SOLVING TECHNIQUES

Problem solving "is a matter of appropriate selection, selection of ultimate solution, or selection of a process leading to a desired explicitly stated goal."[5] In other words, it is a matter of choosing (or even creating) the appropriate tools and methods to be applied in order to answer given questions raised by problematic situations.

Like other problem solvers, public policy analysts have a standard bag of tricks at their disposal—an inventory of readily available problem-solving tools and techniques useful for many of the problems they confront. In later chapters we review models that can be used to explain certain policies: the group theory model, the single elite or pluralist models, incrementalist models, etc.[6] Similarly, in describing foreign policies, commentators and political candidates often apply models of international relations that use such familiar phrases as "balance of power," "detente," or "tripolar world." In most cases, these models are all the policy analyst may need. In such instances, "good" policy analysis is determined by the technical competency of those using the models.

Yet, such a collection of standard problem-solving techniques may prove insufficient at times, for like analysts in other fields, people who think about public policies often face unique questions that current instruments and procedures are incapable of answering. In such circumstances, the policy analyst must be able to create new problem-solving tools and techniques, or adapt old ones to different situations. In this sense, policy analysis is not simply a technical or mechanical task, for it frequently calls upon the imagination and creativeness of the problem solver. It demands openness and flexibility, especially the ability to break out of the conceptual boundaries of everyday life and thought. In approaching a public policy problem, the analyst may have to be innovative, perhaps even radical, in his or her thinking.[7]

As is shown in the next chapter, problem-solving techniques are methods for prying oneself free of the many physical and mental constraints that bind us all. To that extent, the public policy analyst is an innovator, or at least should be if he or she is to be successful. As analysts face increasingly difficult questions, success becomes more a matter of openness and flexibility and less a result of merely learning to apply common tools of the trade. Thus, under those challenging circumstances a "good" policy analyst is not necessarily the one who demonstrates a technical proficiency in quantitative analysis or other sophisticated models. On the contrary, such a person may be regarded as a poor analyst unless he or she can adapt to different challenges. The tools used do not matter as much as the selection and appropriate application of problem-solving techniques. You can be a *good* policy analyst whether you are asking the simple questions of a citizen or dealing with the complex problems of highly skilled professionals. In general, therefore, the good analyst is one who is capable of developing and selecting the right model or other tool to help answer the analytic questions being asked.

BOX 2.2

The fact that policy models are merely potential tools in our effort to understand the world of public policy is sometimes ignored by those who use them. This can have dire consequences. These tools often become "creeds" in the hands of those who fail to comprehend the instrumental nature of their use. This situation is especially common in the area of foreign policy and international relations according to Coplin, McGowan, and O'Leary (p. 219),

> Scholarly frameworks are intended to be used to determine what is true and what is false. However, when these frameworks are adopted by politicians, civil servants, journalists, or laymen and used to form guidelines on how foreign policy ought to be conducted, then scholarly frameworks often become ideologies and are used to justify one value position over another. One way this often happens is that a politician or journalist adopts a . . . framework *describing* the status quo and employs it to argue that the status quo cannot be *changed*. This of course is often a fallacious inference.

Once elevated to the level of ideologies, problem-solving tools can become dangerous implements. They lose their identity as instruments for analytic understanding and instead become unchallengable grounds for policy actions. They become part of how the world is perceived by policymakers and opinion leaders, and the results can prove disastrous.

Again, the principle example is in the area of foreign affairs. John G. Stoessinger has provided us with an insightful and provacative study of relations among the United States, the Soviet Union and China. What he found were three "nations in darkness" whose misperceptions of each other could have catastrophic consequences. Of even greater concern is his conclusion that most policymakers "will not examine their prejudices and stereotypes until they are shaken and shattered into doing so." (p. 220) The desirability of regarding policy analysis models as merely tools rather than as guidelines for action is obvious.

See William D. Coplin, Patrick J. McGowan, and Michael K. O'Leary, *American Foreign Policy: An Introduction to Analysis and Evaluation* (North Scituate, MA: Duxbury Press, 1974); and John G. Stoessinger, *Nations in Darkness: China, Russia, and America*, 2nd edition (New York: Random House, 1975).

To summarize, public policy analysis is the application of problem-solving techniques, and these techniques range from those currently available and in wide use to those that must be created or adapted to new and unique uses. In this sense, the policy analyst is not merely a technician; nor is a good policy analyst one who knows only the current tools of the trade. The key to problem solving, and thus the key to policy thinking, is the development of one's ability to make *appropriate* selections of problem-solving techniques.

THE QUESTIONS OF PUBLIC POLICY ANALYSIS

"If you don't ask the right questions, they don't have to give the right answers." That statement can be adopted as the motto of public policy analysts the world over, for what they do depends on what questions or problems they seek to solve. This is as true for the citizen policy analyst as it is for highly trained experts. Analysis begins with a problem, and the nature of that problem is a crucial determinant of the entire policy analysis enterprise.

The range of policy questions and problems susceptible to analysis is very broad. Which national health insurance plan is best? What would be the impact of a 3 year, 25 percent tax cut on inflation? Under current wage base and coverage rules, what will be per capita costs of Social Security and related programs in the year 2050? What is the most efficient means for reducing traffic fatalities? These and similar queries, covering topics ranging from the mundane (How many snow plows should the city purchase?) to the critical (Should we undertake a preemptive attack on the Soviet Union?) not only deal with a variety of situations and substantive issues, but also reflect the different types of questions that arise. Some questions seek knowledge about the future, what "will be." Other problems to be solved focus on "what is" or "was," while still others are concerned with what "ought to be." To better comprehend the variety of extant policy analyses, we can classify the basic types of problems that public policies pose for analysts into three categories.

At the most basic level, policies are *analytic problems*. That is, they are problems in the sense that we seek to know and understand what governments are saying and doing, why they are doing and saying those things, and with what consequences. Analytic problems are the common grounds for all systematic thinking about public policies, for solutions to them provide the information and raw material needed by all policy analysts whether they be citizens or highly skilled professionals.

At a second level of thinking about public policies, one must deal with them as *judgmental problems*. Put briefly, those who have a basic understanding of government statements and actions may need to decide whether to support a policy or seek changes in it. For these individuals public policy problems involve more than merely comprehending what is happening or why; in addition, these individuals must assess a government statement or action in light or some standard. Thus, having reached a point of knowing about U.S. foreign policy toward Latin America, the policy analyst may have to decide whether our efforts in that arena are worth the costs involved or fit into our overall foreign policy plans. At that point, public policy thinking becomes judgmental.

Finally, public policies may be thought of as *strategic problems* in the sense that they call for the development of new or better government actions and statements. For instance, an analyst may regard poverty policy as a means to an end, that is, a means by which poverty can be eliminated or suffering can be alleviated among those who live on incomes below the poverty level. For that analyst the policy problem to be solved is the development of appropriate government programs to produce the desired goals. To accomplish this, the analyst goes through a number of steps that will lead to a prescriptive choice among several possible means to achieve the desired objective. The approach used begins with a *diagnosis* of the poverty stiuation in America and the *establishment of a goal or objective* that the problem solver wishes to work toward. Following this, the analyst considers what *alternative courses of action* might be taken to bring the current state of affairs in line with the desired one. Using various techniques, the analyst *assesses the costs and benefits* of each alternative and *decides which one should be recommended for adoption* as the best policy choice among those examined. As we will see in the last chapter, for highly trained policy analysts, strategic problems are their central concern.

Thinking about public policies at these different problem levels obviously makes a difference for how the analyst approaches his or her tasks. The fact is, different questions are raised at each level. Analytic problems focus attention on descriptive and explanatory questions as well as those dealing with policy consequences. Judgmental problems shift attention to questions of if and how policies measure up to our standards. And strategic problems make us concentrate on developing and adopting changes in public policies. Since our purposes in this book are neither judgmental nor strategic, we will focus on the three key analytic problems all policy analysts must deal with: What is the policy? Why is the policy? What are the policy's consequences?

What Is the Policy?

All analysts face the task of *describing* what they are dealing with. The phenomenon labeled public policy can be perceived from many different points of view, and (as we see in Chapter 4) choosing a specific framework for describing a given policy can have important consequences for those who use the analyst's results.[8] Consider, for example, the policy of U.S. arms sales to opposing sides in the long-standing Middle East dispute. That policy can be described in terms of some overall objective sought by policymakers, for example, to maintain a balance of military power between Israel and its Arab neighbors or to maintain friendly relations with the leaders of countries in conflict whose cooperation is regarded as important for the United States. That policy can also be described within the context of a more general foreign policy mandate. Thus, we can describe the sale of arms to Saudi Arabia as part of an overall attempt to counter Soviet influence in the region. These arms sales also can be described in historical terms, for example, reflecting a long-standing commitment to Israel's survival. Or they can be described in strictly budgetary terms, that is, X percent of U.S. expenditures for foreign aid. As will be shown in Chapter 4, questions associated with descriptive problems of public policy analysis are extremely important for the analyst to consider in detail. There is a rich inventory of techniques the analyst can apply in answering these questions, and the choice is no inconsequential matter.

Why Is the Policy?

Understanding *what* a policy is, the analyst often turns to the problem of trying *to explain* why the policy is what it is. Different people undertake policy analysis for different reasons. It follows that there are different types of analytic techniques applicable to the distinct explanatory needs of analysts. Explaining U.S. policies in the Middle East is a task for Presidents, Pentagon officials, historians, journalists, social scientists, conservatives, radicals, as well as every other interested citizen. Yet, while each seeks the same objective (to know why these policies are what they were), each will use different analytic approaches in their work and therefore come to different explanations for the policy. In Chapter 6 we will consider some of the alternative approaches applicable to this type of analytic problem.

What Are the Policy's Consequences?

It is important not only to know what a policy is or why it is, but also *what impact* it has had or will have. As discussed in Chapter 8, the problem of analyzing policy consequences takes the form of determining the *specific impacts* of a policy carried out by government officials. Thus, the impact of the Vietnam War can be studied in terms of number of persons killed in action, the amount of human and financial resources diverted from other military or domestic activities, or the extent to which the fabric of U.S. society was damaged by reactions to American involvement in the conflict. Many analysts go beyond the mere *analytic* description of policy consequences to the more *judgmental* task of evaluating the outcomes of government statements and actions. In fact, it is often difficult to distinguish between studies of policy consequences that are either analytic or judgmental, and in Chapter 8 we do not stress the differences except for some introductory comments. However, it should be stressed that judging the impact of the Vietnam War on U.S. society or on the lives of specific groups or individuals is an extremely difficult task, both methodologically and emotionally. Similarly, it may be unlikely that we could reach any conclusions about how effective our Middle East arms sales policy was short of a regional conflict or world war. It may be impossible to develop or apply criteria that would allow the analyst to state with any certainty that a policy was beneficial or costly, good or bad, efficient or inefficient. Nevertheless, steps can be taken in that direction, and if accomplished with an awareness of the limits involved in such analyses, policy evaluation can be a worthwhile endeavor. We explore some of those limits in Chapter 8.

DEALING WITH EXPRESSIONS OF GOVERNMENT INTENTIONS

Expressions of what government intends to do about a public problem come in many forms, some formal or informal, others official or unofficial. Government policy statements are always official when issued as formal documents. Legislatures issue statutes or resolutions, which are "laws" in the most legitimate sense; mayors, governors, and presidents disseminate executive orders, which are enforceable as law; and courts provide written judicial decisions, which have the impact of law. Informally, policy statements can range from the official speech to the unofficial leak. On an official level, informal policy statements have played an important role in American foreign policy, from the Monroe Doctrine asserting the interest of the United States in preserving hegemony in the Western Hemisphere, to President Ford's Pacific Doctrine speech, which expressed a commitment to the "preservation of the sovereignty and the independence of our Asian friends and allies. . . ." Such statements differ substantially, however, from the unofficial comment attributed to a "high-level spokesperson" which expresses the govenment's intention to take certain action (e.g., to cut off military sales or other aid to Israel unless it adjusts its stand on settlements on the West Bank).

Regardless of the specific form of policy statements, what government says it will do is analytically important for two reasons. First, those statements may be indicative of what government actually intends to do. Thus, such statements could provide some insight into the questions of what a policy is, why it is, and what its intended consequences are. For example, if we assume that U.S. policy statements regarding the sale of arms to Israel, Egypt, and Saudi Arabia are valid reflections of the government's intentions, then the analyst's task of answering descriptive, explanatory, and evaluative questions about U.S. policy in the Middle East can be facilitated. The policy analyst would be able to go directly to policy statements to find out what the official or unofficial Middle East policy is, what reasons are given for that policy, and whether those intentions are carried out to the fullest.

A second reason for studying what government says about a public problem is that such statements may be significant in and of themselves; that is, as *symbolic* expressions of intent that do not reflect contemplated government actions but instead act as possible solutions to the policy situation. Policy statements, in other words, may be used as a substitute for policy actions. Talk is a powerful policy tool. "Through language," notes Murray Edelman, "a group can not only achieve an immediate result but also win the acquiescence of those whose lasting support is needed."

> That talk is powerful is not due to any potency in words but to needs and emotions in men. In subtle and obvious ways cultures shape vocabulary and meaning, and men respond to verbal cues. People who share the same role learn to respond in common fashion in particular signs. Specify a role and a political speech, and you can also specify a response with a high measure of confidence. . . .[9]

It follows that a policy statement may be sufficient to satisfy a particular portion of the public concerned with a given problem. The implications of this can lead to a cynical view of public policymaking. Having satisfied the most vocal and politically important groups in this way, the policymaker will probably do little more unless some other factor is driving him or her to do more than make symbolic statements. If what governments say seems to be merely symbolic, then the task of the policy analyst might be to examine not only the content of the statement, but also the reason for its use. For example, who were targets of these statements? What was the impact of the policy statements (e.g., was the target public sufficiently satisfied)? Did the statement have any impact on other publics? If so, was their response positive or negative? These and related questions could produce some very interesting insights into many facets of the policymaking systems as well as the policy issue involved.

BOX 2.3

There are a number of examples of government statements being used as public policy solutions. During the first year of his administration, Jimmy Carter found himself under critical attack from Vernon Jordan, head of the National Urban League. Jordan accused Carter of failing to live up to his campaign pledges regarding jobs for unemployed blacks. Carter seemed to effectively quell those misgivings by appearing before an Urban League Convention and reasserting his policy commitments on minority employment policies. His words were enough to soothe many of the disenchanted. What Carter said, *not what he did,* was an effective policy.

Symbolic policy statements are not only in the province of presidents. The history of Congressional civil rights legislation was, for many years, a history of heavy words and little action. Until the middle 1960s, civil rights acts contained considerable rhetoric backing various minority group claims, but they didn't have much in the way of enforceable "teeth" to back them up. There were commissions and studies and some administrative movements to integrate federal government agencies, but overall civil rights was a policy arena in which symbolic expressions of policy were given the most weight. It wasn't until the Civil Rights Act of 1964 and the Voting Rights Act of 1965 that action began to back up the words.

See Murray Edelman, *The Symbolic Uses of Politics* (Urbana: IL: University of Illinois Press, 1964). On civil rights legislation of the 1950s and 1960s see James L. Sundquist, *Politics and Policy: The Eisenhower, Kennedy and Johnson Years* (Washington, DC: Brookings Institution, 1968), Chapter VI.

Regardless of whether analysts approach formal or informal, official or unofficial policy statements, and no matter if they examine those words as what government actually intends or merely as symbolic expressions, the focus on what government says is a critical topic for analysis. However, it is equally (if not more) important to analyze what government does relative to a public problem—its actions as opposed to its words.

ANALYZING GOVERNMENT ACTIONS

What government does about public problems—its performance[10]—has received a great deal of attention from many analysts in recent years. For example, Ira Sharkansky, a prolific writer who has done a good deal of work in this area, considers public policy as representing "actions taken by government."[11] Yet, while the consideration of government actions has been increasing, not all analysts have focused on similar phenomena. In fact, a review of the work of many public policy analysts indicates three distinct views about what it is they study when they speak of public policy actions.

For some analysts, public policy actions are discrete events or decisions that can be isolated and studied separate from other acts; in other words, a behavior that can be pinpointed and examined as a singular manifestation of some policy statement. By narrowly defining the concept of policy actions in this way, those who study public policies are able to concentrate on describing, explaining, and assessing the consequences a specific event, usually through case studies.[12] For example, one can study President Kennedy's imposition of a naval blockade around Cuba during the 1962 missile crisis,[13] the Federal Trade Commission's 1964 mandate that health warnings be printed on cigarette packages,[14] or the Atomic Energy Commission's 1966 decision to locate its 200 billion electron volts accelerator near Weston, Illinois.[15]

Other analysts focus on discrete events, but not on singular policy actions. These analysts view policy actions in clusters—as performances by government which are related to each other through some common theme or target subject.[16] For example, one can study the U.S.S.R.'s foreign policies in Africa, Ronald Reagan's fiscal policy, Lyndon Johnson's Great Society programs. One can focus on clusters of short-term policies related to health care, education, welfare, or transportation.[17] Or one can examine the United States' Middle East policy or its cold war era policy of containment. What links these actions together is not related policy objectives or policy instruments, but rather some shared point of organization: some common location, some basic policy statement, some historical or cultural tie.

A third perspective, offered by foreign policy analyst James N. Rosenau, is based on the contention that public policy actions are serial, purposeful, and coordinated attempts to deal with a state of affairs. Policy actions are more than distinct responses that can be isolated or pinpointed; rather they are continuous actions taken to maintain or change a situation. Rather than use terms such as "decisions" or "policies," Rosenau chose to label these policies efforts *undertakings*. To paraphrase his defintion, an undertaking is a course of action that duly constituted officials of government pursue in order to preserve or alter a situation in the social system in such a way that the results are consistent with a goal or goals decided upon by them or their predecessors.

> An undertaking begins when a situation arises . . . that officials seek to maintain or change. It is sustained as long as the resources of the society mobilized and directed by officials continue to apply to the situation. It terminates either when the situation comes to an end and obviates the need for further action or when officials conclude that their action cannot alter or preserve the situation and abandon their efforts.[18]

As an example of the difference between these views of policy action, consider how one might approach the study of U.S. policy with regard to Fidel Castro's Cuba. At the discrete event level, one may study a specific occurrence such as the Bay of Pigs invasion, the missile crisis of October 1962, or the negotiation of an antihighjacking agreement between Cuba and the United States. At the level of clusters of policy actions, the concern would be for the relations between the two countries under some specific administration (e.g., Kennedy, Johnson, Nixon, Ford, Carter, or Reagan); or it would focus on some specific matter over a period of time (e.g., trade relations). On the level of undertaking, one can study policy as those actions taken by U.S. administrations to isolate the Castro regime from the rest of the Western Hemisphere. These distinctions are sometimes arbitrary and frequently overlap. Nevertheless, it does make a difference for the policy analyst that one is studying a number of events rather than merely one, or that the events are related by some person or topic of concern.

These three views of public policy activities—as discrete events, as clusters of actions, and as undertakings—provide those who think about public policies with a variety of focal points for raising specific analytic questions and applying appropriate problem-solving techniques. But they reflect only part of the picture when it comes to questions about what government does, for the actions themselves take on different forms in terms of their sources and the functions they perform in the political system. In Chapter 4 we survey several of the many typologies of policy actions that analysts have used to distinguish among the various things that governments do. The point to be stressed here is that when thinking about public policies as forms of government actions, we should be aware of the variety of focal points at our disposal.

POLICY THINKING AND POLICY ANALYSIS

This brief discussion of public policy analysis has pointed out a number of defining characteristics that need to be emphasized. First, public policy analysis is not simply the accumulation knowledge related to a policy. It is primarily the application of thought to that knowledge in order to understand the policy.

Second, what are applied are problem-solving techniques, that is, models, typologies, and conceptual frameworks that help us answer the questions we have about the policy.

Third, those questions can take a variety of forms, but the most fundamental distinction is between analytic, judgmental, and strategic questions. *Analytic questions*, the most basic, are concerned with describing, explaining, and assessing the consequences of a given policy. *Judgmental questions* seek an evaluation of policies based on given standards. *Strategic questions* are prescriptive and seek solutions to problems of developing and choosing among policy alternatives.

Fourth, public policy analysis deals with questions about the formal and informal expression of government intentions. Some of those expressions are *indicative* of what governments intend to do. Others are *symbolic* expressions that have impacts as official or unofficial statements over and above what they reflect about government intentions. Finally, public policy analysis may deal with questions about government actions. Those actions may be *discrete events, clusters of events,* or *undertakings.*

These defining characteristics of public policy analysis give you some taste of what it is that you are about to learn. Public policy analysis encompasses an enormous variety of tasks and approaches. In Chapter 10 we will take a closer look at the career options available to any student who aspires to go beyond the analytic basics we focus on in this book. For now we concentrate on those basics, not only because they are fundamental for learning the more sophisticated forms of public policy analysis, but also because they provide us with the rudimentary tools we should all possess as citizens in a world where what governments do and say means so much.

ENDNOTES

1. See Dickinson McGaw and George Watson, *Political and Social Inquiry* (New York: John Wiley & Sons, Inc., 1976), p. 116.

ENDNOTES

2. See Alan S. Blinder, *Economic Policy and the Great Stagflation* (New York: Academic Press, 1979). Also see discussion on economic policy in Chapter 5.
3. The distinction made here owes much to the work of John Dewey. See his *Experience and Nature* (New York: Dover Publications, Inc., 1929/1958), Chapter IV; also Dewey and Aruthur F. Bentley, *Knowing and the Known* (Boston: Beacon Press, 1949).
4. Moshe F. Rubinstein, *Patterns of Problem Solving* (Englewood Cliffs, NJ: Prentice-Hall, Inc. 1975), p. 7.
5. Ibid., pp. 6–7.
6. See Thomas R. Dye, *Understanding Public Policy*, 3rd edition (Englewood Cliffs, NJ: Prentice-Hall, Inc., 1978); also Peter Woll, *Public Policy* (Cambridge, MA: Winthrop Publishers, Inc., 1974), especially Chapter 2.
7. For a useful introduction to creative thinking see James L. Adams *Conceptual Blockbusting: A Guide to Better Ideas*, 2nd edition (New York: W.W. Norton, & Co., Inc., 1979).
8. See Lewis A. Froman, Jr. "The Categorization of Policy Contents," in Austin Ranney (ed.), *Political Science and Public Policy* (Chicago: Markham Publishing Co., 1968), pp. 41–52.
9. Murray Edelman, *The Symbolic Uses of Politics* (Urbana, IL: University of Illinois Press, 1964), pp. 114–115. Also see Edelman's *Political Language: Words That Succeed and Policies That Fail* (New York: Academic Press, 1977).
10. David Easton, *A Systems Analysis of Political Life* (New York: John Wiley & Sons, 1965), p. 353.
11. Ira Sharkansky, "Environment, Policy, Output and Impact: Problems of Theory and Method in the Analysis of Public Policy," in Ira Sharkansky (ed.), *Policy Analysis in Political Science* (Chicago: IL: Markham Publishing Co., 1970), p. 63.
12. See Raymond A. Bauer and Kenneth J. Gergen (eds.), *The Study of Policy Formation* (New York: The Free Press, 1968) especially Bauer's introductory chapter: "The Study of Policy Formation: An Introduction," pp. 1–26.
13. See Graham T. Allison, *Essence of Decision: Explaining the Cuban Missile Crisis* (Boston, MA: Little, Brown and Co., 1971).
14. See A. Lee Fritschler, *Smoking and Politics: Policymaking and the Federal Bureaucracy*, (Englewood Cliffs, NJ: Prentice-Hall, Inc., 1975).
15. See Theodore J. Lowi, et al., *Poliscide* (New York: Macmillan Publishing Co., Inc., 1976).
16. See the discussion on decision cluster studies in James A. Robinson and R. Roger Majak, "The Theory of Decision-Making," in James C. Charlesworth (ed.), *Contemporary Political Analysis* (New York: The Free Press, 1967).
17. For example, consider the chapter titles given in Fred I. Greenstein and Nelson W. Polsby (eds), *Handbook of Political Science, Volume 6: Policies and Policymaking* (Reading, MA: Addison-Wesley Publishing Co., 1975): "Making Economic Policy . . ."; "Science Policy"; "Welfare Policy"; "Race Policy"; "Comparative Urban Policy . . ."; "Foreign Policy."
18. James N. Rosenau, "Moral Fervor, Systematic Analysis, and Scientific Consciousness in Foreign Policy Research," in Ranney (ed.), *Political Science and Public Policy*, p. 222.

KEY TERMS
Analytic Problems
Clusters of Events
Discrete Events
Indicative Statements
Judgmental Problems
Problem Solving
Public Policy Analysis
Strategic Problems
Symbolic Statements
Undertakings

CHAPTER 3

The Problem-Solving Approach: A Primer

As is clear from our discussion thus far, public policy thinking is essentially a set of problem-solving approaches to questions arising from what governments say and do. For us to develop the analytic capabilities to deal with such problems, we need to understand the task of problem solving and try to relate that understanding to the various issues raised in public policy arenas.

In this chapter we examine human problem solving and consider ways to make the process more effective. In addition, we briefly consider some advice that students of problem solving have offered that might help us use those techniques and deal more effectively with obstacles we might encounter.

We also examine the nature and use of models that can aid in problem solving and discuss how we should evaluate a model's usefulness. Two useful models are examined as examples. We look at model-building and describe six basic steps in that process. In addition, we briefly discuss various sources of potentially useful models and, finally, some guidelines for choosing among alternative ways to solve problems.

Of course, there is no substitute for experience in public policy thinking. This brief introduction to the problem-solving process is a guide for finding and adapting the various tools for policy analysis that are available to you. In later chapters we will examine some of the tools themselves and how they are applied to different policy areas. For now, however, let these ideas help you find new ways to think about public policies.

WHAT WE KNOW ABOUT PROBLEM SOLVING

Social scientists have approached *human problem solving* in two ways. The more controversial perspective is that of the behaviorist school of psychology and its leading proponents, John Watson and B.F. Skinner. According to behaviorists, problem solving is the behavior exhibited by an organism in response to some stimuli. Any factors that cannot be empirically observed—such as "mind," "image," or even "thinking,"—cannot be considered as explanations for the problem solving actions which are observed. Faced with "a question for which there is at the moment no answer" (Skinner's definition of a "problem"), the human subject relies on certain behaviors to find a solution; e.g., calculations, research, or "previously learned answer."[1]

The second approach, known as the information processing perspective, is presented by Allen Newell, Herbert A. Simon, and others. For these researchers, the human problem solver is an information processing system with limited capabilities. For example, it relies on serial processing methods, a small short-term memory capability, and an infinite long-term memory capacity "with fast retrieval but slow storage."[2] As an information processing unit, the human being also has two other qualitites that make it quite successful: first, it is highly adaptive to the demands of its immediate "task environment"; and second, it makes use of specific principles or devices (called heuristics) "which contribute to the reduction in the average search for solutions." Unlike the behaviorists, these scholars believe the key to understanding human problem solving is found in the perceptual and cognitive (heuristic) devices brought to bear in such situations.[3] However both schools of thought agree that human problem solving resembles a search process rather than the rational step-by-step procedure that is usually offered as the ideal model for "good" problem solving. There seems to be a logic involved in this search, but it is limited logic often guided by "extrarational" or nonrational forces.

BOX 3.1

We can perhaps best understand how much the ideal model of rational problem solving differs from the reality by considering some significant cases of problem solving from the annals of science. As we review these cases, remember what you learned about the scientific method in your physics or chemistry classes. Supposedly, scientific problem solving is a rational process whereby a community of researchers observe a situation over a period of time, develop hypotheses based on those observations, structure experiments to test them, replicate those experiments over and over again, and then establish tentative conclusions based on the findings derived from those tests. Discoveries are thus made and knowledge accumulated and verified in science—or so we are taught.

The first case deals with one of the most significant advances in the history of mathematics: the discovery of the Cartesian coordinate system. That system has proven important for at least two reasons: first, it was the foundation for the fusion of algebra and geometry into analytic geometry; and second, it "provided the springboard for Newton that led to his discovery of the Law of Gravitation." All this was the product of the work of René Descartes, a seventeenth century French scientist who has left his mark on our lives in a number of ways. The interesting thing about Descartes' discovery was his claim that it was not the product of scientific observation and the hypothesis-testing procedure; rather, he gives credit to a mystical vision he had one November night in 1619 when an "Angel of Truth" visited him while he was stationed with the army just outside Paris. "The vision was so vivid and compelling," notes E.A. Burtt, "that Descartes in later years could refer to that precise date as the occasion of the great revelation that marked the decisive point in his career." Thus we obtain a view of problem solving quite different from the rational, calculative picture scientific texts seem to stress. For Descartes, at least, discovery was "inspired" in the mystical sense of that term.

The second case of problem solving is found in the experiences of Albert Einstein. If his first major writings on the theory of relativity in any way reflect the process by which he achieved his insights, then we have still another break from the pattern of the rational scientific method of problem solving. According to Moshe F. Rubinstein, the discovery of relativity was the product of metaphorical thinking in which Einstein "reduced his problem to a metaphor involving a train and the observation of bolts of lightning striking at two different points." In this way, Einstein's discovery was not accomplished through "straight" and rational thinking, but rather creative and perhaps even playful thinking. That solutions to problems may be the result of "play" rather than "work" is a thought we must keep in mind as we consider just what the process involves.

Still another example of problem solving is found in the discovery of the structure of DNA by Francis Crick and James D. Watson. The Nobel Prize winning discovery of the double helix, according to Watson, was the end product of a situation characterized not by cooperative and rational scientific research, but by ambition, social pressures, and complex interactions based on a conflict of personalities. The story Watson tells is as dramatic as the discovery was significant and provides but one more example of the forces that seem to underlie problem solving at the higher levels of the scientific community.

See E.A. Burtt, *The Metaphysical Foundations of Modern Science* (Garden City, NY: Doubleday and Co., Inc., 1954), pp. 105–106; also Moshe F. Rubinstein, *Patterns of Problem Solving* (Englewood Cliffs, NJ: Prentice Hall, Inc., 1975), pp. 22–30; and James D. Watson, *The Double Helix: A Personal Account of the Discovery of the Structure of DNA* (New York: New American Library, 1968).

The cases offered in Box 3.1 exemplify how some of the most signficant products of scientific thought do not quite live up to the standards of rational problem-solving methods. They provide us with a number of important lessons about human problem solving. The first is that the process of problem solving is a varied one which can range over a wide variety of approaches. Descriptions of Descartes' mystical inspiration, Einstein's playful use of metaphors, and Crick and Watson's competitive urge driven by ambition are more than mere stories. What makes them important for our purposes is that they contradict the picture of ideal problem solving methods as represented by the scientific approach we are all exposed to early in our classroom experiences. The second lesson of these cases is one expressed by William J. J. Gordon when he notes that "ultimate solutions to problems are rational; the process of finding them is not."[4]

If the rational approach to problem solving is not the most fruitful one, then what approach is? This is a difficult (if not impossible) question to answer. One of the reasons why the scientific method is often promoted is that it is logical, communicable, and thus easily taught and learned. There is no denying these attributes of the scientific method; nor should we assume that the rational and experimental approaches cannot produce useful solutions to certain problems. However, there is a tendency for us to regard the approach as the problem solving method *par excellence* rather than one among many means at our disposal. The same holds true for any distinct problem-solving approach.

What must be emphasized is that problem solving is not a predetermined set of actions or behavior patterns. It is the *interaction between the problem solver and the problematic situation*. Understanding this interaction involves identifying the ingredients that facilitate the process. The primary ingredient is simple; it involves a certain frame of mind or attitude. "Being prepared with *the right attitude* and a frame of useful general ideas," claims Moshe F. Rubinstein, "will help you recognize new patterns of problem solving at the most unusual times as by serendipity."[5]

But what is this "right" attitude, and how does one get it? The correct attitude is difficult to pinpoint, but in its essence it is a condition of being what psychologist Joseph R. Royce has termed "unencapsulated." A person is encapsulated when he or she claims "to have all of the truth" when in fact having only part of it. By encapsulation, we

> mean claiming to have truth without being sufficiently aware of the limitation of one's approach to truth. We mean looking at life partially, but issuing statements concerning the wholeness of living. In its most important sense the term "encapsulation" refers to projecting knowledge of ultimate reality from the perceptual framework of a limited reality image.[6]

Such an attitude will severely limit one's capacity as a problem solver. This is particularly true when applying problem-solving to public policy. Blind adherence to an ideological "faith" prevents the use of many tools or concepts because they are regarded as inappropriate or unacceptable. Conversely, reliance on purely empirical techniques may ignore the value systems that guide policy decisions.

Beyond keeping our minds open and flexible, we need to recognize and compensate for our human inadequacies, such as the limited ability to use all the information available to us. We are, in fact, neurologically limited in our capabilities, at least in terms of short-term endeavors.[7] According to one source, at any point in time humans are capable of handling about seven bits of unrelated information items, plus or minus two.[8] This difficulty has been contended with in several ways, most of which can be reduced to two basic methods: chunking and patterning.[9]

Chunking is a process by which information bits are organized into larger blocks or chunks. It is the process we use when we memorize seven-digit telephone numbers or the many addresses we don't bother to write down. The telephone number, for instance, is usually remembered in two chunks (the first three digits and the second four) and any attempt to recall another chunk (e.g., five digits) is most frustrating. (As an experiment that can help you understand this phenomenon of chunking, ask a friend for the last two digits in his or her telephone number. The reaction is likely to be a stuttering response and only after a few seconds have passed will you get a clear answer. In fact, it is likely that your friend can provide the seven digits of the number faster than just those two.)

Chunking is also a basic tool in concept and language development. For example, instead of speaking about apples, oranges, apricots, and tangerines, we speak of fruit. Similarly, when reporting on the activities of members of Congress, reporters often speak in terms of party labels (Democrats, Republicans) or geographic identifications (Southerners, Northerners, Midwesterners) rather than of individual representatives.

Closely related to chunking is *patterning,* a process by which we put information bits into forms and patterns so that they stand together. Thus, reporters may deal with individual representatives to Congress, but they report on them in terms of the patterns of behavior each demonstrates (e.g., liberal or conservative, hawk or dove, and so on). Theories give us insights into some phenomenon, but more importantly they arrange facts and concepts in an order such that we are able to assimilate them all despite their complexity. In short, by fitting bits of information into patterns we increase our ability to manage a great deal more information than would otherwise be the case. Along with the chunking process, patterning can be regarded as a basic heuristic device (in Newell and Simon's sense) used by humans to overcome severe problem-solving limitations.

There are other limitations besides neurological ones that affect our problem-solving abilities, many of them psychological and social. Even if the problem of information processing capacities were successfully challenged, we would still face barriers imposed through unnecessary constraints—constraints we place on ourselves and which ultimately rest on our ability to encapsulate ourselves. First among these are *constraints of association*. Associational constraints trap us into patterns of thought that are otherwise extremely useful. For example, while calling representative X a liberal or conservative may help a newsreporter (or newspaper reader) deal with an overabundance of information about all legislators and their voting records, it is a costly association for it obscures some of the unique qualities of X and perhaps incorrectly informs us. Thus we start to associate X as a liberal or conservative and orient our electoral activities based on that association rather than other relevant bits of information available to us such as the representative's views on specific issues.

Related to associational constraints are *functional constraints*—those that focus on the functions of an item or person we are dealing with. A shoe is useful for protecting one's foot while walking, just as a physician is the person we call or visit when we are ill. But the shoe and the physician can be used in other ways, at least if we allow ourselves to think outside the functional categories we have created for them. The shoe, for instance, can be a makeshift hammer or a substitute weight under appropriate circumstances; similarly, a physician can serve as a counselor to those who are well or as a tennis partner, if appropriate. There are, of course, obvious limits to the alternative functions one can design for an item (e.g., the shoe would make a lousy tennis racquet). Nevertheless, effective problem solving would entail a willingness to question the current definition of functions commonly used in society.

The functional and associational constraints seem to culminate in a third: the *"world-view" constraint* whereby we imagine the world to be as we intellectually organize it. C. West Churchman demonstrates this constraint with the story of a mathematics professor who was challenged by his students to find the next item in the sequence of 32, 38, 44, 48, 56 and 60. After pondering the problem for hours, the professor gave up in frustration. He was unable to discover the logical sequential rule that governed the series. The answer was "Meadowlark," the commuter railroad stop after 60th Street at which he stopped each day he came to campus.[10] We are all familiar with persons like the mathematics professor; the economist who defines the world's problems in economic terms, the biology instructor who thinks of the university as a living organism, the lawyer who analyzes all social actions in terms of torts and liabilities. They are constrained by a perspective of the world into which they have been thoroughly socialized and within which they find themselves during most of their waking and working hours.

The only good advice to offer for overcoming these unnecessary constraints is to pry loose. That is often easier said than done, of course, but several suggestions can facilitate the task, and each can be seen as an important entry on our list of ingredients for effective problem solving. The first such entry is for the problem solver to remain detached from the problematic situation. *Detachment* is achieved when one is able to stand back from the problem in order to take a good and objective look from outside.

Yet this advice must be qualified almost immediately, for while detachment and objectivity are useful in problem solving, so is a continuous and conscious *involvement*. A problem solver is often aided by being able to become part of the circumstances that surround a problem—being able, in other words, to see the details and get the "feel" for a situation.

The seemingly contradictory advice that a problem solver be both detached and involved might make more sense were we to put it in terms of getting the total picture and avoiding becoming too focused on details or completely immersed in the broadly defined situation. While it might not be possible to be detached and involved simultaneously, the effective problem solver continuously moves from one level to the other in the process of developing solutions. The point is not to get stuck at one level without considering the other.[11]

Still another ingredient for successful problem solving is found in one's ability to *ask the right questions*. Consider, for example, the implications of going to an ear, nose, and throat specialist for a severely ingrown toenail. Relying only on the physician's questions as a means for obtaining a diagnosis, the office visit is bound to be long and frustrating for both of you. As a problem solver (e.g., diagnostician), the specialist asks all the correct questions from his or her point of view, but not necessarily from yours. The questions asked frequently determine the answers provided.[12]

Most students of problem solving agree that *deferment* is an important part of the process, that is, the ability to withhold one's judgment for as long as necessary. "Do not commit yourself too early to a course of action," warns Rubinstein. Premature attempts at the solution must be avoided for the obvious reason that it preempts the exploration not only of alternative answers, but also alternative questions.[13]

Which leads to the next ingredient: the ability to *speculate*, to try "different paths" and various means in trying to develop a solution. This may call for working backwards, generalizing from the specific, following one's intuitive feeling, and otherwise exploring both plausible and questionable directions. In Gordon's terms, it means using one's "recurrent ability to let the mind run free. . . ."[14]

A willingness to *use and change representations* of the world is also crucial in effective problem solving. This involves the frequent use of models, analogies, and metaphors, topics we explore later in this chapter. For now let us just say that models are a great aid in simplifying the world and making reality manageable. And so is the use of metaphors and analogies. We have already seen, for instance, how Einstein used metaphors as problem-solving mechanisms to explain his theory. What these tools do can be summarized briefly: they render the strange more familiar and the familiar strange. In both cases they help us pry loose from our mental constraints. For instance, we have made the strange phenomenon of radio communications familiar by appying the metaphor of waves; and when attempting to explain how electricity moves we often speak in terms of power flowing through wires as if discussing plumbing.

Making the familiar strange is a process by which everyday perspectives are distorted, inverted, or transposed. It involves "an intentionally naive or apparently 'out of focus' look at some aspect of the known world." Picturing oneself as an atom or molecule, converting problematic situations into symbolic representations that can be manipulated mathematically, using fantasies to develop solutions—each of these tactics has been used to obtain insight and to break away from a constraining world view. In each case the problem solver moves away from the object, getting reinvolved at a different level. In each case the world is represented in new and unique ways.[15]

Finally, the problem solver must have a *will to doubt*. Being able to accept premises as tentative, being "flexible and ready to question their credibility," being capable of prying oneself "loose of fixed convictions" and rejecting them when necessary are some of the qualities needed for the effective development of innovative solutions. The will to doubt allows, even encourages, you to reject your own solutions and then should make you wonder if that was the right thing to do. It is the attitude that mandates that a problem solver views every premise skeptically, and that any claim to truth be challenged. This final ingredient brings us full circle to our first one—the need to avoid encapsulation.[16]

In this section we have reviewed some of the basic ingredients most students of human behavior believe make for effective problem solving. These ingredients can be stated in positive terms as *general precepts for problem solving:*

- Avoid encapsulation; remember, there are several paths to truth.
- "Chunk" and "pattern" infomation where feasible and useful.
- Get the total picture through both detachment and involvement in the problem situation.
- Take care to ask the right questions.
- Defer; withhold judgments as long as possible.
- Speculate whenever possible.
- Make use of and be willing to change representations of the world; apply models, metaphors, and analogies to simplify, make the strange familiar, and the familiar strange.
- Maintain the will to doubt at all costs.

ON THE NATURE AND USEFULNESS OF MODELS

The problem-solving approach is particularly appropriate for understanding public policies characterized by complex relationships between government entities, by overlapping goals, and by multilevel activities. In order to identify and analyze such policies, the problem solver can use certain conceptual tools. Among the most useful of these concepts are models, analogies, and other representations of the real world. These tools can help us understand the processes that cause a policy to be adopted, how certain policies affect society or the economy, or the interaction between public goals such as energy independence and air pollution.

According to Richard Rose, a *model* "is a simplified representation of the complexities of the world around us."[17] Moshe Rubinstein notes that we frequently use models to "facilitate understanding and enhance prediction."[18] These specific qualities render models and related tools particularly useful for analysts. In this section we will discuss the nature of such models, their usefulness, and their suitability to public policy problems.

The Functions and Forms of Models

Models facilitate understanding of some phenomenon by placing it within the context of a general pattern of objects, ideas, or acts. They enhance prediction by indicating the relationships among the many factors that might cause or condition that same phenomenon.[19] At times the use of models relies on "novel methods of representation" that provide us with "fresh techniques by which inferences can be drawn." The end result is what scientists term discovery.[20] Yet at other times models can be applied in ways that narrow one's perspective and restricts innovative thinking. Models in short, can be the source of either joy or frustration, creativity or distortion.

All models are abstractions from reality.[21] This particular quality must be emphasized, for consciousness of it allows us to approach the use and manipulation of models with a great deal more openness and flexibility. We often tend to regard simplified representations of the world as reflections of a "true" reality, and to that extent we become reluctant to change and adapt many models to our particular needs. But while models do have a form and content all their own,[22] these qualities should not be confused with the characteristics of the world they are supposed to represent. Rather we must view models as "mental constructs developed for resolutions of empirical or conceptual problems."[23] They are tools we apply to various problematic situations. At times they manifest themselves in material forms—in wood, clay, or steel, or as symbolic markings such as words or numbers set to paper. At other times they are merely idealizations providing cognitive form to the world we live in.[24] (Compare, for instance, the road map of the United States in the glove compartment of your car with the mental map of your neighborhood stored in the recesses of your mind and retrieved unconsciously when it is needed.) In either case, the model should be regarded as a cognitive tool on which we depend in our attempts to contend with a problematic world.

Another distinction can be noted between models "in which actual phenomena are being symbolized" (i.e., *hard* models) and those are representations "of purely theoretical or hypothetical or conceptual matters, of imagined characteristics of some event of our concern" (i.e., *soft* models).[25] For instance, consider the difference between a blueprint that represents a "real" house under construction (hard model) as contrasted with a textbook diagram of the "abstract" economic exchange market that would exist under perfect societal conditions (a soft model). Whether hard or soft or somewhere in between those two extremes, what should be remembered is that *models are themselves abstract representations rather than literal "truths."* That they might reflect empirical reality or a vague idea makes no substantial difference in the fact that models are mental constructs which we use to solve problems.

Evaluating Models

In fact, usefulness, not its material form or its "hardness," is the crucial measure of a model. In basic problem solving as in science, the acceptance of a model is justified by its usefulness, or in Stephen Toulmin's words, its ability to be "deployed."[26] "A good model," notes David Hawkins, "like a good map, is rich: it guides us, under suitable interpretation, to many true statements. Without necessarily consisting of statements at all, or of statements intended as literally true, it facilitates understanding."[27] To the extent it successfully does this, the model is *useful* and thus for our purposes, good.

BOX 3.2

The usefulness of a model may well determine its success regardless of its validity. For example, there have been various models of the astronomical relationships among the stars, planets, and earth throughout the centuries. For many generations the earth was viewed as the center of the universe. The early Greeks saw the stars as "sources of light fastened to a revolving shell of hollow space" with earth at its center. While such models proved sufficient for a period of time, their lack of "utility" (e.g., their inability to account for certain "wandering stars" and the seasonal shift of some heavenly bodies) soon resulted in modifications. New models were developed that allowed for the movements of certain wandering stars (i.e., the planets) and seasonal changes, but the essential view of the universe and the earth's central location remained unchanged.

But these modified models, too, proved less than entirely satisfactory over time, and eventually there developed a model that posited the sun at the center of a solar system of orbiting planets. This discovery by Copernicus (1473–1543) was followed by an even more useful model developed by Kepler (1571–1630) which not only posited elliptical orbits for the planets around the sun, but also allowed astronomers to calculate the maximum distances planets traveled from the sun in their orbit. Newton's (1642–1727) laws of motion and gravity made the model even more "deployable" by placing the solar system within the context of a more general model of the physical universe and the forces that seemed to guide it.

See Moshe F. Rubinstein, *Patterns of Problem Solving* (Englewood Cliffs, NJ: Prentice-Hall, Inc., 1975), pp. 213–215.

Analogies and metaphors are particular forms of models that have proved quite useful. An *analogy* posits as a model for one phenomenon a representation appropriate to another. So, for instance, students of Eastern

European politics have frequently applied a solar system model to describe relationships between the Soviet Union and the states bordering it on the west. The image used is that of a sun surrounded by satellites that behave as if in fixed orbit around their star. None of this is meant literally, of course, but the implications of the analogy are quite interesting, especially in the historical context of the Cold War era.

Metaphors, on the other hand, actually suggest a "literal transference" from one representation of the world to a different situation. For example, the use of the solar system model to describe and explain the construction and behavior of the hydrogen atom was intended as a literal transference. In 1913, Neils Bohr hypothesized that the relationship between the positively charged nucleus of the hydrogen atom and its negatively charged electron was similar to that which the solar system model implied existed between the sun and one of the orbiting planets. This transposition of the characteristics of one model to a different situation eventually led to the development of quantum mechanics.[28]

Thus the Copernican-Keplerian-Newtonian model has proven itself highly deployable not only as a representation of the solar system, but also as an analogy and metaphor put to use in unique and creative ways. In this sense we regard analogies and metaphors as types of problem-solving models.

If we are to make extensive use of models in problem solving generally and public policy thinking specifically, we must somehow develop criteria for further evaluating the usefulness of models. One generally accepted rule on this matter is that to evaluate a model you should "test derivations rather than assumptions. . . ."[29] That is, a model must be assessed in terms of its ability to provide us with a useful understanding of the world, not only in terms of how closely it resembles reality. Following this logic, *the greater the number of useful derivations one can obtain from a model, the greater its value relative to alternative models.* The model of Eastern European relationships as a solar system has given U.S. foreign affairs analysts some insight into the relationships within that region, but the model is less useful for explaining relationships in other parts of the globe. In contrast, a pluralistic international model that emphasizes the historic and political interests of nations provides a better understanding of antagonisms within the communist bloc as well as in Southeast Asia and the Middle East.

The key questions to ask of any model are: Does it simplify and clarify our thinking? Does it identify important forces in the environment? Does it allow us to communicate a comprehension of the world or that particular part of interest to us? Does it facilitate inquiry and suggest solutions where needed? These are some of the concerns we must keep in mind in choosing and using models.

Two Useful Models

To better understand what characterizes good and useful models, let us consider two that have proven extremely successful for problem solvers in several fields, including the study of public policy. These are the system and market exchange models.

The System Model. The definition applied to systems is extremely broad. In its most basic form, a system is any set of elements standing in relation to one another, that is, a pattern of interrelationships.[30] Given this broad view, almost everything is a system of some sort. Systems can be found at various levels and include atoms, clocks, thermostats, biological circulatory systems, the human being, legislatures, entire societies, language, and so on *ad infinitum*.

But not all systems are alike. One basic distinction can be made between those that are static and others that are dynamic. *Static systems* are relatively unaffected by changes in their surroundings. The word "relatively" is important here for there is probably no system that is completely divorced from its surroundings. Nevertheless, the brick and mortar structure (i.e., system) of the building you live in is extremely stable and not likely to change in any substantial way under normal circumstances. *Dynamic systems*, on the other hand, depend on external conditions to determine their state of being. In other words, they change in response to externally derived inputs, which tend to vary. These variations effect the system which, in turn, influence its outputs or production.

Still a further elaboration of the model occurs when we consider representations of a dynamic system in which the output has an impact on the system's input. This is not characteristic of all dynamic systems; for example, clocks and simple machines traditionally do not react to their own output. However, there are many systems that do, and this reaction is accomplished through a mechanism called the *feedback loop*. A common example of such a system is the home thermostat, which triggers a heating system when the temperature (input) of a house falls below a pre-set level and shuts off that system when the heat (output) has raised the room temperature to a desired level. The thermostat acts as the "brain" of the system, issuing instructions to the furnace in order to maintain the preferred temperature. The study of such self-controlling mechanisms is called *cybernetics*.[31] The human body is another example of a dynamic system. An increase in the temperature of its environment causes the body to sweat in order to cool the body; exposure to cold temperature causes the blood vessels to constrict, conserving body heat. These changes in body function in response to inputs are controlled by the central nervous system, acting without our consciousness.

Dynamic system models vary in complexity from the extremely basic to the highly sophisticated. They have proved useful in fields such as engineering, computer technology, and the social sciences. In political science, the system model has been adapted to study both the political processes of a single nation as well as the interactions between many actors. One of the best known formulations is that proposed by David Easton who defines the *political system* as including all actions, activities, and relationships that are concerned with "the authoritative allocation of values." The political system (essentially all political and governmental actions) exists within an environment that is both domestic and international. The inputs to the system are demands by the citizens as well as from abroad for public action aimed at resolving problems. The system also receives "support" from the citizens in the form of loyalty, participation, and law-abiding behavior. The political authority, as shown in Figure 3.1, responds to the demands by formulating laws, taking actions, and making other policy decisions. The feedback loop represents the capacity of the people to evaluate the impact of these outputs and to provide support or press for further change. The political system model has proved fruitful in generating new theoretical insights into the process of political development and by its easy adaptation for use in studying other political practices.

The Market Model. The market model represents a simple view of economic decisions. The economist's model of market exchange is a form of dynamic system, but it has intellectual roots and historical development that are quite distinct from the system model. In its most basic form,[32] the market model represents exchange behavior between two parties: a household possessing fundamental factors of production (i.e., land, labor, and capital), and a

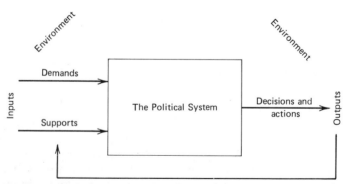

Figure 3.1. Simplified model of a political system. (Adapted from David Easton, *A Framework for Political Analysis,* Englewood Cliffs, NJ: Prentice-Hall, Inc., 1965, p. 112.)

ON THE NATURE AND USEFULNESS OF MODELS 41

business with the technology to convert those factors into consumable products.

Households are regarded in the market model as signal decision-making units that have as their objective the maximization of whatever satisfaction (called utility) they can derive from the exchange of the factors they have to offer. In other words, households do not hold on to the factors of production, but rather exchange them for rent (land), wages (labor), or interest (capital) which can then be used to purchase products from which the individual households can derive utility. The decisions households make, therefore, are how to earn and spend their incomes.

Business units possessing the technology by which the factors of production can be converted into consumable products also have a goal, but in this case it is the maximization of surplus value, or profit. Profit is the amount of value left by the sale of a consumable product after costs have been met. Thus, the business will try to charge as much as it can get for its product over costs. Those costs are determined by what the business unit must pay to households in the form of rents, wages, and interest. What they must decide is (1) what they wish to produce, (2) how they are to produce it, and (3) what resources they will use in the production process.

At the heart of the market model is the interaction between these two parties. The interaction takes place in marketplaces, of which there are at least two. First, there is the factor market, where households offer their respective capabilities to business. Households come to this market with a supply of production factors they are willing to exchange in certain quantities at certain prices. The general rule is that their willingness to supply a factor will vary directly with the price a business is willing to pay in rent, wages, or interest. This is represented in Figure 3.2a as the *supply curve*.

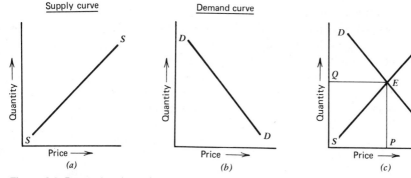

Figure 3.2. Demand and supply curves.

Business comes to that same market with a schedule of demands; that is, they are willing to pay a certain price for a given supply of factors. The rule governing their demands is that the greater the price for a factor, the lower the quantity demanded. The resulting *demand curve* is illustrated in Figure 3.2 b.

Given the differences in supply and demand schedules involved, the interaction among the parties takes the form of give-and-take bargaining, which eventually resolves itself in an agreement (see Figure 3.2c) where a certain quantity of a factor Q is supplied for a given price P. The agreement thus achieved represents an equilibrium position E for the exchange where both parties are reasonably satisfied with the outcome. The dynamic behind this exchange process is called the law of supply and demand.

Similar interactions take place in the product market. In this market, however, the positions of households and businesses are turned about. The households play the role of demanders here, for they seek to purchase products the businesses are supplying. Again there are schedules of supply and demand, and again the law of supply and demand brings about a satisfactory solution in the form of equilibrium exchange.

There are, however, certain conditions that must be met before the exchange between businesses and households can take place:

1. The condition of *increasing cost*. Under all circumstances the cost of producing or supplying each additional unit must be greater than the last. It must cost a household more to supply an additional unit of land, labor, or capital, and it must cost a business more to produce the second item than the first. If this were not the case—if in other words, there was a situation of "decreasing costs" or "economies of scale"—there would be a tendency toward monopoloy.

2. The need for *perfect competition* in all markets. Where any particular demander (monopsony) or supplier (monopoly) is able to arbitrarily control an aspect of an exchange (for example, price or wages) the market will not be capable of reaching a solution satisfactory to both sides. A *monopoly* exists when a single economic unit controls the supply of goods or services; a *monopsony* exists when a single unit controls demand.

3. The *exclusion principle*. All factors of production, technologies being applied to them, and transactions between buyers and sellers in a given market must belong exclusively to the individual parties involved and no one else. If not, the result would be what economists call spillovers, that is, effects (both positive and negative) that some third party (some other household or business) is neither paying nor being reimbursed for. Thus, auto emissions

impose *spillover costs* on a household's neighbors for they do not receive full compensation for the damage being done to their lungs. It is also possible that *spillover benefits* result, for the car might provide a household with an alternative means of transportation and thus relieve some of the pressure on local buses or commuter railroads that serve the society of households or businesses.
4. The *absence of public goods*. *Public goods* are extreme cases of spillover effects. The most commonly cited examples of public goods are ocean lighthouses and national defense. These are products that cannot be packaged and sold as units, yet they may also be necessary to the sufficient functioning of a society.
5. *Complete and total knowledge and mobility* among all parties to a market exchange. All buyers and sellers must be fully aware of their alternatives and those of others in the marketplace. In addition, each must be able to move with the trends that the marketplace's law of supply and demand mandates.

It should be obvious that the model of the market exchange used by economists is an unrealistic one given the conditions it demands. The low costs of mass production, the lack of perfect competition, the inability to create exclusiveness of possession or to eliminate the need for public goods, and the inevitable presence of market ignorance and immobility are common to real-life economic exchanges. But if the model is so far from reality, why has it been so successful? One reason is found in the model's ability to provide useful insights into the actual functions of markets. Economic analysis, built on the foundation provided by this simple market model, has proven extremely useful not only among students of private sector exchanges, but also among those who focus on public policy decisions regarding government taxation and spending, interest rates, and the availability of money.

Despite their limitations dynamic system models and the market exchange constructs have been successful. We will be able to apply variants of these two models to some of the analytic problems of public policy that this book examines. Not all the models we apply in this book are derived from system or market constructs, but many are related or can be used in tangent with them. Ultimately, what makes them successful is their usefulness for solving the analytic problems we face.

MODEL-BUILDING

The major role played by models in problem solving raises the question of how these useful representations of the world are derived. If we assume the perspective of the information processing school of thought, models can be regarded as part and parcel of human thinking and are therefore inherent to us all. "Every person approaches . . . problems . . . with the help of models."[33] At times these models take the form of subconsciously applied mental constructs; at other times they are used formally and explicitly. *The conscious use of models and awareness of the assumptions they reflect is the key to understanding public policies.* As was noted in Chapter 2, public policy thinking involves the application of problem-solving techniques to questions relevant to policy. What must be stressed is that the application process is accomplished with eyes (and mind) wide open.

There are essentially two sources of problem-solving models, and both are relevant to the policy thinker's tasks. First, the problem solver can construct a model from scratch. Second, the problem solver may reach into the current inventory of available models and adapt some of them for use in a given situation.

The difficulty of *model-building* varies according to the nature of the problem being faced. Obviously, a complex or ambiguous problem will be more difficult to handle than one that is simple and clear. But the inherent difficulty of a problem is not the only determinant of how easy the modeling process will prove to be. As with problem solving in general, model-building depends on the attitude and orientation of the model-builder. The ability to think abstractly, to use existing models, to see derivations from a model, and to evaluate the model's usefulness are all-important skills.

We use a famous attempt at world modeling to illustrate the task involved in each of the six steps in model construction. Our examples are drawn from the study titled *The Limits to Growth,* published in 1972.[34] Sponsored by the prestigious Club of Rome, this study presents the work of a team of scholars from Massachusetts Institute of Technology (MIT) who tried to predict trends in world resources. Although the conclusions and methods of *The Limits to Growth* study have been challenged, the study itself does provide us with an excellent example of modeling.

Step 1. Examine the problematic phenomenon or situation carefully and proceed to factor (i.e., divide) it into simpler, more manageable problems.[35] This first step is intended to keep the problem solver from addressing a problem too complex to be modeled, as well as to render the problem more manageable. The Club of Rome study, for instance, was initially defined in terms of a general "world problematique" which plagues humankind. "The intent of the project," noted William Watts, "is to examine the complex of problems troubling men of all nations: poverty in the midst of plenty; degradation of the environment; loss of faith in institutions; uncontrolled urban spread; insecurity of employment; alienation of youth; rejection of traditional values; and inflation and other monetary and economic disruptions."[36]

MODEL-BUILDING

This broadly defined problem would be difficult (if not impossible) to approach were it not for the fact that it could be factored into smaller problem "packages." In fact, the MIT team redefined the problem into five distinct yet interrelated packages: "accelerating industrialization, rapid population growth, widespread malnutrition, depletion of nonrenewable resources, and a deteriorating environment."[37] As we will see, dividing the general "world problematique" into these smaller packages does not mean the more general problem was obscured. On the contrary, through their modeling approach, the MIT team tied these separate problems back together to create a single dynamic system model based on many relationships.

Step 2. Establish the purpose of the model.[38] What do you want it to do? Should it describe? Explain? Forecast? Judge? Prescribe solutions? There are any number of uses for different models, but *no single model is appropriate to all uses*. Because a model in one form may be appropriate for describing, we should not assume it will suffice for any other purpose. Therefore, as early as possible one must make an explicit statement of the objectives to be achieved through the model's application.

In *The Limits to Growth*, the MIT team set forth its purpose quite early: to understand the causes of various problematic trends (as defined in step 1), to uncover the interrelations among them, and to determine "the implications as much as one hundred years in the future."[39] In this way they were able to specify some explanatory, descriptive, and predictive objectives for which their models were to be constructed. This awareness plays a crucial role in the steps that follow.

Step 3. Observe facts relevant to the problematic phenomenon or situation.[40] While this might seem too obvious to warrant separate standing, it is a major step—one too critical in the model-building process to leave unstated. Problems are all too frequently perceived and defined without reference to the empirical facts of a situation. The problem solver must first decide what facts are needed to study a given problem and then acquire that information. It is impossible to construct a model about, say, criminal activity in Houston without knowing the patterns of arrests, crimes, victims, weapons, and demographic information.

Members of the MIT team identified and collected facts relevant to an analysis of world growth. They predicted the rate of growth for the world's industrial production (about 5 percent annually) and for the world's populations (double in 33 years). They noted that the present world population growth rate is 2.1 percent per year, occurring to a considerable degree in less developed countries and "corresponding to a doubling time of 33 years." They also considered trends in available levels of foods, nonrenewable resources, and pollution, and found that projecting these into the future indicated patterns that do not look promising for humankind.[41] This data was presented in such a way as to fit the various facts together into larger chunks of information that indicate interrelationships among the various parts. In this sense, the MIT team not only presented their readers with "observed facts," but simultaneously demonstrated the next two steps in modeling.

Step 4. List the elements that may relate to the model's purpose. Select those that are believed to be the most relevant to the problem at hand. Arrange these relevant elements into chunks or clusters that reflect "strong structural, functional, or interactive connections. . . . . ."[42] Observations made in step three should not only provide the model-builder with bits of information, but also give some insight into the many elements that make up a problematic situation or phenomenon.

The MIT team examined numerous elements of problems they had defined in their first step. For instance, they took special note of population size, birth rates, death rates, population age, food produced per capita, food consumed per capita, capital investment growth rates per capita, industrial capital growth, nutritional composition of the human diet, flows of DDT in the environment, copper and steel production, oil and natural gas consumption rates, and on and on through numerous factors. Of course, in presenting their list of relevant elements in *The Limits to Growth,* the MIT team only incidentally commented on the total number of possibly related elements and those dropped from the potential model as being not quite as important as those included. But of the elements remaining, all were aggregated into factors and subgroupings of factors based on reasonably strong relationships. At the apex of these various aggregations were five major clusters of factored variables: population, capital, food, natural resources, and pollution. With the help of computer technology, the MIT team was able to perform the complex data analysis of the numerous components to the problem.[43]

Step 5. Consider these aggregates and the facts they represent relative to the purpose of your proposed model. Try to find patterns or relationships among these factors that will aid you in fulfilling that purpose. Use analogies and other methods to facilitate the task.[44] Here is where speculation, creativity, and "brainstorming" come into play. There are several means for completing this step. We have already considered the use of analogies and metaphors in previous discussions. But analogies are only the beginning, for several other techniques might prove useful in uncovering various patterns and relationships. For example, after establishing various relationships between major elements, some previously unconsidered linkages among factors might show up.

The MIT team demonstrate this approach when it considered the factors that compose the aggregate of world population size. That aggregate reflects interactions between three factors: population size at the beginning of a given period; births in that period; and deaths during that same period. The number of births in a given year depends on the fertility rate and the actual size of the population. If births exceed deaths, the world population grows.[45] The MIT team also used simple graphic depictions to portray relationships between elements in the model as well as between the five main components of the world system. Such figures can be easily translated into mathematical calculations that can be carried out by a computer. The actual projections of *The Limits to Growth* project were produced this way.

In Figure 3.3a, the simple relationships between population size and food per capita are illustrated using arrows to indicate patterns of influence. The closed circle in the diagram demonstrates that this is a dynamic system with a pattern of feedback. Any growth in population reduces the amount of food per capita, as a result mortality increases, thus decreasing the total population.[46] However, the world model is concerned with the behavior of conscious beings who try to alter their circumstances. In Figure 3.3b, we see another feedback loop related to the first. If less food per capita is available than people want, then more capital is devoted to agricultural production to produce more food per capita, thus mortality rates fall, probably leading to increased population. The MIT group built similar models for many relationships within the world model.

Still another aid for accomplishing Step 5 is for the model-builder to write down (in symbolic form if possible) obvious points of information about the factors involved and the relationships among them. This exercise can prove highly suggestive, for often there are things we take for granted that, under scrutiny, can lead to many important insights. For example, we

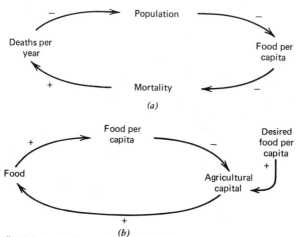

Figure 3.3. Feedback loops in the world model. *(a)* Food supply and mortality. *(b)* Food supply and production increases. (Source: Meadows, et. al., *The Limits to Growth*, 2nd edition, New York: Universe Books, 1974, p. 99.)

know population will increase if birth rates rise and mortality rates remain constant for the same period. But take another point of view. Does the increase in population size affect births per year? If so, under what circumstances? Immediately? In ten years, or twenty? What if the death rate increases? What impact will a war have? Or a fatal epidemic among teenagers? Or an increase in pollution-related mortality? All these questions—and perhaps some answers relevant to the model—can be generated by merely considering what would otherwise be dismissed as obvious information.

Step 5 can also be achieved if the model-builder considers specific historical examples of some of the relationships or patterns being examined. Using such empirical references, the model-builder can obtain factual insights based on both sense data and historical records. In assessing the "world problematique" for example, we might consider the impact of the potato famine in Ireland as an example of the relationship between food and population size; or we could look to the growing population of India for lessons concerning the influence of population on food supply. These explorations of empirical examples can pay off in other ways, for example, by supplying analogies that may be explored in considerable detail. In short, there are many paths for the model-builder to explore in the search for a useful simplification of reality.

Step 6. Elaborate upon the constructed model where necessary; simplify where possible.[47] A model is supposed to make a complex world more manageable for the problem solver; so the ultimate objective is to develop a model that fulfills its objective by applying the simplest possible form. Still, simplification should not take priority over the need to develop a model that is at least useful for those who apply it. This may mean that the resulting construct might seem unwieldy and complex, although it is perhaps pared down to basics. For instance, the complete "World Model" developed by the MIT team included over 100 variables, with multiple interrelationships and dozens of feedback loops.

The six steps elaborated here and the example of The Club of Rome study speak to the fact that model-building can be difficult and time consuming. And even when undertaken by experts, the results are bound to be less than ideal. "The model we have constructed," confesses the MIT team, "is, like every other model, imperfect, oversimplified, and unfinished."[48] So it would be with "every other model." Yet even imperfect and unfinished models will probably be used and reused by other model-builders.

SOURCES OF MODELS

If we had to begin all problem solving from "scratch," this would indeed be a difficult world to live in. Luckily, we are a species of learners—

individually as well as collectively. That is, once we develop an appropriate tool or process for doing something, we tend to retain that means (or its idea) for future use or reference. We don't reinvent the hammer if there is a nail to be driven. Instead, we reach into a tool box and draw upon its accumulated resources for our tasks. Sometimes we make use of those tools in a way that is out of the ordinary—as when we use a hammer to shatter a glass. At other times we substitute alternative tools for accomplishing the hammer's function—as when we use a brick, board, or shoe to drive in a nail.

Models are the tools of problem solving. Like the woodworker's tools, models are products of human inventiveness, and they can be valued for their utility. Also like such tools, they come in a variety of forms and can range from those applicable in only a limited number of specific situations (e.g., the Phillipshead screwdriver) to the multipurpose types (e.g., the standard hammer). They can be adapted like some tools to a variety of situations, and it is not out of the question to find substitutes for any particular model among all those available.

Unlike woodworker's tools, which necessarily take a "hard" form (because they contend with a "hard" reality, e.g., nails and screws), models are tools of the mind, heuristic devices used to solve specific problems. Thus they can exist apart from any empirical reality. To be sure, many models are rendered empirically "hard" when they are verbalized, transcribed into symbolic (i.e., mathematical) form, or represented by some physical construct (e.g., when an engineer or architect exhibits a scale model of some project). Taking these forms, models are likely to be recorded and communicated among those who might have some use for them. In this way they become part of a body of knowledge and can be stored until retrieved for dissemination and possible use in problematic situations.

However, the storage of models is far from uniform and systematic. There are no model banks, libraries, or catalogues to which we can refer given a specific problem. Instead, there are a multitude of diverse sources from which one obtains information on portions of the total model inventory at our disposal.

University instruction is one important source. Lectures and textbooks in disciplines from electrical engineering to biology to anthropology to political science devote a great deal of time and space to describing and demonstrating the use of models commonly used to study the subject. The classroom dissemination of information on models and their use may not be explicit; in fact, it may not even be intentional. Yet, to a considerable degree, that is one of the primary functions of university teaching: to provide students with the basic conceptual and cognitive tools (e.g., models) that will help them analyze issues that they will confront in the future.

Still another source of models are the voluminous collections of manuals, handbooks, and guidebooks used by professionals in their respective fields. For every professional—from accountants to auto mechanics, from city planners to plumbers, from physicians to bus drivers—models play a crucial role in carrying out their jobs. Information about these models and their application are often made explicit in instruction manuals or similar forms of occupational reference aids.

Of course, there is always the primary storehouse of models: the human mind. As learning creatures we have a phenomenal capacity to accumulate and hold for future use various models of reality. Some of these are directly related to our everyday activities, such as the model or map of the geographic area we traverse to get from home to class. While we use these all the time, we give them little thought after they have been committed to memory—that is, until some event makes it necessary for us to consider alternate routes. When detours become necessary, we are forced to explore models (maps) which we have not used for a time, but which have been stored in our subconscious for a long period. In such situations, you might say we have reached back into our mental "tool boxes" and retrieved a model that might prove useful in dealing with a unique situation.

To summarize, there are a multitude of models already developed and available for use, but they are stored in locations so diverse and scattered that it would be impossible to consider (or even attempt to know) the entire inventory. The dilemma we face, therefore, is developing a model-selecting capability to complement our knowledge of model-building.

CHOOSING A MODEL

While the ultimate basis for selecting a model is its usefulness, other criteria can be applied even before one begins to test for utility. There are likely to be situations where one faces the possibility of applying several models to a problem, but due to limited resources or time, it is necessary to concentrate on only one or two of the available constructs. Under such conditions one can ask a series of basic questions about each model and rank them based on the answers obtained.[49]

To what extent does each model address facts of the problem under consideration? That is, how relevant is the model to the problematic situation being tackled? The greater its *relevance,* the more preference it should be given.

In some situations the choice among alternative models will seem obvious at first glance. For example, when dealing with the issues of government regulation of railroads, it is clear that the economic market model is more relevant than a model of the solar system. There are also situations where the choice is extremely difficult. For example, there are several models applicable to the problem of poverty in the United States.

CHOOSING A MODEL 51

One of these models focuses on the impoverished persons of this country, another concentrates on the factors in the economy that perpetuate poverty, while still one other speaks to the "poverty bureaucracy." Each is relevant to a different facet of the poverty policy problem, yet each gives a different picture of the situation. As long as a problem is generally defined, selecting appropriate models will be difficult. The more specific the stated problem (e.g., What causes poverty to be passed on from one generation to the next?) the more likely one will be able to apply the relevance criterion to the selection of appropriate models.

To what extent does the model bring to bear known solutions to the problem at hand? Preference should be given to models with demonstrated effectiveness.

Although previous successes do not guarantee present or future success, one may use the past as an indicator of a model's usefulness. What worked before might just work again. The solar system model was used over and over again by both journalists and scholars who studied the relations among Eastern European states during the early part of the Cold War era. It seemed useful as both an explanation and predictor of the foreign policy behavior of the U.S.S.R. and its "satellite" countries. It was right, therefore, for many of those analysts to use that model as a primary tool whenever possible. However, even such useful tools wear out and must be replaced.

How adaptable is the model? Preference should be given to models that are flexible when faced with new or changing circumstances.

A model of a constantly changing world will itself have to be in motion, or at least be flexible enough to maintain some relation to a turbulent environment. In this sense, an open model is more valuable than one that closely resembles some specific situation. A model of the U.S. economy that assumes that inflation and rising unemployment are mutually exclusive conditions inversely related to each other must be regarded as inflexible in this day and age when the problem of stagflation combines both trends in one time period. A flexible model of the economy would leave such a condition neither undescribed nor unexplained.

How rich is the model? Is the model fertile enough to generate interesting insights when applied to problem solving?

Certain models used by social science today are so rich that they often become causes unto themselves. The Marxist perspective of capitalist society is such a model, for its application to a policy issue or public problem can tell a great deal about the forces that may determine a current state of affairs. We shall see this fertile model at work in a later chapter. The market model is also valuable in this sense. Suffice it to say for now that highly fertile models will likely prove more useful than those that do not.

How simple is the model? The smaller the number of assumptions used in the model, the better. This criterion must be seen in light of the usefulness a model must have, for it is not simplicity in the narrow or arbitrary sense that is intended. Rather, it is a matter of keeping the complexity of a model's assumptionns down to a minimum given a certain level of usefulness. Another assumption or given should be added to a model if the construct becomes more useful with the addition; otherwise, one is merely wasting time and energy. Thus, we can now develop a model that can predict a voter's party identification with some degree of certainty. With such a model we accomplish that task without considering events in a voter's life; that is, all we need is data on his or her background (e.g., parent party identification, income, education, place of residence). Information on how the voter feels today can be taken into account, but such considerations do not add much to the usefulness of the model.

How easily can the model be enriched? A model that can be modified and further elaborated in interesting directions should be preferred.

This is one of the great attributes of the economist's market model, for its simple form provides a base on which many elaborations can be structured. Actors (e.g., government or firms) can be added or subtracted; conditions can be changed; market pressures manipulated at will. This is also among the best qualities of the Copernican solar system model which was enriched by Kepler and Newton and the many astronomers who have followed in their footsteps.

Are the assertions made by the model testable? The more one is able to verify or disprove statements derived from a model's assumptions, the more that model is to be preferred.

Not all models are valued for the quality of their derivations and predictions. Some models are quite sufficient as idealizations and pure abstract categorizations of phenomena. But where models are the source of assertions and hypotheses, one should insist that these be susceptible to empirical testing. Thus, models of poverty in America that attribute impoverishment to the misallocation of capital investment to non-poverty areas of the country should be preferred to models that attribute poverty to the "will of God." The latter is untestable and thus does us no good, while the former can be examined for its credibility.

These seven criteria cannot and will not provide us with sufficient grounds for adopting a particular model for a problem solving situation. Each indicates what kind of model is *likely* to be of greater use, but none of these actually measures usefulness. That can only be known when the model is selected and at least partially applied. This means that to a considerable extent, the process of model selection for policy analysis (or any kind of problem solving situation where a specific model is not predetermined to be the solution) is a risky undertaking. The choice of an appropriate model is a difficult task, one that can consume much time and effort for those who are uninformed about the models most commonly used in given problematic situations.

The last point is extremely important, for the ability to select from among the enormous variety of potentially useful models is limited at the onset by our inability to know all relevant models. In this book we will make use of many of the most common models applied by public policy thinkers. In doing so, it is hoped that you not only become familiar with the problem-solving approach to public policy studies, but also that you develop a sense of the range of tools available for analyzing policy.

To summarize, models relevant to studying public policy take a variety of forms and come from a number of disciplines. Complete, representational models of structures and processes such as the system or market models, are only one model type. Sometimes models take the form of classification schemes or typologies based on certain characteristics, while others are more closely related to maps and blueprints. Some models represent mental processes like the "scientific method," or "cost-benefit analysis," and can be applied to many different activities in the public sphere. In the chapters that follow, we consider models that can be used to describe, explain, and evaluate public policies. Each of these makes a distinctive contribution to our understanding of policies. They are not mutually exclusive, for you will see that the lines between description, explanation, and evaluation are not hard and fast. However, it is the thesis of this approach that all three kinds of analysis are necessary to completely understand any public policy. By adopting the problem-solving perspective, we can choose and construct appropriate models for understanding broad or narrow questions of public policy.

ENDNOTES

1. Moshe F. Rubinstein, *Patterns of Problem Solving* (Englewood Cliffs, NJ: Prentice-Hall, 1975), pp. 2–3; also see Marc Belth, *The Process of Thinking* (New York: David McKay Co., Inc., 1977), pp. 15–19.
2. Herbert A. Simon and Allen Newell, "Human Problem Solving: The State of the Theory in 1970," *American Psychologist*, 26 (February 1971), p. 149.
3. Ibid., pp. 149–153; also see A. J. Newell, J. C. Shaw, and H. A. Simon, *The Processes of Creating Thinking* (Santa Monica, CA: The RAND Corporation, 1959); and Herbert A. Simon, *Administrative Behavior: A Study of Decision-Making Processes in Administrative Organizations*, 2nd edition (New York: The Free Press, 1957), Chapter 7.
4. See William J. J. Gordon, *Synectics: The Development of Creative Capacity* (New York: Collier Books, 1961), p. 11.

5. Rubinstein, *Patterns of Problem Solving*, p. 8 (emphasis added).
6. Joseph R. Royce, *The Encapsulated Man: An Interdisciplinary Essay on the Search for Meaning* (New York: Van Nostrand Rheinhold Co., 1964), p. 30.
7. For a well-written and informative exploration of human intelligence, see Carl Sagan, *The Dragons of Eden: Speculations on the Evolution of Human Intelligence* (New York: Random House, 1977).
8. This is despite the fact that the human brain is capable of holding trillions of information bits. See George Miller, "The Magical Number Seven, Plus or Minus Two," *Psychological Review* (1956), cited in Rubinstein, *Patterns of Problem Solving*, p. 8. Also see Sagan, *The Dragons of Eden*, pp. 40–43.
9. Most of the discussion on chunking and patterning is derived from Rubinstein, *Patterns of Problem Solving*, pp. 8–13.
10. Cited in ibid., p. 13.
11. Ibid., p. 14; also see Gordon, *Synectics*, p. 18.
12. Rubinstein, *Patterns of Problem Solving*, pp. 16–17.
13. Ibid., p. 14; Gordon, *Synectics*, pp. 18–19.
14. Gordon, *Synectics*, p. 19; also Rubinstein, *Patterns of Problem Solving*, pp. 19–21.
15. Rubinstein, *Patterns of Problem Solving*, pp. 14–16; see Gordon, *Synectics*, Chapter Two.
16. Rubinstein, *Patterns of Problem Solving*, pp. 17–19.
17. Richard Rose, *What Is Governing?: Purpose and Policy in Washington* (Englewood Cliffs, NJ: Prentice-Hall, Inc., 1978), p. 15.
18. Rubinstein, *Patterns of Problem Solving*, p. 19.
19. Ibid., pp. 193–196.
20. Stephen Toulmin, *The Philosophy of Science: An Introduction* (New York: Harper and Row, Publishers, 1960), pp. 34–35.
21. Simon and Newell note that models take three basic forms: verbal, mathematical, and analogical. In each form models take on "distances" from the reality they represent. See Herbert A. Simon and Allen Newell, "Models: Their Uses and Limitations," in Leonard D. White (ed.), *The State of the Social Sciences* (Chicago: University of Chicago Press, 1956), pp. 66–83. Also see the discussion in Rubinstein, *Patterns of Problem Solving*, pp. 294–208.
22. Simon and Newell, "Models," p. 67.
23. Belth, *The Process of Thinking*, p. 57.
24. See Kenneth E. Boulding, *The Image: Knowledge in Life and Society* (Ann Arbor, MI: The University of Michigan Press, 1956.)
25. The distinction is developed in Belth, *The Process of Thinking*, especially pp. 66–67.
26. Toulmin, *The Philosophy of Science*, pp. 36–37.
27. David Hawkins, *The Language of Nature: An Essay in the Philosophy of Science* (Garden City, NY: Doubleday and Co., Inc., 1967), pp. 38–39.
28. Rubinstein, *Patterns of Problem Solving*, pp. 217–219.
29. Charles A. Lave and James G. March, *An Introduction to Models in the Social Sciences* (New York: Harper and Row, Publishers, 1975), p. 53.
30. This basic definition is adapted from Ludwig von Bertalanffy, *General System Theory: Foundations, Development, Applications* (New York: George Braziller,

KEY TERMS

Inc., 1968), Chapter 1. For a related definition of system, see Rubinstein, *Pattens of Problem Solving*, p. 409.
31. On general system theory, see von Bertalanffy, *General System Theory* and the work of Kenneth E. Boulding. On cybernetics, see the work of Norbert Wiener, especially *The Human Use of Human Beings: Cybernetics and Society* (New York: Avon Books, 1967).
32. Much of what follows is from Robert H. Haveman, *The Economics of the Public Sector*, 2nd edition (Santa Barbara, CA: John Wiley & Sons, Inc., 1976), Chapters 2 and 3. Also see the two-volume work by Kenneth E. Boulding, *Economic Analysis*, 4th edition (New York: Harper and Row, Publishers, 1966); and C. E. Ferguson and S. Charles Maurice, *Economic Analysis*, revised edition (Homewood, IL: Richard D. Irwin, Inc., 1974).
33. Lave and March, *An Introduction to Models in the Social Sciences*, p. 4.
34. Donella H. Meadows et al., *The Limits to Growth: A Report For The Club of Rome's Project on the Predicament of Mankind*, 2nd edition (New York: Universe Books, 1974), p. 26.
35. See William T. Morris, "On the Art of Modeling," in Ralph M. Stogdill (ed.), *The Process of Model-Building in the Behavioral Sciences* (New York: W. W. Norton and Co., 1970), pp. 83–84.
36. From the Foreword in Meadows et al., *The Limits to Growth*, p. x.
37. Ibid., p. 21.
38. Morris, "On the Art of Modeling," p. 84; Rubinstein, *Patterns of Problem Solving*, p. 197.
39. Meadows et al., *The Limits to Growth*, p. 21.
40. Lave and March, *An Introduction to Models in the Social Sciences*, p. 19.
41. Meadows et al., *The Limits to Growth*, Chapters I and II.
42. Rubinstein, *Patterns of Problem Solving*, p. 197.
43. Meadows et al., *The Limits to Growth*, Chapter III.
44. Lave and March, *An Introduction to Models in the Social Sciences*, p. 20; Morris, "On the Art of Modeling," pp. 84–85.
45. Meadows et al., *The Limits to Growth*, p. 96.
46. Meadows et al., ibid., pp. 98–99.
47. Morris, "On the Art of Modeling," p. 91.
48. Meadows et al., *The Limits to Growth*, p. 21.
49. See Lave and March, *An Introduction to Models in the Social Sciences*, Chapter Three; also Morris, "On the Art of Modeling."

KEY TERMS
Analogies
Associational Constraints
Behaviorist Perspective
Chunking
Deployability
Dynamic Systems
Exclusion Principle

Functional Constraints
"Hard" Models
Heuristics
Information-processing Perspective
Inputs/Outputs
Law of Supply and Demand
Market Model
Metaphors
Model
Model-building (six steps)
Model-selection (seven criteria)
Monopoly
Monopsony
Patterning
Perfect Competition
Political System
Public Goods
Rational-problem Solving Approach
"Soft" Models
Spillover Costs and Benefits
Static Systems
System Model
"World-view" Constraints

CHAPTER 4

Policy Description

THE NATURE OF DESCRIPTION

Policy description is the most paradoxical among all analytic tasks. Although it can be the simplest task, it can also prove to be the most crucial step in thinking about government statements and actions. It can be simple because it usually involves the application of familiar concepts and categories to a public policy. In addition, suitable descriptive models—typologies—are relatively easy to develop once the analyst is aware of the problems and issues involved. As will become increasingly evident, when compared with policy explanation (see Chapter 6) or the assessment of policy consequences (see Chapter 8), the development and application of descriptive techniques may not be as demanding as the other tasks. In other words, it is generally easier to describe a policy to someone than it is to explain it or determine its impact.

At the same time the task of description is by far the most important any policy analyst will face. The description provides the foundation on which all further study is built; if that foundation is weak, the analysis that follows will be weak. Obviously the explanation of a government statement will be meaningless unless we understand the statement. For example, we cannot expect to explain a foreign policy before we know what it is. Nor can we get around description in our efforts at determining a policy's consequences. In addition, if we are to judge the impact of a government action or statement, we must be clear about what it entailed. Most significantly, descriptions can also determine the "direction" of an analysis, for example, whether it will focus on social or political factors or economic or cultural variables.

Implied in this perspective is the fact that there is no such thing as an objective policy description. Description is often mistakenly perceived as a mechanical and unbiased act—a process in which one merely sets forth in words "a graphic or detailed account of a person, thing, scene, etc." or marks out "qualities or features" that can be attributed to an object.[1] There are two compelling reasons for challenging this view. First, our perceptions are constantly filtered through a conceptual "screen" which differs from person to person and culture to culture.[2] The description of public policy is not exempt from this natural imposition of subjectivity.

The second source of bias is the purposive nature of policy description. That is, there is always a reason behind any description of a government statement or action. These reasons may not be clearly and openly stated. Nor are policy thinkers always conscious of the purposes of their work. Yet, because all policy thinkers have specific goals in mind, their descriptions may focus on certain aspects of a government activity while ignoring or playing down the significance of other factors. *The ends sought by the analyst strongly influences the question asked and the approaches used to establish certain answers.* In this sense no policy description is objective or mechanical; it is far from an unbiased act.

Because of these biases, we must pay careful attention to the purpose behind any policy description. This means that in applying problem-solving techniques to the analysis of government statements and actions there are two distinct traps we should avoid. First, we must be aware of our own biases. This does not mean we can hope to eliminate bias, but we can remain conscious of, and perhaps even control, its presence. To combat our own biases we must follow the key precept of problem solving discussed earlier; maintain the will to doubt.

Beyond the trap set by our own preferences, we must remain constantly skeptical of the work of others. No matter how sophisticated an analyst's techniques or approaches, some bias is inevitable. When reading a policy description you should always ask yourself what underlying assumptions or motivations produced the analysis. What purposes, goals, or values are supported by the descriptive framework? For example, the system model is widely used in political science as a framework for the empirical investigation of the political process. Critics of that model point to the underlying assumptions of system persistence or stability as an inherent source of bias in that analytical scheme. Another example is the U.S. budget. As we will see later in this chapter, if we regard budget documents as a description of national public policy, we will obtain a biased view of what Washington is and ought to be doing. In both cases, one cannot deny these criticisms. But that does not mean we need to avoid using such biased descriptions. What it does mean is that we should use such material with a skeptic's awareness of those biases.

Finding that a policy description is biased need not render it useless for you. Later in this chapter we review a variety of criteria to apply when you are assessing a descriptive typology. While the degree of bias in any typology is a major criterion, you should still evaluate policy descriptions and the methods used to carry them out in light of the use you want to make of them. Will they answer a question you have raised about a policy? Will they, in short, solve the problem at hand? Keep in mind that *utility* is the key.

TYPOLOGIES AND POLICY DESCRIPTION

Underlying every policy description is a simple and fundamental form of an analytic model: the *typology*. Typologies are the basic ingredients for descriptions because they provide the classification schemes into which those things we term public policies may be categorized. Some students of language believe such a classification process is at the very heart of all language and meaning. "When we name something," states semanticist (and former U.S. Senator) S.I. Hayakawa, "then, we are classifying. *The individual object or event we are naming, of course, has no name and belongs to no class until we put it in one.* . . . Classification is not a matter of identifying 'essences,' as is widely believed. It is simply a reflection of social convenience and necessity—and different necessities are always producing different classifications."[3]

Just as classifications are at the base of language and thought, so typologies, which provide a basis for the categorization of public policies, are the foundation of policy description. For this reason it is necessary for policy thinkers to develop an awareness of and familiarity with the process of creating and applying various classification schemes appropriate for the task of describing government actions or statements.

This is not asking much, for the classification of public policies is something we do frequently and quite naturally in our day-to-day conversations. When discussing a city's tax policy, a state's education policy, or a President's foreign policy, we are in fact using classification systems as means for labeling and thus describing specific policies. Consciously or unconsciously, we continuously characterize policies in terms of typological categories, and these in turn allow us to describe a government statement or action by associating it with the qualities highlighted by the typology.

Simply put, *typologies are the means by which we set forth similarities and differences among a group of objects or things.* They are tools for organizing and guiding thought in general, and policy descriptions in particular. Typologies are themselves the product of two organizing and guiding activities: classification and assignment.[4]

Classification calls for the ordering of concepts into categories or sets reflecting associations among them. It is a theoretical process based on abstraction and conceptualization; that is, it is inherently a thinking rather than a physical or mechanical procedure. *Assignment*, on the other hand, is a more physical operation demanding the identification of real world objects or situations that fit into the developed categories created through the classification process. The entire procedure is, of course, very flexible and allows for the continual reconsideration of both classification and assignment acts.

BOX 4.1

As an example, consider the conceptually simple yet often applied distinction between domestic and foreign policy. Together these two categories provide an all-encompassing typology for U.S. government activities. Individually, each type covers a substantial portion of government statements and actions. Nevertheless, anyone carefully examining these categories soon discovers at least one major drawback: assignment to one does not imply exclusion from assignment to the other. For that reason we might modify the typology to reflect these categoric overlaps. For example, we could attempt a typology containing three categories: one holding policies that are essentially domestic in nature; one focusing on policies that are basically foreign; and one type reflecting a mixture of both. To carry our task even further, we could decide on an assignment rule that any given policy is to be placed in one of these types according to what the analyst perceives as the explicit and direct intention and target group for the government activity. A domestic policy can be defined as one demonstrating an explicit intention to directly influence a sector of American society while intending no such direct impact on parties outside the U.S. social structure. Following the same logic, a foreign policy would be characterized as having the explicit intent of influencing conditions or forces outside U.S. society while having only a secondary or indirect impact internal affairs or actors. It follows, of course, that mixed policies are characterized by a combination of explicit and direct domestic and foreign impacts.

After conceptualizing the typology in this rather loose manner, we next attempt to identify given policies accordingly. For instance, a policy promoting or setting a highway speed limit of 55 miles per hour for the nation is obviously domestic. It is characterized under our typological scheme by an intention to directly and explicitly affect motorists. A policy of price supports and similar cash subsidies to American farmers is also identifiable as domestic according to this classification arrangement. This is not to imply that these policies have no significance for those residing outside the United States; nor should we assume that these policies were not meant to have a "foreign" impact. After all, much of the rationale underlying the movement to reduce highway speed came from concerns generated by the energy crisis and America's increasing dependence on foreign oil supplies during the early 1970s. Similarly, farm price supports and related policies are often reactions to competition from agricultural imports. Despite these important qualifications, it is probably still valid to hold that speed limits and farm policy are matters that are essentially domestic as we have used the term here.

On the other side of our typological picture are government statements or actions that directly affect foreign actors. During the Cuban missile crisis of October 1962 the United States imposed a naval blockade on ships headed for Castro's island with the objective of halting shipment of certain offensive weapons to that nation. While those actions had repercussions both within the United States as well as outside, the direct and intended targets were leaders of certain foreign governments. The same can be said for U.S. policies regarding arms control, white rule in South Africa, or the establishment of formal relations with Mainland China. While each has implications that spill over into the domestic arena, they are essentially foreign policies in light of our typology.

There are, of course, policies that can be classified in a mixed category reflecting their having explicit and direct impact on both domestic and foreign actors. The raising and lowering of import duties or quotas is one example of policies fitting this middle category. Faced with strong competition from abroad, many parts of America's industrial complex have sought "protection" in the form of tariffs or other import restricting policies, effectively raising the price of imported merchandise and thus reducing competition. This protectionist policy has been successfully obtained by some industries (e.g., in the past oil and sugar provided two excellent examples) while others still seek such actions on their behalf (e.g., the American steel and shoe industries have been battling for higher tariffs since the middle 1950s). From the perspective of these industries, tariff policies are domestic—that is, their primary function is to influence parts of the U.S. domestic economy. However, from the viewpoint of certain foreign actors and perhaps the State Department, these policies are directly and quite explicitly related to individuals, firms, and nations outside the United States. For examples, Venezuela, Saudi Arabia, and Nigeria would be the victims of proposed reductions in oil imports; Japan and the Common Market will directly feel the impact of price restrictions on imported steel; and Japan, Taiwan, Italy, Spain, and Brazil would regard themselves as the explicit target of trade restrictions on footwear.

This typology is not a very efficient or tight scheme, and there will certainly be those who argue that the definitions being applied are too vague and that the process of identifying and assigning a particular policy to one of the categories is too ambiguous. Policy thinkers from other nations may feel that much of U.S. domestic policy is essentially foreign and political experts would note that any given foreign policy may become a domestic issue particularly during an election campaign. Those faults cannot and should not be denied. While we all realize typologies such as this are imperfect, we must also keep in mind that what we are looking for is not the ideal descriptive model, but rather one that is useful. In this sense the threefold classification scheme developed here might prove relevant and useful for many policy thinkers.

If typologies are the key to description, then the question we must consider next is how one constructs a typology that might prove useful for describing various aspects of public policies. Actually, the process is so common that we often do not realize we are creating and applying categories when we speak of government statements and actions. Were we to concentrate on the process we would discover that it relies on three basic approaches to conceptualization: observations of the world, idealizations, and a combination of the two.[5]

Sometimes the concepts we use are derived from our observations of the world. Building on perceptions of the world around us, we learn and develop classification schemes to help organize our lives (e.g., kitchen versus workshop tools, luxury purchases versus necessities, and good neighbors versus uncooperative ones). We examine the "facts" and find the patterns or clusters that form bases for our categories and typologies. On a more complex level, we develop certain classifications about political events and persons. For example, by monitoring the news and experiencing political campaigns we classify certain policies, viewpoints, and actors as typically Republican or Democrat. We may categorize foreign nations as friendly or hostile, stable or revolutionary, or developed or underdeveloped on the basis of news reports. On a more sophisticated level, political analysts have developed systematic techniques for identifying certain clusters (i.e., categories) of policy issues, such as civil rights and social welfare, which are related to Congressional voting patterns.[6]

A second form of typology is built on conceptualizations derived from idealizations. We often think of the world in terms of ideal types or generalizable models, rather than empircally induced perceptions. At times these ideal types are useful in developing descriptive classification schemes. For example, in describing an act of government we might classify it as "capitalist" or "socialist" and use some idealization of what those categories mean to determine where the policy belongs. Of course, the characteristics of a capitalist or socialist policy are rooted in abstract theories rather than observed realities (see Chapter 5). However, empirical validity should not be the measure of the model. Instead we must again look to usefulness as the key.

Finally, a third approach combines qualities of the first two by relying on concepts rooted both in *ideal characteristics and empirical observations*. Our attempt to build the foreign-domestic policy typology illustrated in Box 4.1 exemplifies this strategy. We first defined the characteristics of the ideal case for each of the polar types and then modified the scheme with a mixed category and useful assignment rule when it became evident that the real world did not fit the categories as originally constructed. This is probably the way most analysts develop typologies for most descriptive analysis. They begin with categoric abstractions and attempt to apply them to real-world phenomena. It soon becomes evident, however, that the typology must be adapted to reflect the realities of the world. In this way some very clear and neat schemes may be destroyed or at least their luster as a classification scheme is likely to be tarnished. Nevertheless, what results from such modifications is a more useful model for policy description; and that, after all, is the point of the analysis.

WHAT TO DESCRIBE: THE ATTRIBUTES OF PUBLIC POLICY

One very significant factor in describing public policy is the focus of the description. Public policies are not isolated things with one-dimensional characteristics. They are often very complex actions and statements characterized by a variety of attributes, many of which might be of interest to the policy thinker. Given the fact that policies have so many attributes, we must ask how an analyst chooses a particular attribute (or set of attributes) to study.

It may be useful to distinguish between two types of policy characteristics: intrinsic and extrinsic attributes. Intrinsic attributes are characteristics inherent to the policy being examined, while extrinsic attributes are those characterizing a policy's relationship to external factors.

Intrinsic attributes are the internalized qualities of a public policy. Such qualities are often central to our daily conversations about government actions or statements. We are discussing intrinsic attributes when we classify or label policies according to the substantive issues they address. Thus, the policies we read about in our daily newspapers are described as "economic policy," "abortion policy," "civil rights policy," and so forth. Here the subject matter addressed by the policy provides our categories.

And even within these substantive issue classifications we can discuss subcategories further reflecting qualitative distinctions. For instance, when we divide economic policy into fiscal, monetary, and incomes policies (see Chapter 5) we are highlighting the means intrinsic to the government action or statement rather than the issues involved. Fiscal economic policies are those using public sector taxing and spending mechanisms to bring about desired objectives, while monetary policies use the supply of money, and incomes policies rely on the control or manipulation of prices, wages, and profits.

Other intrinsic attributes of public policy useful to a policy thinker are those focusing on subject populations or policy objectives. Foreign policies are often categorized according to the specific country or geographic area on which they are intended to have an impact. Thus we have a China policy, a Latin American policy, or a Southeast Asia policy. Related to these qualities are those focusing on targeted population groups such as Vietnamese refugee policies, policies on Third World nations, or policies regarding the Organization of Petroleum Exporting Countries (OPEC). Policy objectives also provide an intrinsic foundation for our descriptive classification schemes. Policies are often described as "anti-inflationary" or "pro-life" or "anti-pornography"—each label reflecting the goal of the government action or statement.[7]

Extrinsic attributes concentrate not on static qualities of public policies, but on the way government actions and statements relate to their surroundings. Here we stress the dynamic characteristics of public policies and consider patterns of relationships between policies and their environments.

A major example of a descriptive scheme based on the extrinsic attributes of public policies is one used by political scientists to discuss functions performed by political systems. This scheme usually includes four such policy types: allocative, extractive, control, and symbolic.[8]

Allocative policies are those involving the "allocation of goods, services, honors, statutes, and opportunities of various kinds from the political system to individuals and groups in the society."[9] These policies can have direct or indirect effects; that is, government can provide the benefits of its allocative activities directly or indirectly to the beneficiary. Students, for instance, receive the direct benefits of governmental investments in education; the community as a whole also receives benefits (so it is usually argued) from these investments, but indirectly through the improvement of knowledge, the development of a more intelligent citizenry, and so on.

Extractive policies draw "material and human resources" from the environment and apply them in a deliberate way.[10] The most common form of extraction in the United States occurs through taxation, although these activities take other forms as well. For example, highway tolls and user fees at local beaches or parks are extractive policy actions. Sometimes they involve more than taking money, for government can also expropriate private property through its power of eminent domain or draft human beings through the selective service system. If allocations distribute benefits, then extractions impose costs; and as with allocative actions, these impositions can be either direct (e.g., the personal income tax, the draft) or indirect (e.g., when the burden of the federal corporate profits tax is passed on to consumers in the form of increased prices).

Control policies are found in the laws, rules, and regulations which exercise "control over the behavior of individuals and groups."[11] Regulations affect a variety of activities, from the act of murder to the maintenance of a marriage contract to the rates a transporter can charge for hauling avocados from California to Boston. In this sense, control policies are activities wherein government draws boundary lines around certain behaviors and requires that citizens, corporations, or groups remain within those lines. Such activities are often related to other policy statements or actions. For example, your failure to respond to an attempt by the Internal Revenue Service to obtain overdue back taxes would mean that you have interfered with a control policy as well as an extractive one, and the control mechanisms of public policy will probably be activated.

There are several notable characteristics of control policies.[12] First, the controls imposed by public policy activities may be direct or indirect. For instance, the daily commuter traveling by private car from the suburbs to a job in the central city must contend with all sorts of traffic controls, ranging from signs to lights to police officers giving directions. The commuter is in constant direct contact with regulations almost every moment. On the other hand, the resident of a central city neighborhood who is seeking a loan to build a home in the suburban fringe is facing controls as well. These can be zoning and land use controls, which limit the availability of property for residential construction, or controls imposed through the Federal Reserve Bank's manipulation of prime interest rates which effect the willingness of local banks to finance a home purchase through mortgage contracts. Both indirectly regulate that central city resident.

A second important characteristic of control policy actions is that they can be based on either positive or negative sanctions. Controls are effective because they are backed by either rewards or punishments, and public policies will differ according to whether they impose controls through the use of "carrots" (incentives) or "sticks" (disincentives). Criminal laws are enforced through negative sanctions—when you commit a crime, the policy reaction is to imprison you and take away your rights for a period of time. Positive sanctions take several forms, ranging from the bestowing of honors on heroes to the presentation of monetary rewards. For example, in 1978 a passenger riding a commuter train in Chicago noticed a hairline crack in a primary support beam over which elevated trains ran every few minutes. Investigations by trained engineers indicated that the crack was a critical structural flaw, and tragedy could have resulted had not this citizen (a civil engineer by trade) reported his observations. The commuter line was shut down for a week while repairs were undertaken, and the observant passenger was rewarded with medals and accolades from the mayor of Chicago in a mass media event. In a similar vein, bounties in the form of monetary rewards have a long history in this country, especially in law enforcement and animal control policies. Positive sanctions also take the form of special tax incentives for certain types of investment, such as the tax deduction for interest paid on a home mortgage.

Symbolic policies involve the manipulation of symbols to control the response of given audiences. As noted in our discussion of symbolic policy statements in Chapter 2, these policies can influence a given audience in a certain way according to the cultural meanings that audience attaches to certain words or phrases. It would follow that a given audience can be aroused or rendered acquiescent through the manipulation of these linguistic symbols. Symbolic policies may involve more than mere words; they may also deal with the manipulation of material symbols (e.g., flags, troops) or other human and physical resources (e.g., famous persons, reports) to produce similar effects; that is, to calm or excite given audiences.[13]

Symbolic policies are often directly relevant to the public morale during a period of crisis and may be seen in activities such as parading the troops, waving the flag, or broadcasting patriotic speeches. For example, a "fireside chat" by a President wearing a cardigan sweater in front of the White House fireplace may help dramatize the importance of individual energy conservation efforts. At other times, however, symbolic policy actions are used to divert attention from an issue or otherwise buy time for policymakers who would rather not take action at a given time. Such a tactic has been used widely by presidents from Eisenhower to Reagan. Two examples stand out. In his presidential campaign of 1952, Eisenhower endorsed the concept of federal aid to education in order to help states and communities meet the critical shortages of school facilities. After two years of inaction and under increasing pressure to do something, Eisenhower made his move in the form of convening White House Conferences on federal aid to education throughout the country in 1955. While these conferences were rationalized as means for obtaining better policy input and more careful study, for the opposition Democrats in Congress "the conferences looked suspiciously like a scheme for delaying action for three years while the school 'crisis' worsened."[14] Lyndon Johnson faced a different situation during his administration. When ghetto areas exploded in riots throughout the country, he desperately needed to demonstrate to the American people that the government was doing something, and doing it *now*. It was this desperation which led to the creation of the National Advisory Commission on Civil Disorder (the Kerner Commission), which was essentially a symbolic action, as most special presidential commissions seem to be.

This typology is only one of several schemes used by policy thinkers to describe government actions or statements that is based on extrinsic attributes. For example, Richard Rose has developed a classification of policies that focuses on how a policy or set of policies relates to its environment over a given period of time (see Box 4.2).

BOX 4.2

As Richard Rose classifies them, policies can be found to be one of four types during any given period of time: static, cyclical, linear progressive, or discontinuous. A *static policy* (see Figure 4.1a) exists when a government's influence maintains a given condition over the time period in question; that is, the policy works to promote the status quo rather than any changes during that time. Like a heating system in winter which is tied into a thermostat set constantly at 68° F., the policy stays on target as time progresses. The U.S. government has pursued such a policy during the 1960s and 1970s with regard to Social Security pensions, increasing the monthly benefit checks to keep pace with inflation but making few alterations in the goals or methods of the program.

In contrast to this model is the *cyclical policy,* one characterized by a regular and consistent fluctuation of policy objectives over time (Figure 4.1b). We can view contemporary economic policies in this way. Typically (or at least according to modern economic theory) an economy will cyclically range from points of relatively high unemployment and low inflation to high inflation and low unemployment. If this is the case (and we shall see in Chapter 5 that it has not been so in

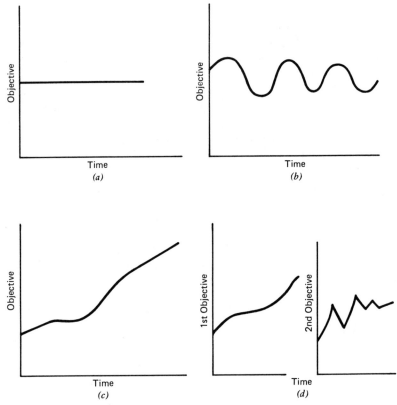

Figure 4.1. Four types of public policy. *(a)* Static. *(b)* Cyclical. *(c)* Linear progress. *(d)* Discontinuous. (Source: Richard Rose, "Models of Change," in R. Rose (ed.) *The Dynamics of Public Policy*, Beverly Hills, CA: Sage Publications, 1976, p. 17.)

recent years) then government policy should act to counter the adverse inclinations of both trends. This means fighting inflation when it is on the rise or unemployment when it begins to increase beyond acceptable levels.

In Rose's typology, a *linear progress* policy is one that increases in a fairly steady fashion toward expansion of a program, either by including more persons or achieving an expanding objective (see Figure 4.1c). His example of such a policy is that of public health programs in which governments attempt each year to provide greater protection from communicable diseases to a larger proportion of the population. Another example of this type of policy would be the continually increasing educational levels of the American population as the percentage of children of school age in attendance increases and more people stay in school longer.

WHAT TO DESCRIBE: THE ATTRIBUTES OF PUBLIC POLICY

> Finally, Rose designates a type of policy that goes through a radical change in direction or pattern during the time period in question. These *discontinuous policies* (see Figure 4.1*d*) are sometimes the product of a change in administration or attitude. Nixon's *de facto* recognition of Mainland China and Carter's formal recognition in late 1978 are clear examples. From a static policy of Cold War antagonism to a linear progressive policy of increasing contact between the two powers, the opening of an official link represents a major discontinuity in American foreign policy since the Korean War. On the domestic front, the U.S. Supreme Court overrules prior cases of constitutional standing very infrequently, but in 1954 it did so in the *Brown v. the Board of Education* case and thus not only broke with a long-standing precedent favoring "separate but equal" public school systems but also caused a major discontinuity in social policy. Another example is the major shift in U.S. fiscal policy that took place when Ronald Reagan became President in 1981. In the words of a White House press release of February 18 of that year, the Reagan program "calls for a *fundamental redirection* in the role of the federal government . . ." (emphasis added). The growing spending policies of the past were suddenly and (in some cases) drastically turned around as "Reaganomics" came to Washington.
>
> Rose's typology is both interesting and useful, but it is not ideal. Nonetheless, Rose's typology does allow us to describe government statements or actions with respect to dynamic changes in coverage and direction over time and to compare these patterns of change.
>
> See Richard Rose (ed.), *The Dynamics of Public Policy: A Comparative Analysis* (London: Sage Publications, 1976).

Of course, there are some policy description typologies that combine intrinsic and extrinsic attributes. One example popular among analysts is a scheme developed by Theodore J. Lowi. In his initial delineation of his typology,[15] Lowi distinguished among three types of policies: distributive, regulatory, and redistributive. On the one hand, how a policy is classified in Lowi's scheme depends on whether its benefits or costs can be divided and packaged by distribution or not. In this sense, Lowi's typology is based on the intrinsic qualities of a policy. On the other hand, Lowi believes major differences among public policies can be linked to the different "arenas of power" in which they operate; that is, how they interact with their surroundings.

For example, *distributive policies* under Lowi's typology are "characterized by the ease with which they can be disaggregated and dispensed unit by small unit, each unit more or less is in isolation from other units and from any general rule." At the same time, distributive policies are those that emerge from a political arena in which power is not concentrated in the hands of a few, but rather is distributed among many organized interests. Under such conditions "politics works in the short run; and in the short run certain kinds of policies can be made without regard to limited resources." Governments will opt for "policies that are virtually not policies at all, but are highly individualized decisions that only by accumulation can be called a policy." Lowi's primary examples are political patronage appointments and "pork barrel" policies which deliver defense installations to some congressional districts and water reclamation projects to others. They are "policies in which the indulged and deprived, the loser and the recipient, need never come into direct confrontation."[16]

Regulatory policies in Lowi's typology lack at least one of the two key attributes of distributive policies. On the one hand, they may be intrinsically less disaggregatable. On the other hand, they may be implemented in an arena of power where confrontations between winners and losers are unavoidable. Typically, regulatory policies involve a situation in which some valued but limited resource (e.g., an exclusive franchise or license for broadcasting over a given radio or T.V. frequency) is to be assigned to one of several competing applicants. This is the situation that the Federal Communications Commission (FCC) faces in making its licensing decisions. They must make direct and somewhat explicit choices in the short run "as to who will be indulged and who deprived."[17]

Redistributive policies also call upon government to make direct choices between winners and losers, but under conditions quite different from regulatory decisions. Redistributive policies involve resources that are so limited that they must be extracted from some group in society in order to satisfy others. Thus, intrinsically we are dealing with extremely scarce and highly valued policy resources. Extrinsically, redistributive policies generate strong reactions from both those from whom they are taken and those who gain as a result.[18]

In theory, the progressive income tax is supposedly redistributive. Through such a tax those who make more income pay at a higher rate (percentage) than those who make less. For example, someone who reports an income of $10,000 might pay at a rate of 15 percent while a person who makes $100,000 might pay closer to 50 percent in taxes. However, through various loopholes and exemptions—each an example of distributive policies—the redistributive impact of the current U.S. personal income tax is not at all strong. If there are any truly redistributive policies in the United States, they are found in the extremely controversial and ever expanding "transfer" programs of the federal government. Under these programs, monies collected in general or special funds from taxpayers are converted

WHAT TO DESCRIBE: THE ATTRIBUTES OF PUBLIC POLICY 71

into benefits for certain groups. Some of these benefits are in the form of cash transfers, as in Aid to Families with Dependent Children and Unemployment Compensation. Others are transfers in kind as in food stamp and public housing programs. In any case, redistributive policies are characterized by acts that take resources from one major segment of society and give it to another.[19]

The basis of Lowi's typology of public policies, distinguishing among regulatory, distributive, and redistributive policies, lies in both the intrinsic and extrinsic nature of such policies. Each is defined in terms of the perceived interaction of a policy with the status and influence of groups and sectors within society.

BOX 4.3

Lowi's typology of public policies has proven quite popular since its introduction in 1964. One measure of that popularity is the variety of modified versions that have emerged over the past several years. Lowi himself has modified the scheme by adding a fourth category he calls *constituent policies*. Intrinsically, these policies are like distributive policies in seeming to be disaggregatable; that is, an individual can get a sense of having gained or lost something when a constituent policy is passed. For example, if you are a veteran and it was announced tomorrow morning that the Veteran's Administration was being shut down in an economy move, you are likely to feel adversely affected. If you are a Vietnam veteran and a new special agency for you was being created to serve the needs of Vietnam era veterans, once again you would have a sense of impact, although this time of a positive sort. Extrinsically, however, constituent policies are like redistributive policies in generating reactions among large classes of individuals. Veterans are not only a significant group in terms of absolute numbers; they also have a great deal of emotional support within our society and any general policies affecting them can stimulate a great deal of activity among large segments of the American citizenry. The same holds true for the elderly, the handicapped, and other groups that have the support of the general public.

Another modification of the Lowi typology has been provided by a student of comparative public policies. T. Alexander Smith uses a four-fold typology to compare policies in the United States, France, Great Britain, Canada, and West Germany. His categories include:

1. *Distributive* policies [which] display little, if any, conflict and are settled quietly in executive and/or legislative committees. Party discipline is unaffected.
2. *Sectorally fragmented* policies [which] display moderate conflict among interests representing primary economic sectors and are resolved on the legislative floor by coalitions of legislator bargaining with ministers or other bureaucrats who oversee the particular sectors. Party discipline remains relatively strong in most cases.
3. *Emotive symbolic* policies display[ing] wide conflicts of deep intensity over "way-of-life" issues in which governments refuse to stake out positions and in which individual legislators reject leadership controls over their actions. Party discipline is virtually nonexistent.
4. *Redistributive* policies [which] display wide conflicts of deep intensity between classes and are settled by "peak" associations of labor and management negotiating with presidents and prime ministers (legislatures are relatively quiescent). Party discipline is relatively high.

Other modifications of the Lowi typology include changes offered by Randall B. Ripley and Grace A. Franklin. They have made two noteworthy adjustments. First, they have distinguished between domestic and nondomestic (defense and foreign) policies and in the process created three new categories to deal with the latter. Thus, they discuss *structural policies* which "aim primarily at procuring, deploying, and organizing military personnel and material . . ."; *strategic policies* which "assert and implement the basic military and foreign policy stance of the United States toward other nations . . ."; and *crisis policies* which are "short-run responses to immediate problems" that are regarded as serious but for which policy makers were unprepared. As second change is a distinction between competitive and protective regulatory policies. *Competitive regulatory policies* impose limits on the provision of specific goods and services so that there are definite winners and losers. *Protective regulatory policies* "are developed to protect the public by setting the conditions under which various private activities can be undertaken." Taken all together, the Ripley-Franklin typology expands Lowi's initial three categories to seven.

These modifications of Lowi's basic descriptive classifications reflect both the limits and potential fertility of any basic model or typology. From a relatively simple scheme of three policy types has emerged an entire literature that has greatly influenced policy thinking for many people.

> See Theodore J. Lowi, "Four Systems of Policy, Politics, and Choice," *Public Administration Review*, 32, no. 4 (July/August 1972), pp. 298–310; T. Alexander Smith, *The Comparative Policy Process* (Santa Barbara, CA: ABC-Clio, Inc., 1975), especially pp. 7–8; and Randall B. Ripley and Grace A. Franklin, *Congress, The Bureaucracy, and Public Policy* revised edition (Homewood, IL: The Dorsey Press, 1980).

EVALUATING DESCRIPTIVE TYPOLOGIES

What is a "good" typology and what is not? What criteria should we use in evaluating the many typologies and classification schemes that make up the inventory of such descriptive tools? This is a difficult question to answer, but political scientist Lewis A. Froman, Jr. took on the task. In a 1968 article he specified several factors one must take into account when evaluating various policy typologies.[20] Briefly summarized, these factors included:

Inclusiveness

In applying this criterion, the greater a typology's comprehensiveness, the better. In short, the ideal classification scheme should cover all possible policy forms in its categories. There should be no policy that remains "unclassified" because it does not fit. The example we developed earlier, which permitted us to categorize policies as domestic, foreign, or mixed, would meet this specification. Most of the modifications made to Lowi's typology (Box 4.3) are attempts at making amends for a lack of inclusiveness. For example, the addition of three modified types for foreign policy in Ripley and Franklin's model is meant to answer for the lack of inclusiveness in the original scheme.

Mutual exclusivity

Are the categories sufficiently distinct so as to avoid any possibility of overlap among two or more policies? The potential for overlap is frequently overlooked in policy typologies. Historically, we have a tendency to link certain policies to particular Presidential administrations or to specific "courts" (e.g., the "Marshall Court" or "Warren Court"). By structuring our categories in this way, we come close to establishing mutually exclusive categories. *Marbury* v. *Madison* and *McCulloch* v. *Maryland* were products of the Marshall Court, while *Brown* v. *Board of Education of Topeka,*

Escobedo v. *Illinois, Mapp* v. *Ohio* and other significant cases are linked to the Warren Court. However, it is doubtful that the assignment of national domestic policies to specific Presidential administrations is as valid as associating certain decisions with the Chief Justice sitting when the decision was handed down. Unlike Court decisions, many Executive Branch policies originated or were first proposed by Presidents years before. Few would question that the Highway Beautification Act or the War on Poverty bears the Johnson Administration's distinctive stamp, but the Medicare bill, also advocated and signed by Johnson, was first proposed by Harry Truman, and some would even argue it originated as part of Franklin Roosevelt's social security proposal.

Hugh Heclo takes Richard Rose's temporal typology (see Box 4.2) to task on just this point. Recall that Rose held that over time a policy can be classified as static, cyclical, linear progressive, or discontinuous—four types posited as seemingly mutually exclusive categories. But as Heclo points out, a more careful look at the typology would indicate that there is considerable overlap among the four types. He suggests that what Rose has developed is best perceived as a continuum along which the four categories of policies can be placed as "ideal types" against which a given policy at a given time can be measured.[21]

Validity

One may also evaluate policy categories by asking whether the concept used to differentiate among government actions and statements actually defines "what it says it does." How valid, for example, are the institutional categories used when we classify a policy as presidential, congressional, or judicial; or as state, local, or federal? Exactly what do we mean by these labels? Is a policy generated within the Interior Department a presidential policy since it comes from the Executive Branch? Or are presidential policies just those that have the official sanction and blessing of the White House? Is the policy of a congressional committee chairperson or specific legislative leader equivalent to a policy of Congress? It is obvious that these categories lack the distinctiveness and clarity that would enhance their validity, and this is something Froman feels we should seek in our descriptive models.

Reliability

The creator of a descriptive typology knows what is meant by the concepts used in the model and therefore can apply it with relative ease. But can the typology be replicated by others? That is, is it possible for a researcher to come along in 1984 and use Lowi's categories the same way they were used in 1964? As Froman puts the question, "Is there a high level of agreement among independent researchers on what specific policies fall into what categories?" If so, then the typology is reliable.

In Heclo's critique of Rose's temporal typology of public policies, for example, he points out that there may be some problems along these lines. What may be seen as a static policy from one perspective may be regarded as cyclical or linear progressive from another. This Heclo terms the "perceptual relativity of policy change," and given this quality the Rose typology would rank rather low in reliability unless all the reseachers who use it approach a given policy using the same temporal framework.[22]

In Box 4.2 we used the example of U.S. policy toward China as becoming "discontinuous" during the Nixon administration's opening of relationships. If we judge the relationships over a longer time span, from the first arrival of Americans in China early in our history as a republic until the establishment of formal diplomatic relations under the Carter Administration in 1979, the policy would appear to be cyclical, with America alternately becoming involved in China and then withdrawing. Looking only at post-Korean War contacts, China policy may well be described as linear progress, particularly if a scholar could obtain records of the decade of secret contacts before the Nixon initiative. Thus, changing the perspective of the analysis alters the classification of the policy in the Rose typology.

Level of Measurement

The concern here is for the development of categories appropriate to the measurement needs of the professionally trained analyst and the data available. While most of us may never be concerned with measurement issues when we think about public policies, it is still useful to consider how well a typology will do when put to the test of more sophisticated policy thinking. Descriptive typologies can reflect three different levels of measurement, each susceptible to statistical manipulation in varying degrees. Some classification schemes, for example, allow us merely to type a policy according to some attribute or set of characteristics for which we have established a particular label. This is the case for our classification of domestic, mixed, and foreign policies—a scheme calling for the labeling of a policy according to some defining characteristics but stating nothing more than the fact that policies placed in one category are different from those in another. These are termed nominal categories and involve the use of *nominal levels of measurement.*

Other typologies allow us not only to distinguish between classes of policies, but also order them in terms of having more or less of some attribute. Such models are susceptible to *ordinal levels of measurement* and are common in instances when we call one policy more liberal, more inflationary, or more "hawkish" than another.

Finally, in some typologies we cannot only distinguish between nominal characteristics and their ordinal placement, but also specify the size of the intervals that separate the ordered types. These are descriptive models based on *interval or ratio levels of measurement,* so-called because the placement also indicates the relative distance of policies from each other or from a position relative to some absolute base point. This is most often used when policies are described in fiscal terms, that is, how much money is being spent on the government activity. To say that the federal government is spending 40 times more on national defense than space exploration is an example of using an interval scale of measurement. To show that same information in terms of dollars expended (i.e., $200 billion for national defense and $5 billion for space exploration) is to present the same information on a ratio scale.

Returning to the criteria Froman sets forth, his point is that each descriptive model has its own level of measurement. At the nominal level all the analyst can do is *classify* a policy. At the ordinal level an analyst can *order* as well as classify. At the interval/ratio level the analyst can work with policies in terms of *their relative (and measurable) distance* to some base point as well as classify and order them. For some analysts nominal level capabilities are sufficient, but for others the ability to order or to work at the interval/ratio levels is crucial. Each level, in short, can be used to evaluate a particular descriptive scheme and the typological model on which it is built.

Ease of Operationalization

It is just as important to ask whether a policy can actually be measured in regards to a set of attributes as it is to determine at what level it is being measured. In other words, how difficult is it to empirically assign a policy into one category or another? For some typologies and some policies the assignment task is easy. For others it is difficult. Froman calls this process operationalization. Policies that raise revenue for government, for example, can be operationalized rather easily. Using a ratio scale based on $0, one can describe different revenue-raising policies by placing them at that point on the scale that reflects the amount of current dollars raised. The same can be done for expenditures, and the resulting description is found in various budget document tables.

But, while monetary units facilitate the operationalization of certain policies (e.g., those dealing with the raising of revenue or the expenditure of funds), other policies cannot be described in monetary terms. For example, the policies of many regulatory agencies such as the Food and Drug Administration (FDA) or the Securities and Exchange Commission (SEC) cannot be described entirely in monetary values, and thus cannot be easily operationalized. Both the FDA and the SEC expend funds, but their activities cannot be summarized in monetary terms. And there are the obvious difficulties of "monetizing" policy statements and symbolic activities. Thus the ratio scale used in the budget documents cannot be used for a significant portion of U.S. public policy.

Other typological models have the opposite problem. That is, while they cover an extremely broad spectrum of public policies, it is often difficult to designate policies as belonging to one type or another. This is the case with our domestic-mixed-foreign typology and with Lowi's widely used categories and the modifications that have followed it. What makes a policy regulatory rather than distributive or redistributive? What attribute places a policy in the foreign rather than the domestic or mixed categories? These typologies are more difficult to operationalize than others, and it is this very difficulty to which Froman calls our attention.

Differentiation

This final criteria developed by Froman for the evaluation of descriptive policy typologies is perhaps the most abstract and, for many readers, will be the least significant. However it can prove important for those interested in more advanced studies of public policy. By citing differentiation, Froman asks to what extent the categories being used are theoretically fruitful and significant. That is, how much do we find out about a policy when we know that it is regulatory or distributive or redistributive? Is the fact that a policy is foreign rather than domestic important in that it also indicates to us other attributes of the policy that are not outwardly clear? Does the knowledge that the United States may spend over 40 times as much for national defense as it does for space exploration tell us much more about national defense and our other priorities? These are some of the questions raised when we assess any descriptive typology on the basis of this criterion. As Froman puts the question of differentiation, "Do the categories correlate with other phenomena, and if so, to what extent?"

Each of Froman's seven criteria raises interesting questions regarding the classification schemes we use to describe public policies. Ideally, of course, we would like to develop and apply descriptions that score high on each point. However, it is unlikely that any current or future policy typology can come close to meeting that ideal, and so we must settle for less. How much less? To a considerable extent that is a matter for each policy analyst to determine when approaching a descriptive policy problem. As we mentioned earlier, the *usefulness* of a given model in solving the problem at hand should be the critical measure.

Many analysts, for example, have welcomed Lowi's initial three-fold classification despite its many limits and drawbacks. Why? First, the typology has been adaptable to their particular needs in many instances. Second, it does possess a relatively high degree of what Froman called "differentiation." But most important of all is the fact that it has proven useful to many policy thinkers in both its original and modified forms. The distinction between regulatory, distributive, redistributive, and other policies is weak on a number of points. It is not completely inclusive; the categories lack mutual exclusivity and score low on reliability. Nor do they provide more than a nominal level of measurement, or minimal ease of operationalization. Yet it is still an exciting typology to work with. Those who use it are aware of its weaknesses but continue to apply it—with caution. Like any other typology they might choose, they realize it is not perfect, but what tool is? This attitude is one you should keep in mind as you approach the task of policy description.

THE U.S. BUDGET AS A "CONCRETE" POLICY DESCRIPTION

As important as description is for the policy thinker, a great deal of thought ought to be given to selecting the right type of policy description. This is as true for those who seek out policy descriptions as it is for those who present them. For example, consider the annual U.S. Budget documents issued each year by the White House. At the beginning of each year the President of the United States provides the Congress with the details of what is being spent on public policies by agencies under his jurisdiction and what he and his administration believes ought to be spent on those policies in the forthcoming fiscal year.[23] In fact, what the President is giving the Congress is a description of U.S. public policy as his administration sees it.

As a policy description that offers the White House's views of current and future activities, the budget's presentation is an important factor in any administration's success. Therefore a great deal of attention is given to its presentation as well as its preparation. That is, the administration will present its policy descriptions in a way that highlights the President's programs and policy objectives. Anyone familiar with the changes found in the presentation of the U.S. budget from year to year and administration to administration would not be surprised at this manipulation.

For example, consider the design of the specific documents we call the U.S. Budget. Throughout the presidencies of Johnson, Nixon, Ford, and Carter the U.S. Budget had been presented in four basic volumes. The basic document was *The Budget of the United States Government—Fiscal Year 19——*. Usually running over 500 pages, this volume contained the Presidential "Budget Message" and an overview of the details of spending and taxing proposals as well as explanations for them. It is a description intended for people who have a more than passing interest in the budget. A second volume, *The Budget of the United States Government, 19——, Appendix,* is the size of a metropolitan area telephone directory and offers a great deal more detail about allocation of budgeted funds to government agencies and how they are to be spent. It is so detailed and lacking in interesting narrative that it is used by only the most involved of budget analysts. A third volume, *The United States Budget in Brief, 19——,* provides an easy-to-read 90-page general overview of the presidential proposals for a given fiscal year. Filled with colorful illustrations and brief narratives, this document is intended for general public consumption. Finally, each administration has issued a bound volume of *Special Analyses, Budget of the United States Government, 19—,* containing ten to twenty detailed studies of certain parts of the budget which are mandated by Congress or the White House wishes to highlight.

This multivolume format for presenting the U.S. Budget has emerged over several decades and reflects the need to provide detailed information to Congress and the American people. But the policy descriptions offered in these documents also reflect the need for presidents to give the public and its representatives the special view of American public policy from the White House. The organization and content of the budget documents are carefully developed to accomplish that objective.

The four-volume format was a standard for many years—until the fiscal year 1983 (FY83) budget issued by Ronald Reagan. In that presentation two basic changes were evident. First, the *Special Analyses* were presented in eleven unbound pamphlets. Second, and more significantly, a new document was added. Titled *Major Themes and Additional Budget Details,* this nearly 300-page book was intended to explain and justify the administration's proposals. Most Washington budget-watchers noted that this new document was a highly partisan presentation and defense of the President's budgetary programs. But while it may have been a more explicit and obvious example of biased policy description, it was no different from the other budget volumes in emphasizing policy facts and trends that presented the administration's efforts and proposals in a good light.

Given this situation, those who use the policy descriptions provided in U.S. Budget documents need to read that information carefully. Reading the budget presentations is not like reading the daily newspaper. The presentation is often filled with tables and graphs that indicate "factual" patterns and trends about past, current, and projected spending and economic conditions. However, such presentations are often permeated with questionable or partisan assumptions that may need to be approached cautiously by the reader. The good policy analyst will take care not to accept such policy descriptions on face value. Instead, he or she should learn to examine such policy descriptions systematically and with the skepticism of someone who understands the biased nature of policy description.[24]

TYPES OF POLICY DESCRIPTIONS

It is one thing to understand the nature and limits of policy description, but it is quite another to comprehend the different forms that policy descriptions take. Descriptive typologies are not difficult to develop, and there are an almost infinite variety of categories and labels used to describe what governments say and do. We have already explored some major typologies in our discussion of the attributes of policies on which policy descriptions focus. In this section we try to gain understanding of the many types of descriptive frameworks available to policy thinkers. The result is a typology of policy description typologies, and like all such classification schemes it is intended to be a useful tool in helping you sort out the many alternatives you have when thinking about public policies.

As we have already noted, some descriptive categories stress the intrinsic objectives of government actions and statements. Thus, we often hear policies described in terms of "stopping" inflation, "increasing" employment opportunities, "eliminating" poverty, or "achieving" energy independence. These we will call *intentional descriptions,* and what they have in common is the belief that policies can be classified according to their explicitly stated purposes. On the other side of the coin is a different type of policy description that focuses on what government actions or statements accomplish, regardless of any explicitly stated intentions. These we will call *functional descriptions* for they stress the roles and functions that a policy ends up fulfilling.

Intentional descriptions stress the rationales for policy development and implementation. The nationwide 55-mile-per-hour speed limit was instituted after the first major OPEC oil embargo in 1973 with the expressed purpose of conserving energy resources. The space program of the National Aeronautics and Space Administration (NASA) was established in the early 1960s in order to fulfill President Kennedy's stated goal of putting a man on the moon by 1970. The level of interest rates was kept high by the Federal Reserve Board in the early 1980s in order to help reduce inflation. In each instance, the policies could be identified by the stated intentions of the policymakers: energy independence, preeminance in the "race for space" with the Soviets, and stopping rampant inflation.

Functionally, those same policies served goals and objectives beyond those they were expressly intended to serve. The 55-mile-per-hour speed limit has helped save lives on the highway; the space program has enhanced our technological and defense capabilities; and high interest rates have dampened the 1970s boom in the housing and real estate markets. Functional classifications may contain "unintended" as well as "intended" categories. It was not the purpose of the Federal Reserve Board to damage home-building industries, but that was a function performed by that policy. On a more positive note, the reduction in highway deaths was a nice (and not necessarily unexpected) benefit of lowered speed limits.

A variation on both intentional and functional descriptions are those that focus on segments of the population affected by a policy. *Population-focused descriptions* see government actions and statements in terms of the specific groups in the environment that benefit or are harmed. We frequently read or hear about policies which are pro- or anti-labor, pro- or anti-business, for or against the farmer, for or against the consumer, and so on. Describing policies in these terms provides the policy thinker with a common thread that ties together many diverse public sector activities. Sometimes a policy is easy to categorize using this approach, especially when it is an action that is intentionally developed to have an effect on a particular group. American farmers are the intended beneficiaries of commodity price supports and other subsidy programs. These are usually labeled "agricultural" policies, the implication being that they most directly affect the national farming community. Similarly we hear policies labeled as "consumer protection" or, in the foreign policy arena, according to country or geographic region (e.g., Latin American policies, Eastern European policies, etc.).

The population-focused approach is a little more awkward when we take into account the many groups that may be indirectly or unintentionally affected by policies. Thus, as a group, U.S. homeowners are affected by a wide range of policies from local, state, and federal tax laws to the Federal Reserve's policies on interest rates to policies concerning the disposal of hazardous waste (e.g., the Love Canal tragedy which left many homeowners in the New York community homeless). Are these all to be categorized as "homeowner policies"? In a world where all facets of social life are increasingly linked to one another, a population-focused typology may be more difficult to develop and less useful to policy thinkers.

Developmental descriptions provide an historical picture of public policies. Public policies are rarely "new" in the sense of having no roots to or links with policies of the past. Those linkages may, in fact, provide us with a much better understanding of current policies. If we were to accept the view of public policies as "undertakings" (see Chapter 2), then developmental descriptions make even greater sense since a policy is what government does over time to solve some problem or attain some objective. U.S. policy toward the Republic of South Korea may not be usefully described unless if seen in the context of the entire post-World War II period. Nor can many of our social welfare policies (e.g., Social Security) be described in terms that stress only explicit intentions or population focus. As we will see in Chapter 9, the evolution of these policies is often the key to understanding them.

One useful form that developmental descriptions take is illustrated in Figures 4.2 and 4.3. Using fiscal years as basic descriptive categories, these graphs chart the historical paths of federal spending and taxing policies for given periods.[25] Such illustrations give us a view of government activities in these areas which would be missing if we relied only on information about expenditure or revenues for individual fiscal years. Of course, the same approach can be taken to describe any policy area where money or some other interval is involved.

Programmatic descriptions place specific policies within the context of some more general "package." Often such a package is consciously developed by the policymaker, as in the case of Lyndon Johnson's War on Poverty.[26] At other times they are perceived as a package from a vantage point other than the policymaker's, e.g., when the media looks at "Reagan's budget-cutting policy" or a historian reconsiders "Roosevelt's New Deal." When placed within such contexts, public policies take on a more general

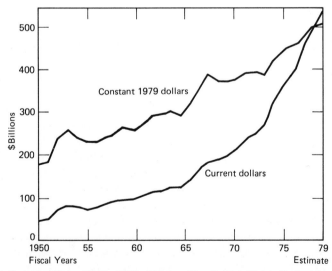

Figure 4.2. Budget outlays, 1950–1979. (Source: *The United States Budget in Brief, Fiscal Year 1979,* Washington, DC: Office of Management and Budget, 1978, p. 2.)

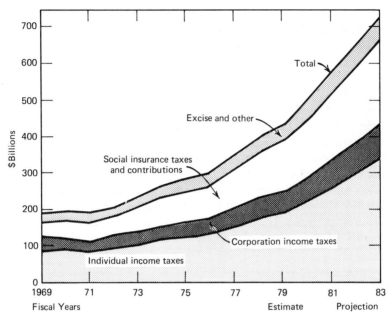

Figure 4.3. Budget receipts, 1969–1983. (Source: *The United States Budget in Brief, Fiscal Year 1979,* Washington, DC: Office of Management and Budget, 1978, p. 19.)

identity and thus come to be regarded as integral to the program rather than as unique or separate programs. The War on Poverty provided such identification to operations like the Headstart pre-school program and the Job Corps training program for unskilled youth. When the Nixon Administration announced plans to end the Office of Economic Opportunity (the administering agency for the War on Poverty), its supporters immediately suspected that all of the programs would be destroyed. In fact, some were ended but others were transferred to regular Executive Branch departments where the emphasis became departmental objectives rather than the goals of the Johnson program.

Comparative descriptions are to a great extent built on many of the types already discussed. Any of the factors listed to this point—intentions, functions, developmental trends, programmatic contexts—can be used for comparing one policy with another. The "other policy" involved may be an action of the same government or some other political system; it may be different policies or a comparison of the same policy at different times. Typical comparisons might be the health insurance policies of the United States, Canada, and Great Britain or the economic policies of Presidents Ford, Carter, and Reagan. Regardless of the object being used for comparison, the purpose is to describe the policy being analyzed, and the analyst approaches the task with that in mind.

As with the other forms of common policy description, examples abound. Economic policies, for example, can be compared in terms of their objectives: Are they aimed at promoting economic growth or financial stability? Are they to deal with problems of unemployment among factory workers or inflation for consumers? Or policies may be compared in terms of different functions: Is a tariff on imported shoes used to raise revenue or to protect a troubled American industry? Similarly, a comparative description may concentrate on developmental trends. We might, for example, compare how much difference there has been over the past two decades between spending for social programs and defense spending. Such a developmental comparison shows that, at least until the Reagan administration, an increasing proportion of the U.S. budget was given to social programs. Between 1951 and 1953 defense purchases by the federal government accounted for 10.9 percent of the U.S. gross national product (GNP), while its spending on nondefense purchases, grants-in-aid to state and local governments, and domestic transfer programs (e.g., Social Security) stood at 5 percent of GNP. In the years 1971–1973 the same figures were 6.4 percent for defense purchases and 12 percent for the other categories. By 1981 the percentages were 5.1 for defense and 15.3 for the nondefense-grants-domestic transfer categories. Finally, a comparison can also be undertaken describing a given policy in terms of its programmatic relationship to other policies. Thus, we can make comparisons between Reagan's policies on economic recovery and his administration's defense program.

The six policy description types discussed in this section (see Table 4.1) do not, of course, cover the entire spectrum. There are many other forms of description in addition to these common types. For example, policies are sometimes examined and described in terms of the policymaking body responsible for their formulation or eventual passage. Thus we often distinguish between presidential policies (such as *Johnson's* War on Poverty) and congressional policies (such as the many "pork barrel" public works programs that pass through the legislative process year after year). This *institutional description* approach is also useful in pointing out significant differences among national civil rights policies that have played a prominent role in U.S. politics since 1954. In that year the Supreme Court handed down the precedent-setting decision in *Brown v. Board of Education of Topeka,* which declared de jure segregation (racial segregation sanctioned "by law") unconstitutional. Over the next quarter century the Court built upon that initial decision to create a *judicial policy* which continues in the direction set forth in 1954. In addition there have been *congressional* civil rights policies such as the 1964 and 1968 Civil Rights Acts and *presidential*

Table 4.1 Common Types of Policy Description Used By Analysts

Description Type	Policy Perceived As:
1. Intentional	1. Purposes, goals, policymaker objectives.
2. Functional	2. Roles or services performed for society or some social sector.
3. Population-focused	3. Actions and statements that benefit or harm specific groups in the environment.
4. Developmental	4. Evolving statement or act; part of an emerging trend or historical movement.
5. Programmatic	5. Part of a "package" of similiar or related policies.
6. Comparative	6. Comparable to other policies or programs.

civil rights policies such as the executive orders designed to integrate U.S. government agencies and entities dealing with them.[27]

Still other types of description focus on factors such as the *time period* involved (e.g., antebellum, postwar, Nixon years) or the *arena of activity* (e.g., the classic and frequently applied distinction between foreign and domestic policy). The point here is not to provide you with an endless list of description types, but to indicate some of the more common approaches and the impact each has on how policies are perceived. In the next chapter we see how some variations of these types are used in a specific area— economic policies.

ENDNOTES

1. These are typical examples of definitions found in the *Oxford English Dictionary*.
2. See Kenneth E. Boulding, *The Image: Knowledge in Life and Society* (Ann Arbor: The University of Michigan Press, 1956).
3. S.I. Hayakawa, *Language in Thought and Action,* 4th edition (New York: Harcourt Brace Jovanovich, Inc., 1978), p. 201; emphasis in original.
4. See Robert S. Sokal and Peter H. A. Sneath, *Principles of Numerical Taxonomy* (San Francisco: W. H. Freeman, 1963).
5. Kenneth D. Bailey, "Monothetic and Polythetic Typologies and their Relations to Conceptualization, Measurement and Scaling," *American Sociological Review,* 38 (February, 1973), pp. 12–21.

6. See Aage R. Clausen, *How Congressmen Decide: A Policy Focus*, (New York: St. Martin's Press, 1973).
7. As is evident from several of these examples, some of these labels have considerable emotional weight (e.g., "pro-life," "anti-pornography"), which should be taken into account when establishing descriptive categories.
8. Gabriel A. Almond and G. Bingham Powell, Jr., *Comparative Politics: A Developmental Approach* (Boston, MA: Little, Brown and Co., 1966), Chapter VIII.
9. Ibid., p. 198; the label "distributive" is used synonomously with "allocative" by Almond and Powell. We restrict ourselves to the "allocative" label since the term "distributive" is also associated with Lowi's typology discussed below.
10. Ibid., pp. 195–196. Also see Larry L. Wade, *The Elements of Public Policy* (Columbia, OH: Charles E. Merrill Publishing Co., 1972), pp. 12–13; L. L. Wade and R. L. Curry, Jr., *A Logic of Public Policy: Aspects of Political Economy* (Belmont, CA: Wadsworth Publishing Co., Inc., 1970), p. 7; and Robert H. Haveman, *The Economics of the Public Sector*, 2nd edition (Santa Barbara, CA: John Wiley & Sons, 1976), Chapter 5.
11. Almond and Powell, *Comparative Politics*, pp. 196–197; Wade and Curry, *A Logic of Public Policy*, pp. 7–8; and Wade, *The Elements of Public Policy*, pp. 13–14. The term "control" is used here instead of "regulatory" in light of the use of the latter term in Lowi's typology (see below).
12. See Joyce M. Mitchell and William G. Mitchell, *Politics: Problems and Outcomes* (Chicago: Rand McNally and Co., 1971), Chapter 6; Also Robert A. Dahl and Charles E. Lindblom, *Politics, Economics, and Welfare: Planning and Politico-Economic Systems Resolved into Basic Social Processes* (New York: Harper and Row, Publishers, 1953).
13. See Almond and Powell, *Comparative Politics*, pp. 199–201; also Mitchell and Mitchell, *Politics*, Chapter 4; and Wade, *The Elements of Public Policy*, p. 14.
14. James L. Sundquist, *Politics and Policy: The Eisenhower, Kennedy, and Johnson Years* (Washington, DC: The Brookings Institution, 1968), pp. 157–161.
15. See Theodore J. Lowi, "American Business, Public Policy, Case-Studies, and Political Theory," *World Politics*, 16 (July, 1964), pp. 677–715.
16. Ibid., p. 690.
17. Ibid., pp. 690–691. On the FCC policymaking process, see Erwin G. Krasnow, Lawrence D. Longley, and Herbert A. Terry, *The Politics of Broadcast Regulation*, 3rd edition (New York: St. Martin's Press, 1982).
18. Lowi, "American Business, Public Policy, Case-Studies, and Political Theory," p. 691.
19. For a review of the transfer programs aimed at lower income Americans, see Robert Plotnick and Felicity Skidmore, *Progress Against Poverty* (New York: Academic Press, 1975). Also see Chapter 9.
20. Lewis A. Froman, Jr., "The Categorization of Policy Contents," in Austin Ranney, ed., *Political Science and Public Policy* (Chicago: Markham Publishing Co., 1968), especially pp. 46–48.
21. See Hugh Heclo, "Conclusion: Policy Dynamics," in Richard Rose, ed., *The Dynamics of Public Policy: A Comparative Analysis* (London: Sage Publications, Ltd., 1976), pp. 237–266.

KEY TERMS 87

22. Ibid., p. 238.
23. A "fiscal year" is the period a corporate or government unit uses for budget purposes. Until recently the typical fiscal year ran from July 1 to June 30. While this is still the case for most political jurisdictions, the federal government changed their fiscal year to October 1 to September 30.
24. For a useful introduction to U.S. budget reading, see Stanley E. Collender, *The Guide to the Federal Budget: Fiscal 1983 Edition* (n.p.: The Northeast-Midwest Institute, 1982). For a detailed review of the budgetary process, see Dennis S. Ippolito, *The Budget and National Politics* (San Francisco: W.H. Freeman and Company, 1978).
25. "Current" dollar figures in Figure 4.2 are those representing the value of items at levels of the specific year being cited; "constant" dollars, on the other hand, translate those values to a level reflecting a "base" year. Thus, something that costs us $2.50 today in *current* dollars might cost us $1.50 in *constant* 1967 dollars. Among other things, this permits better comparisons and is also an indicator of price inflation.
26. For a study of how the War on Poverty "package" developed, see Robert Haveman, ed. *A Decade of Federal Anti-poverty Programs* (New York: Academic Press, 1977).
27. An in-depth study of the development of a judicial Civil Rights policy, see Richard Kluger, *Simple Justice* (New York: Alfred E. Knopf, 1976). On congressional policies in this area, see Sundquist,*Politics and Policy*,Chapter VI.

KEY TERMS
Allocative Policies
Assignment
Classification
Comparative Descriptions
Competitive Regulatory Policies
Constituent Policies
Control Policies
Crisis Policies
Cyclical Policies
Developmental Descriptions
Differentiation
Discontinuous Policies
Distributive Policies
Ease of Operationalization
Emotive Symbolic Policies
Extractive Policies
Extrinsic Policy Attributes
Functional Descriptions
Inclusiveness

Intentional Descriptions
Interval Levels
Intrinsic Policy Attributes
Level of Measurement
Linear Progress Policies
Mutual Exclusiveness
Nominal Levels
Ordinal Levels
Population-focused Descriptions
Programmatic Descriptions
Protective Regulatory Policies
Ratio Levels
Redistributive Policies
Regulatory Policies
Reliability
Sectorally Fragmented Policies
Static Policies
Strategic Policies
Structural Policies
Symbolic Policies
Typology
Validity

CHAPTER 5

Describing Economic Policies

UNDERSTANDING THE "PERSPECTIVE"

Economic policy is perhaps the most discussed and analyzed subject in America today. The 1970s and early 1980s has been a period of economic turbulance, a time when most other issues (e.g., social welfare and foreign policy) took a back seat to more basic "pocket book" concerns. Yet, despite its importance for most of us, relatively few Americans actually understand what current economic policies are or how they can deal with them. We frequently think about economic policies, but often we lack knowledge of analytic techniques that is crucial to comprehending what governments do and say. In this chapter we use the area of economic policy as an example of policy descriptions not only because of its special jargon and descriptive typologies, but also because of its salience to us all. We begin by discussing the specific "biases" that are common to economic policy thinking and providing an alternative perspective that might improve how we approach the topic. In the rest of the chapter we survey a variety of typologies frequently used in describing economic policies.

Describing economic policies essentially means examining government's role in the economy and its policies toward business. For a variety of reasons, these are topics usually approached either reluctantly or cynically by most students of American public policy. This is due, in part, to the fact that many policy analysts were weaned on an ideological diet stressing the virtues of an unencumbered marketplace and the inherent and inevitable inefficiencies of government "intervention" or "interference" with the free exchange of goods and services. That same view allows for government action, but primarily as a less-than-desirable means for dealing with market imperfections and abuses within an otherwise "healthy" private sector.[1] Thomas Paine described government as a "necessary evil," a burden we may have to endure, but not one to be endorsed.[2] Given this assumption, public policies toward business and the general economy are typically regarded as analogous to remedies or "treatments"[3] that a physician might prescribe for an ill patient. Although often welcome and even praised, such treatments are rarely viewed as anything other than indications of a systematic illness and attempts to cure or alleviate the pain associated with an unhealthy condition.[4]

We noted earlier that a good policy analysis is one who takes the bias of policy analyses into account, whether those biases are personal or those of other analysts. The "illness" metaphors and analyses associated with most economic policy thinking in the U.S. today provide an interesting example. They are models, and as such should be judged according to their usefulness. Whether this particular image of economic public policies is valid is not questioned here. Nor can we dismiss the "illness" metaphor on grounds that it lacks analytic usefulness. Nevertheless, we can posit a different perspective, one that may more closely reflect current relationships between economic and political systems. For despite claims or desires to the contrary, government's role in the American economic order is a fundamental fact of life. In the words of Robert A. Dahl and Charles E. Lindblom, "economic life in the real world today constitutes a *political* economy."[5] In fact, it can be argued that the political system is not only a major dimension in present-day economic concerns, but has a long-standing history evident in the activities of American governments dating back to colonial times and even the initial periods of exploration and settlement. "Laissez faire was always more a prescriptive than a descriptive slogan," notes Michael D. Reagan.

> The vaunted separation of business from government never was, nor could be, complete. At the very minimum, government had to provide a legal framework (e.g., laws of contract, of bankruptcy) and a monetary system for even the freest of free enterprise systems to operate. And American government always in fact intervened beyond this minimum to promote business and to act negatively, through the courts, against challenges to laissez faire from labor unions and humanitarian reformers.[6]

Individually, we may continue to regard any government intervention as inefficient, ineffective, distorting, and in fundamental opposition to what is unique about our market-oriented society.[7] However, regardless of such "feelings," the fact remains that economic public policies are and have long been evident in the United States and elsewhere. In our approach to economic policy thinking we take that as a "given." In other words, we make it our explicit "bias."

The viewpoint we assume for our discussion of economic policy is that government–marketplace relationships occur within the context of an ongoing *political economy*. What is a political economy? For present purposes, a political economy is composed of those social means and mechanisms through which human groups seek to solve the problems of production and distribution.[8] To fully understand the implications of this perspective, let us consider the main characteristics of the political economy as we have defined it.

1. The political economy is a *social* response to specific problems. It involves individual and group (e.g., "class") actions that directly or indirectly affect other members of society. Whether one acts as an independent entity or in concert with others, there is inevitably a social relationship involved. In a world of scarce resources, one person's attempts to fulfill a need or desire will invariably detract or overlap with that of another person. The apple I take off a tree is one less apple for you to consume or to even consider consuming. In short, in a finite world there are few if any actions I can take or choices I can make which will not alter your condition or opportunities. My individual actions spill over—they have "social" ramifications.

These social implications become more obvious if and when we cooperate with one another. That cooperation may come about accidentally or voluntarily; or it might be forced on us by some external actor or condition. In any case, the social basis of political economic relationships must be assumed.

2. The political economy uses a variety of *means and mechanisms* in solving the problems of production and distribution. No social group known to modern historians or contemporary chroniclers has yet devised a single solution to these problems, and it is unlikely that any ever will. But that has not stopped some from trying. Either intentionally or subconsciously, societies have always developed and implemented mechanisms and strategies for meeting the challenges of production and distribution. These have taken a variety of forms which, Lindblom notes, are "numerous beyond count."[9] Yet, at an abstract level we can discuss four "types" of mechanisms used by most human groups: exchange, authoritative-command, persuasion, and tradition.[10]

Exchange mechanisms are based on interactions among those who possess scarce yet desired resources. In its simplest form, exchange involves barter or trade between two parties, each possessing some good or service the other wishes to have. For example, as a farmer in a small community isolated from the modern commercial world, you might find yourself with a surplus of wheat after a good harvest. With that surplus crop you go to town and visit the local blacksmith to "deal" for needed farming implements and services. Offering a certain amount of wheat for those items, you begin the bargaining process that is the foundation for exchange. The blacksmith responds with a counteroffer, and the interaction continues until mutually acceptable terms are reached, a trade is established, and a physical exchange of goods and services occurs.

In contemporary mass societies the exchange process is institutionalized in a variety of ways. Exchanges take place in a marketplace where buyers and sellers meet to make demands and offer supplies in varying quantities and qualities (see the market model described in Chapter 3). Procedurally, marketplace exchanges are facilitated by the establishment and enforcement of rules and regulations as well as a medium of exchange (e.g., money), two items typically provided by governments.

Exchange systems differ substantially from *authoritative-command* mechanisms wherein some individual or group makes decisions for others. Through such means parents provide for their offspring's needs and wants. But the use of authority and command is not limited to the care of infants or adolescents. In fact, these mechanisms are widely used both in social systems the world over to implement planning directives, and in many large business firms where what is done by individuals "on the line" depends on orders from a manager.

BOX 5.1

When examining the application of authoritative-command mechanisms, we should take care to avoid three otherwise widely accepted assumptions. First, there is a tendency to believe that systems based on authority or command are "imposed" from above or outside the system. It is difficult for many of us to believe that this hierarchical approach could be established internally and accepted willingly by those who would be commanded. Yet that is often the case. When faced with a serious problem, it is sometimes more effective, less expensive, and more efficient to defer to some person or persons who might provide "better" direction and coordination due to their expert knowledge, strategic position, or other relevant resource. Thus, authoritative leadership is frequently sought from within rather than imposed from without.

> Second, we also tend to associate authority and command mechanisms with force, coercion, and the abusive application of power. While this can be and has been the case, it often is not. Due to the deference to authority usually granted by those subject to it (i.e., authority is frequently regarded as "legitimate"), the need to use coercion or other forms of power-based influence and force is generally minimized. Think of how often you obey the law because it is a law. When all is said and done, your ultimate reason for obedience might be fear of capture and threat of punishment, but there is no doubt that you do many things because it is "right" to obey the law and not only because someone is holding a gun to your head.
>
> Third and finally, we sometimes too easily adopt the assumption that authoritative-command mechanisms are inherently inefficient and automatically less desirable as a problem-solving approach than other means, especially marketplace exchange. Again, while this may be true in many cases, it is also possible that authoritative-command may be a viable, if not the only feasible, solution to certain problems. Various means of obtaining goods and services (e.g., through fraud or thievery) are outlawed by command, and other types of behavior may be mandated in a similar fashion (e.g., you must obtain a license to operate a nuclear power plant, or demonstrate the safety and efficacy of a new drug before you can market it). In the long run, the question of whether authoritative-command is an appropriate and warranted means for solving social problems is an empirical one. One should not automatically assume that it is any better or worse than an alternative approach.
>
> See Charles E. Lindblom, *Politics and Markets: The World's Political-Economic Systems* (New York: Basic Books, 1977), Part II.

In addition to exchange and authoritative-command, societies often rely on various methods of *persuasion*. There are times when we are presented with arguments attempting to persuade us to adopt or avoid certain types of behavior. In fact, we sometimes become so convinced that there may seem little or no need for making trades or mandating behavior through hierarchical commands. Because persuasion can be so effective, it is possible that a society can consciously employ persuasion to achieve certain objectives.

The forms of persuasion range from educational techniques (stressing a conscious and rational basis for action) and highly subjective approaches (relying on subconscious or emotional drives) to ideologically rooted indoctrinations which seek to alter the perceptions of those involved. Thus, being "persuaded" should not be confused or equated with necessarily being "sold a bill of goods" or being "conned." Although there are many instances where these persuasive mechanisms can be abusively applied (e.g., mass media advertising "blitzes" promoting the sale of everything from soup to nuts to nuclear disarmament treaties and presidents), they can just as easily be cited as effective means for facilitating or improving solutions to some of society's most stubborn dilemmas.

Finally, solutions to production and distribution problems can be based in *tradition* and rely on custom and choices rooted in social habits and "proven ways" demonstrated by previous generations. Societies relying heavily on tradition might be regarded by some as primitive or undeveloped, but few would accuse them of taking consciously risky behavior. In fact, what makes dependence on traditions seem undesirable to some is not that it is an ineffective means for solving some key societal problems, but that the results typically do not measure up to "modern" standards calling for economic growth and constant social change.

But tradition is not absent from modern political economies. While market prices, government directives, and persuasive arguments play large roles in our industrial societies, long-standing tastes, customs, and inherited behavioral propensities help determine many political and economic choices. The impact of family and peer influences, which perpetuate the transfer of behavior and preferences from generation to generation, should not be overestimated, but neither can it be ignored. There are many instances where tradition leads us into certain vocations, toward certain purchases, and for or against certain political decisions. Not only is tradition a "possible" solution to social problems, it is a factor constantly with us as we work out our day-to-day dilemmas.

Table 5.1 provides a summary of these four types of political economy mechanisms and the characteristics usually associated with each. It should be obvious that there are few political economies based exclusively on one or even two of these mechanisms. The particular mixture found in a given society will reflect explicit and conscious choices as well as those implicit in a system and evolved over a long period. In our survey of how policy thinkers describe economic public policy we can focus on these various mechanisms and how they are used in the American political economy.

3. Political economies deal with the social *problems of production and distribution*. What are these problems? The answer depends on who you're asking. If you ask most economists, they would respond by noting that any society must solve several basic dilemmas. First, it must "devise social institutions that mobilize human energy (and other resources) for productive purposes." Second, it must simultaneously "assure a viable allocation" of productive effort so that the "right" goods are produced. And third, it must arrange for those products to be parcelled out "in a fashion that will maintain

Table 5.1 Types of Political Economy Mechanisms

Type	Associated Characteristics
1. Exchange	1. Marketplace; trades based on bargaining
2. Authoritative-command	2. Hierarchical relationship; directives
3. Persuasion	3. Convincing arguments; use of education, advertising, propaganda, indoctrination
4. Tradition	4. Reliance on custom, established means; passed from generation to generation.

not only the capacity but the willingness" to continue that productive effort. For Robert L. Heilbroner the first two dilemmas pose the fundamental *production* problem for society, while the third represents the *distribution* problem.[11]

Although this definition of production and distribution problems is useful and sufficient for economists, it is too limited for policy analysts using the political economy approach. From the perspective of economists like Heilbroner, production and distribution problems are merely technical dilemmas. From the political economy viewpoint, however, they also involve a dimension of political and social choice. There are a number of decisions any society must make to solve even the most technical of production and distribution problems. For example, determinations must be made regarding what is to be produced, and how, in what quantitites, of what qualities, by whom, using which resources, for whom. These are obviously just as crucial as the technical problems that follow them, and they are often more difficult to solve.

BOX 5.2

On an individual level, nontechnical choices are typically made in four general ways: (1) by simple preference based on given priorities and tastes; (2) through a complex judgment reflecting a consideration of facts, estimates, and analysis; (3) according to some moral or ethical rule; and (4) by some irrational or nonrational reaction. We are all familiar with each of these through personal experience, and no doubt each of us depends on all four when making decisions concerning what we will do on a given day, what we will purchase or consume, who we will see, how we will vote, and so on. And while there are innumerable instances when such choices are made at the individual level, there are just as many examples of such decisions being made collectively. However, collective enterprises, whether they are small groups or whole societies, are less likely to rely on some of the paths of choice open to individuals facing production or distribution problems.

In the first place, unless the members of the collective are extremely cooperative or very much alike, it is unlikely that a single preference or taste could be found. On making complex judgments, here too the likelihood of obtaining identical or even similar conclusions from a group of diverse individuals is also very low. Similar difficulties would arise in attempting to establish a basic set of rules—moral or ethical—by which choices could be made. And in situations where one is dealing with several irrational or nonrational parties to a decision, collective agreement would seem out of the question. In short, collective decisions on production and distribution choices seem extremely difficult.

This situation is further aggravated once we add the factor of time. Groups might be able to overcome the problems of making collective choices on a given issue at a given time. It is possible that, faced with a crisis or other important dilemma, members of a group might put aside their differences and agree on a solution or some rule by which to decide. But over any extended period of time, a group or society is likely to face a series of production and distribution problems, some quite different from others. Such situations lead groups to establish social institutions that may facilitate such decision-making tasks for it.

These institutions may come in a variety of forms, but in the long run they reflect the four types of political economy mechanisms discussed above. The institution may be a marketplace where individual values and preferences are "exchanged" until a single choice emerges, or a system of voting in which individual choices are aggregated through a poll of the group's membership. Or it may be an organization (e.g., government) where choices are made by an authority who commands obedience either out of respect or coercion through a series of hierarchical relationships. There is also the possibility of institutionalizing a process of choice based on persuasion and relying on educational, propaganda, and indoctrinating mechanisms (e.g., the school, the media, the party, the church). Finally, choice mechanisms can be rooted in a traditional code that a group might turn to, or a set of accepted conventions that direct it to make its decisions in a particular way. Whatever mechanism or combination of institutions are developed, they are intended as means for contending with the basic nontechnical choices facing any group which must overcome the problems of production and distribution.

> On marketplace and voting mechanisms for collective choice, see Kenneth J. Arrow, *Social Choice and Individual Values*, 2nd edition (New Haven, CT: Yale University Press, 1963) and Norman Frohlich and Joe Oppenheimer, *Modern Political Economy* (Englewood Cliffs, NJ: Prentice Hall, Inc., 1978). On hierarchies and organizations, see Kenneth J. Arrow, *The Limits of Organization* (New York: W.W. Norton and Co., 1974) and Victor A. Thompson, *Modern Organization*, 2nd edition (University, AL: University of Alabama Press, 1977). On persuasion see Charles E. Lindblom, *Politics and Markets: The World's Political-Economic Systems* (New York: Basic Books, 1977). On the use of tradition, see David E. Apter, *The Politics of Modernization* (Chicago: The University of Chicago Press, 1965), esp. Chapter 3.

The complex nature of the problems faced by political economies is summarized in Figure 5.1. That figure illustrates not only the two dimensions to production and distribution problems, but also the fact that the solutions involved are interrelated. That is, solutions to the technical problems of production and distribution cannot be developed, implemented, or analyzed separately from the related problems of political and social choice. That is

Technical Problems:

	(a) Production	(b) Distribution
Problems of Political and Social Choice:		
(c) Production	What should be produced *(c)* and how *(a)*?	What should be produced *(c)* and how should it be distributed *(b)*?
(d) Distribution	How should it be produced *(a)*, and to whom should it distributed *(d)*?	How *(b)* and to whom *(d)* should products be distributed?

Figure 5.1. Economic problems.

the principal bias emerging from the political economy perspective. Rather than viewing government activities in the economy as an indication of illness, this approach puts stress on the public sector's inherent ties to the economy.

How does this bias relate to the study of American economic policies? As we examine what governments do and say about the economic and business problems that plague the United States, we will notice that those actions and statements are but a portion of our society's response to the technical and nontechnical problems of production and distribution. Thus, public policies are not some external intervention or interference with natural marketplace activities, but rather part of a general and continuous social effort to solve public problems in this policy arena. Viewed in this manner, the description of economic public policies can be more systematic and perhaps less ideological.

STRATEGIC ECONOMIC POLICY DESCRIPTIONS

There is probably no area of government activity for which there are more descriptively ambiguous labels than economic public policies. We are constantly bombarded with the terms. We hear them every day on TV and radio and read them in daily headlines: fiscal, inflationary, monetary, regulatory, and so on. We see them so often that their significance frequently escapes us and their meaning generally eludes our intellectual senses. They are perceived as the specialized jargon of economists and policymakers, and the job of the journalist is often that of a "translator" who takes these terms and puts them into words and pictures that allows the average listener or reader to comprehend what is happening.

But those labels and terms are more than merely jargon. For the informed policy analyst they represent meaningful concepts and typologies relevant to public policy. They are important because in a few words they may effectively describe what a government is doing or saying about a given policy issue. To know this jargon and understand its meaning is therefore a significant first step in comprehending economic public policy in America.

To begin to appreciate these labels as descriptive typologies, we should put them in proper perspective and demonstrate how they relate to each other. For that purpose we need to classify the labels according to what they describe, and in the analysis of economic public policies we find five relevant means for categorizing descriptive typologies: (1) *strategic* categories reflecting the orientation of policies to the solution of economic problems; (2) categories concerned with the *purpose or function* of economic public policies; (3) a scheme in which policies are categorized according to the *level of activity* being contended with by the government action or statement; (4) categories based on the *tools* used by government; and (5) a broad arrangement wherein economic policies are classified according to the *specific activities* of the government.

In the economic policy area, theory and ideology have played an important role in determining how societies act to solve their production and distribution problems. These theories prove extremely useful when we seek explanations of government policies. But they also play a common descriptive role due to the substantial influence they have had in determining government *strategies* for dealing with the problems of political economy. This fact is most often reflected in the tendency of many policy thinkers to describe public policies as capitalist, socialist, communist, Keynesian, and so forth.

In the United States it is common to hear people describe policies as capitalist or socialist, and in fewer instances does one hear the terms mercantilist or Keynesian. Still, all four terms play a major role in the description of contemporary economic policies and thus will constitute the four types we focus on. Of course, each is looked upon quite differently by the general public. The capitalist view is held in high regard by most Americans, thus providing the capitalist category with an emotional advantage over the others. But for the moment we will disregard the subjective weight given to various labels and concentrate instead on what they represent as strategic descriptions of economic public policies.

Capitalist Policies

Policies that are strategically *capitalist* can best be summarized in terms of both the objectives they seek and fundamental standards for achieving them. Put briefly, capitalist policies seek an efficient allocation of productive resources throughout society, while simultaneously maximizing the freedom of individuals within society to do as they please with a minimum of governmental interference. On a theoretical level, capitalist strategy sees these objectives as so complementary that they cannot be considered separately when developing public policies. This is the message built into the work of capitalism's philosophic founder, Adam Smith,[12] as well as its most prominent contemporary spokesperson, Milton Friedman.[13] The essentials of capitalist thought are that the production and distribution problems of society can best be solved by relying as much as possible on exchange mechanisms and, therefore, the values and judgments of those who come to the marketplace.

Social actions taken to fulfill those objectives have to meet three basic standards. First, the end result of those actions must be products and product distribution in which the benefits received exceed the expended costs. In short, the action must ensure that what is most wanted by consumers gets produced and distributed to them. Second, what gets produced must be produced in the most efficient (i.e., least costly) way. That is, available resources should be employed in ways that maximize the benefits of what is being provided through them and their use. Finally, the distribution of benefits and costs to individuals should reflect their contribution to the solution of production and distribution problems.[14] Any actions, public or private, meeting these standards while achieving the objectives set forth by capitalists, can be termed capitalist.

Obviously, both theoretically and historically, many more private actions than public ones can be described as capitalist. Yet there are public policies that fit into this model. Adam Smith, for example, posited three areas of public activity acceptable within the context of capitalist strategy:

> first, the duty of protecting the society from the violence and invasion of other independent societies; secondly, the duty of protecting, as far as possible, every member of the society from injustice or oppression of every other member of it, or the duty of establishing an exact administration of justice; and thirdly, the duty of erecting and maintaining certain public institutions, which can never be for the interest of any individual, or small number of individuals, to erect and maintain. . . .[15]

And Nobel laureate Friedman emphasizes that "a consistent liberal [capitalist] is not an anarchist." Rather he or she backs a

> government which maintained law and order, defined property rights, served as a means whereby we could modify property rights and other rules of the economic game, adjudicated disputes about the interpretation of rules, enforced contracts, promoted competition, provided a monetary framework, engaged in activities to counter technical monopolies and to overcome . . . [adverse spillover] effects widely regarded as sufficiently important to justify government intervention, and which supplemented private charity and the private family in protecting the irresponsible, whether madman or child. . . ."[16]

In short, there is room for public policies within the capitalist strategy. Thus, it is possible to describe some economic public policies as capitalist. Whether a given government activity or statement fits this category will depend, of course, on its applicability to the means and ends set forth in capitalist theories. They are policies carrying four major assumptions about the way an economy should work. Foremost among these is *individualism* and the belief that each person is the best judge of what he or she desires. What is produced must reflect those judgments.

Second, the primary and best social mechanism for expressing those judgments and fulfilling them is assumed to be the *marketplace* and related exchange-based institutions. Other mechanisms may at times be necessary, but they are inherently less desirable since they each rely on substitutes for individual judgments (e.g., government or tradition) or create an "artificial" desire (through command or persuasion) and therefore provide poor solutions to the problems.

Linked to this is a third assumption holding that any necessary intervention by government should be based on the *rule of law*. By this the capitalist strategy calls for reliance on policies that avoid ambiguous interpretations or arbitrary implementation. This assumption, by necessity, provided for minimal government activity by restricting policies to those areas where non-arbitrary and unambiguous actions and statements are possible.[17]

The fourth assumption is the need for an effectively maintained institution of *private property*. Without the provision of such an institution both the productive and distributive efficiency of the marketplace would be adversely affected, and individual freedom, which the capitalist holds in high esteem, would be limited. The need to legally sanctify and uphold private property is based on the incentive it provides individuals involved in marketplace exchanges. Were these individuals without such incentives, their involvement would be less than total and the result would be a less than efficient solution to the problems of political economy.

In summary, for a policy action or statement to be described as capitalist it must: (1) seek efficient production and distribution solutions while maximizing individual freedom; (2) use means that produce what is desired by consumers, utilizing the most efficient combination of resources, and distributing those products in an equitable fashion; while (3) assuming the primacy of individualism, the marketplace, rule of law, and private property.

Socialist Policies

An alternative category for describing economic public policies is that associated with the concepts of *socialism*. Contrary to popular belief in the United States, socialism is not inherently in opposition to the forms or results of capitalist approaches. In fact, the socialist approach has a great deal in common with capitalism. In almost every form it has taken, socialist strategy accepts the goal of efficient production and many of the standards and assumptions attached to that objective. Its primary difference from capitalism is found in socialism's reaction to (and rejection of) the types of economic freedom posited by capitalist strategies. Freedom does play a role in socialist strategies, but it is secondary to the goal of economic justice.

To understand the goals of the socialist model, we must briefly turn to its classic exposition in the work of Karl Marx. There is a direct link between capitalism and socialism found in Marx's writings. ". . . Marx's critique of capitalism was based on the assumptions of classical economics [i.e., capitalist theory] itself . . . . He used the weapons of the dominant ideology to attack the very system those weapons defended."[18] In the process, Marx observes that solutions to the problems of production and distribution involved two struggles: First, the "struggle of people against nature to obtain subsistence and ease" and, second, "the struggle of people against people."[19] It was the analysis of that second struggle that separated Marx from the capitalists, and it is the objective implied in that struggle—the elimination of human exploitation and class domination—which provides the socialist view of economic justice.[20]

Given these objectives, the standards applied to socialist public policies are both similar to and distinct from their capitalist counterparts. As in capitalism, socialist policies are to produce what consumers want, but with the qualification that the consumer's desires be "true" rather than artificially imposed or manipulated through false advertising or other deceptive practices. Socialist strategy also calls for the optimal use of available resources, but denies that this can be accomplished mainly through uncontrolled market mechanisms. For the socialist, a policy permitting unrestricted exchange is not the most rational approach and is open to both waste and corruption. And the socialist believes a good policy is one leading to an equitable distribution of goods and services, but their view of equity is closer to the concept of providing people with what they need rather than rewarding them on the basis of their individual contribution to productive processes. The often cited passage from Marx's work expressing this standard is "from each according to his abilities, to each according to his needs."

Taken together, these standards and the goals they reflect necessarily lead the socialist to advocate policies relying less on market mechanisms and more on those contributing greater control in society's efforts to solve production problems, that is, on authoritative-command mechanisms. Thus, in place of capitalist policy assumptions focused on private property, individualism, the rule of law, and the market, socialists posit *property redistribution, community values, rational policymaking*, and the *use of a central authority* to bring about policy ends. Property is still important in the socialist production process, but its private possession is not sanctified. Instead, society (through government) assumes the right to redistribute property to accomplish its objectives. The individual is not ignored in socialist strategies, but instead finds a place and value within the community which, in turn, takes priority. As for the rule of law, it is replaced by a belief in the rational capabilities of policymakers and their experts. Finally, the marketplace gives way to centralized authority and its capacity to decide and act in a rational and coordinated fashion.[21] These are the premises for socialist policies, and taken together with socialist goals and standards they form the basis for this category in our classification of economic policies.

Mercantilist Policies

If socialism was historically a reaction to capitalism, then capitalism was historically a reaction to *mercantilism*. Yet, as a policy description, mercantilism may have more to offer today's analyst than merely the satisfaction of historical curiosity. As the dominant European approach to economic policy before capitalism emerged in the late 1700s, mercantilism reflected the monarchial state's goals of developing internal national unity and an external international strength. These goals of nationalism and national power manifested themselves in policies aimed both at commercial self-sufficiency and a supporting colonial system which spread European influence throughout the world.[22] To accomplish these ends, public policies were designed to promote certain interests and prevent the rise of others.

> Manufacturing was encouraged by subsidies, special privileges, patents, and monopolies. Foreign trade was stimulated by acquisition of colonies and efforts to keep wages down and regulated by tariffs, navigation laws, and trade restrictions. Agriculture was fostered by a variety of policies; in England imports of food were taxed in order to keep out foreign competition, while in France exports of agricultural products were taxed in order to keep domestic production at home. In particular, the munitions industries were promoted—guns, gunpowder, ships, and supplies.[23]

Today, certain government activities strategically closely resemble traditional mercantilism. Some of the rationales for these policies have changed. At least in industrial economies, the problem of national unity is not as crucial as that of political stability. No doubt, for some nations there remains the fear of national disunity, which constantly plagued Europe as it evolved from the feudal society of the middle ages. However, today's leaders regard political turmoil and extremist movements as a greater source of concern, and mercantilist policy has been employed to limit such turmoil. Internationally, mercantilism is still concerned with obtaining and maintaining national power, but the stress today is on economic rather than military capabilities. These differences from the historical pattern of mercantilism have led analysts to discuss the approach as new or neomercantilism.[24]

Given the objectives of national unity, political stability, and national power in the global arena, mercantilist policies must meet four interrelated standards to be regarded as acceptable. First, they must help establish a *national self-sufficiency*, particularly in critical natural resources such as fuels and metals.[25] Second, they should provide the country with an *advantageous trade position* in world markets, the ultimate measure being a large balance-of-payments surplus. Third, they push governments in the direction of *protectionist policies* aimed at keeping profits, jobs, and investments at home. Fourth and simultaneously, the new mercantilism seeks to *attract foreign investment* with special attention to policies that give the receiving nation some control over how those investments are made and where subsequent earnings will be funneled.[26]

The assumptions mercantilist policies are based on combine a number of capitalist and socialist policy premises. Markets and other exchange mechanisms are sanctioned, as long as they produce mercantilist results. This is usually guaranteed by assuming that an active authoritative-command mechanism (i.e., government) is monitoring market activities and manipulating or controlling them where necessary. Brought together with the assumed priority of national interest, the results are contemporary policies not very different from the mercantilist policies of old.[27]

Keynesian Policies

We now turn to a fourth descriptive category, one that arises frequently in discussions of economic public policies. Like other models based on strategy, *Keynesianism* is a reaction of sorts. It is most often regarded as a variant of classical capitalism, but it is also a response to the possibility of socialism. Its roots are in the work of British economist, John Maynard Keynes,[28] although some argue that the "Keynesianist" policy approach cannot be directly derived from his writings.[29]

Relative to classical capitalism, Keynes provides an alternative to what has been known as *Say's Law of Markets*. Developed by French economist Jean Baptiste Say in a work published in 1803, this law held that, in the long run, production creates its own demand. The doctrine itself was a response to early critics of Adam Smith's work who claimed that government activity was necessary to help avoid business depressions and the economic disorder accompanying them. These critics believed the free marketplace incapable of handling such downturns on its own. Say's retort was based on the idea that the production of one item meant resources were being diverted from production of another item. If this use of productive resources was an incorrect reading of consumer desires, then the overabundance of the produced item will generate demand for under-supplied goods and services. Producers will eventually readjust to the new demand and thus whatever business slump had been developed earlier would be short-lived and self-correcting.

> Say argued that there could never be a general deficiency of demand or a general glut of commodities throughout the whole economy. Certain industries or sec-

tors of industry might be plagued by overproduction due to miscalculation and excessive allocation of resources to those types of production, but elsewhere in the economy there would inevitably be shortages. The consequent fall of prices in one area and their rise in others would induce business firms to shift production, and the imbalances would be quickly corrected.[30]

Say's Law proved sufficient for the capitalist perspective and its goals of efficient production and economic freedom.[31] However it was also based on a number of implicit assumptions, the most questionable being the finite nature of available resources.[32] The key to the generation of demand in Say's Law is that the production of one item detracts from resources available to produce another. But what if available resources or productive capabilities can be expanded? Would not the "self-correcting" mechanisms be distorted and made ineffective? If so, would it not be better to rely on government and related mechanisms to assure that this expansion is managed to the benefit of society? These were the questions addressed by Keynes in his economic theories, and the answers he provided offer the foundation for contemporary Keynesian policy strategies.[33]

The objectives of Keynesian economic policy are economic stability and economic growth. The goal of stability developed from both a general adversity to the prospect of society continually suffering from boom-and-bust business cycles common to a market system, and a specific fear of a long-term business downturn such as the Great Depression. It reflected a belief that economic instability can be avoided through "fine tuning" maneuvers based on strategies derived from Keynes' theories.[34] The goal of economic growth, while somewhat qualified in the writings of Keynesianists,[35] is rooted in a fear that the specter of poverty predicted by early capitalist theorists (e.g., Thomas Malthus) might come to pass unless a continuous effort is made to expand available resources. In a growing, continuously expanding economy, the Keynesian sees not only the potential for avoiding severe economic downturns, but also the possibility for directing that growth into socially beneficial channels.

When translated into criteria for classifying policy actions, Keynesian objectives reflect a desire to achieve certain quantifiable goals. Heavy emphasis, for instance, is placed on achieving and maintaining a low level of unemployment. During the height of Keynesian influence during the 1960s that standard was specifically set at a *full employment* goal of 4-percent unemployment.[36] Today that target remains as a widely accepted goal, but there also seems a greater willingness to settle for a higher figure such as 6 percent.[37] Another standard is *economic growth rate* which is usually reflected in the expansion of the gross national product (GNP), that is, the market value of all goods and services produced in an economy over a given period of time. The precise level of growth sought under the Keynesian approach would vary depending on the effort needed to achieve full employment, but an annual real growth rate of between 4 and 4½ percent has generally been regarded as desirable by their leading spokesperson.[38] And a third major standard, a low inflation rate, is related to the Keynesian concern for *price stability*. The typical measures for inflation have been the consumer price index and the wholesale price index (recently renamed the "producer price index"), and while there was a period in the early 1960s when the U.S. economy achieved an inflation rate of less than 2 percent annually,[39] more recent goals have been to keep inflation to 7 percent or at least below the "double digit" levels which were common in the late 1970s.[40]

Keynesian assumptions are both conceptually and theoretically close to those accepted by capitalists. For one thing, the market exchange system is accepted, and only its ability to function smoothly in the absence of rational intervention by government is questioned. Thus, Keynesians generally accept a role for command mechanisms, but not to the extent advocated by socialists and mercantilists. Government's role is more in the order of a manipulator rather than a commander, and its primary purpose is to fine tune the amount of aggregate demand that provides the dynamic for the economy. Underlying this view is the assumption that the key to manipulating aggregate demand is total spending in the economy, and this in turn is dependent on consumer spending and business investment. It is in respect to these last two variables that government policy has leverage. Keynesianists believe that through a variety of policies, from direct government expenditure to the control of interest rates and the supply of money, governments can promote economic growth, smooth out cyclical business patterns, and maintain price stability. Such are the theoretical underpinnings of the Keynesian perspective.

BOX 5.3

In the late 1970s and early 1980s, a challenge to the dominance of the Keynesian policy approach emerged in the form of "supply side economics" (or "Reaganomics" since it was closely associated with the policies of the Reagan Administration). Central to this important challenge was the reassertion of the same Say's Law of Markets, the doctrine Keynes had attacked in his work.

Say's Law holds that production and not aggregate demand is the critical variable in determining economic activity. To briefly restate Say's theorem, over the long run and across an entire economy, the unencumbered marketplace will effectively and efficiently correct for any oversupply of goods and services in the economy if allowed to do so. Of course, this view is in direct contrast to the Keynesian belief that a laissez faire economy will necessarily produce a supply glut and thereby invariably create the conditions for economic crises. And while Keynesians are convinced that aggregate demand can be manipulated to stimulate aggregate supply, the supply siders remain convinced that the opposite is true. "The essential thesis of Say's Law remains true," argues supply side advocate George Gilder: "supply creates demand."

> There can be no such thing as a general glut of goods. There can be glut of "bads," but in a world of necessary scarcity in which the very science of economics finds its meaning, an apparent glut of all goods merely signifies a dearth of creative production, a lack of new supplies and fresh demands.
> . . .

Accordingly, any obstacles to the development of "creative production," "new supplies" or "fresh demands" will prove disastrous for the modern economy. It is the contention of Gilder and other supply siders that current Keynesian government policies is full of such obstacles.

Marxist critics Harry Magdoff and Paul M. Sweezy have offered an interesting analogy to help summarize the debate between the Keynesians and supply siders. It is worth quoting at length.

> The trouble with supply-side economics, to use a homely analogy, is that it operates on the principle of moving a string by pushing on one of the ends. The string stands for the economy: one end is labeled supply, the other demand. The supply-siders propose to move the whole piece ahead by pushing on the supply end. The result of course is not to move the string but to mess it up.
>
> . . . The . . . Keynesian recipe for moving the string is to take hold of the demand end and pull it along. This makes more sense, and up to a point it works, as wartime experiences have frequently demonstrated. But if the string is pulled too hard and too long, it breaks at various weak points, and repairs cannot be made from either the supply or the demand ends.

On the supply side position, see George Gilder, *Wealth and Poverty* (New York: Basic Books, 1981), Chapter 4. For a more detailed yet well-written explication of the supply side view, see Jude Wanniski, *The Way the World Works* (New York: Basic Books, 1978). The Marxist critique is from Harry Magdoff and Paul M. Sweezy, *The Deepening Crisis of U.S. Capitalism* (New York: Monthly Review Press, 1981), Chapter 20.

Table 5.2 summarizes the four strategic approaches discussed in this section. While there are areas of overlap and agreement, each is generally regarded as a distinctive approach by which one can describe contemporary political economy policies. While these categories are frequently used to describe economic policies, their value is somewhat limited. As noted in Box 5.4, they are somewhat ambiguous and perhaps irrelevant. Yet they reflect historical, ideological, and philosophic traditions that have given shape to contemporary economic public policies through the provision of strategic perspectives. Therefore, it might be more useful to apply these descriptive categories to clusters of policy statements or actions rather than to individual acts.

For example, in 1979 the British electorate chose a Conservative government headed by Prime Minister Margaret Thatcher. Unlike previously elected Conservative administrations, Thatcher's was politically committed to a strategy of "capitalism" as we have described above. In light of that commitment, the British government's sale of its interest in such enterprises as British Airways and British Aerospace can be labeled as capitalist policies. However, early in its tenure, the Thatcher government also decided to continue full support for two ailing corporate grants, BL Limited (British Leyland) and Rolls-Royce, Limited. Were we to focus on those supportive policies, Thatcher's government could be said to advocate and promote mercantilist or socialist policies. Yet, stepping back from that narrow view one can see those as instances of policies based on economic expediency which detracted only slightly from the general capitalist thrust of Thatcher's program.[41]

BOX 5.4

Strategic categories no doubt represent popular labels. They are frequently applied in daily conversations and newspaper columns as a short-hand description of what government is doing or plans to do. Yet as descriptive categories they have many limitations and flaws, two of which must be stressed. First, these are essentially ambiguous labels in the sense that they mean different things to different people and lack the precision and detail that might render them more useful. These ambiguities are linked both to each other and their common ideological source. Because the meaning of each strategic type varies from analyst to analyst, it is impossible to establish the details necessary to make them useful for the uninformed. There are, for example, several varieties of socialism, ranging from a state-controlled and centralized system involving public ownership of all producing and distributing mechanisms to democratic socialism, which tends to apply the system as a liberal, humane, worker-controlled and decentralized approach. This, in turn, is due to the fact that what makes a policy or set of policies strategically socialist, capitalist, Keynesian, or whatever are common historical roots and not fundamental agreements on specific issues. Thus we must be cautious when using these broad and ambiguous classifications of economic public policies.

Second, an argument can be made that these labels are actually irrelevant for the contemporary analyst and instead are merely artifacts of an era when broad strategic categories had clear meaning and policy significance. As Robert A. Dahl and Charles E. Lindblom argued in 1953, "techniques and not 'isms' are the kernel of rational social action in the Western world."

> Both socialism and capitalism are dead. The politico-economic systems of the United States and Britain differ in important respects, to be sure; yet both major parties in both countries are attacking their economic problems with fundamentally the same kind of techniques. Ideological differences . . . themselves are significant in affecting the choice of techniques, but policy in any case is technique-minded, and it is becoming increasingly difficult in both countries to argue policy in terms of the mythical grand alternatives.

Similarly, it is difficult to describe policies in terms of the strategic categories developed along lines provided by those "mythical grand alternatives." Yet despite the possible irrelevance of these labels, or their vagueness, they have been found of some use by policy thinkers the world over. For that reason we will consider them as manifested in several prominent forms.

See Robert A. Dahl and Charles E. Lindblom, *Politics, Economics and Welfare: Planning and Politico-Economic Systems Resolved into Basic Social Processes* (New York: Harper Torchbooks, 1953), p. 16.

An additional problem with this descriptive categorization scheme is that certain specific policy moves are so new or unique that they can fit in none or all of the categories. For example, consider decisions of the U.S. government in the late 1970s to guarantee bank loans to Lockheed and Chrysler, or the special tax breaks provided for American Motors and other ailing industrial giants. Are these capitalist politics? Socialist? Mercantilist? Keynesian? It seems one can develop a rationale for such policies from each strategy approach. In short, while commonly heard and applied, beware of these popular descriptive labels.

Table 5.2 Strategic Policy Models

Policy	Goals	Standards	Assumptions
Capitalist	1. Efficient production and distribution 2. Maximum freedom for individuals	1. Benefits received must exceed cost of production 2. "Optional" use of available resources 3. Distribution based on value of contribution	1. Individualism 2. Marketplace is stressed 3. Minimal government intervention 4. System of private property
Socialist	1. Efficient production and distribution 2. Economic justice	1. Produce according to "true" needs of consumer 2. "Rational" use of available resources 3. Distribution based on need	1. Community values have priority 2. Use of centralized authoritative command mechanisms 3. Property redistribution 4. Rational policy making and planning.

Mercantilist	1. Political stability (internal unity) 2. National power	1. National self-sufficiency 2. Advantageous international trade position 3. Protectionism 4. Attraction of foreign investment	1. Priority of national interest. 2. Use of any exchange mechanisms to achieve ends. 3. Active (and guiding) government.
Keynesianist	1. Economic stability 2. Economic growth	1. Low unemployment 2. High economic growth 3. Price stability	1. Reliance on market mechanism. 2. Government manipulation to enhance control over aggregate demand created by consumer spending and business investment.

DESCRIPTIONS BASED ON "PURPOSE"

Another commonly used set of labels for public policies dealing with political economic problems concentrates on the *purpose* of government actions and statements. As with strategic categories, descriptions implied by these labels are rarely expressed in technical terms. But unlike the strategic categories discussed above, there is little in the way of a fully developed formal literature backing up these constructs. Rather, they seem directly related to the intended objectives of the policy, regardless of the strategic orientation involved or the specific tools and techniques being applied.

Focusing on policy purposes, these descriptions can be reduced to categories representing six types of activities: stimulation, stablization, protection, promotion, prevention, and restoration. *Stimulative* economic policies are those intended to generate activity in an area of production or distribution characterized as sluggish by the policymaker. If consumer spending is regarded as too low or otherwise below potential, policies will be advocated or implemented to increase retail sales. This can be accomplished through a variety of mechanisms, such as tax cuts or rebates or policies that act to lower prices on specific items such as automobiles and major appliances. If trade is perceived to be unfavorable, policymakers can make tariff adjustments, offer special subsidies, or give special loans or loan guarantees to provide stimulus to relevant industries.

Stabilization policies are not quite the opposite of stimulative activities, although their general impact is to "cool down" what is perceived as overactive economic variables. As we have seen in the brief description of the Keynesian model, many economists and policymakers are as concerned with economic stability as they are with growth or some other objective. Stabilization, however, need not be regarded as the antithesis to growth. In fact, it would help to think of two types of stabilizing policies: first, those representing a preoccupation with smooth business cycles, and second, those reflecting a desire to establish an economic growth pattern with minimal disturbance to productive and distributive mechanisms. During the first half of the 1960s American economic policy was primarily concerned with stable growth in the economy.[42] However, by the last half of the 1970s it was evident that our national policy was primarily concerned with avoiding explosive inflation rates or a steep business downturn. The key words were no longer "stable growth," but rather "mild recession."[43] In either case, the objectives of stabilizing policies are not necessarily to stop increases in population, prices, or other variables, but to control or restrict their growth. Thus, in the period of high inflation during the late 1970s and early 1980s, policymakers would have been satisfied if the annual increase in the consumer price index was held to less than 7 percent. There was never any talk of (or hope for) an overall decrease in price levels, and there was perhaps even a fear that falling prices would indicate a severe recession. Thus, Reagan Administration officials were quite pleased when the overall inflation rate remained below 10 percent throughout 1982. In other words, to stabilize does not necessarily mean to stop or negate economic activity. It does imply a desire to control or smooth out that activity.

Some stabilization polices are built into the economic system. Called *automatic stabilizers*, these policies are triggered by economic conditions and have the effect of partially offsetting their impacts. For example, when unemployment increases so do claims on the unemployment compensation system, thus automatically generating government activity at a time when stability is needed (see Chapter 6 for more information).

Protective policies are moves by governments to enhance the potential of sectors of the economy by creating an environment these sectors perceive as "safe." Protection, as used here, indicates activities that impose trade barriers to competitors, either foreign or domestic depending on the economic sector or industry in question. They also indicate policies, such as government loan guarantees or special tax credits, that might save businesses from bankruptcy. And it also indicates some forms of government subsidies or favorable treatment, such as mandates that only U.S. merchant ships haul commodities purchased by or under U.S. foreign aid programs.

Promotional policies are closely related to protective government activities for the obvious reason that "safe" environments are conducive to the expansion of specific industries or economic sectors. Yet to protect is not necessarily to promote, for promotion implies policies that render an economic enterprise more healthy and valuable rather than merely "safe." Promotional policies come in the form of government purchases, subsidies, loans, or substantial tax incentives.

BOX 5.5

A significant example of promotional tactics was President Carter's "synfuel" policy proposals announced in mid-July of 1979. In response to an energy crisis based on the politics of the Organization of Petroleum Exporting Countries and an increasing awareness that world oil reserves were limited, the U.S. government turned toward policies intended to develop alternative energy sources for the future. In the early 1970s an effort was made to enhance the nuclear power and coal industries, but these efforts proved disappointing. By 1979 a new strategy was called for, and this led Carter to propose a set of policies promoting the establishment of a synthetic fuels, or synfuel, industry.

Among his plans was the creation of an Energy Security Corporation charged with investing upwards of $88 billion to generate by 1990 the equivalent of 2.5 million barrels of oil per day from domestic shale and coal sources. To this was added a proposal for an Energy Mobilization Board with powers to accelerate synfuel industry development by getting around, preempting, or speeding up actions by state boards and federal agencies which deal with environmental protection. All this was in addition to related promotional activities, including the decontrol of domestic oil and natural gas prices (which would rise and therefore make higher cost synfuels a more attractive investment), mandates for the automobile industry to produce more fuel-efficient vehicles, tax incentives to stimulate conservation and conversion to non-petroleum fuels, and increased federal investment in research dealing with alternative fuel sources. And even with these proposals and policies, there was considerable discussion of further measures to promote synfuel development, measures such as government guaranteed markets and prices, as well as tax breaks significantly larger than those already proposed. Although the Reagan Administration dismantled many of these programs, they still represent a classic example of promotional economic policies.

See "The Oil Crisis Is Real This Time," *Business Week* (July 30, 1979), pp. 44–60.

Preventative policies are often of a different nature than those discussed to this point. For one thing, preventative policies are not concerned with getting the economy as a whole or specific firms to do something or creating safe environments for industries. On the contrary, they are oriented toward stopping types of economic activity regarded as dangerous, unfair, or in some other way undesirable. Thus there is a second distinction between preventative policies and those previously discussed: the existence of a set of standards or criteria reflecting what the policymaker views as a desirable or worthwhile situation, Put briefly, preventative policies assume the existence of good and bad, desirable and undesirable, states of affairs. Given this assumption, preventative policies are intended to stop the political economy from generating the bad or undesirable conditions.

For example, where policymakers perceive occupational safety as desirable, they might formulate and implement policies intended to prevent accidents in the workplace. Where they regard environmental pollution as a threat to the health or aesthetic senses of their constituents, they might impose regulations to stop further or future polluting by industry and others involved in environmental degradation. And where monopolies and dominating cartels are regarded as detrimental to the economic well-being of the public, policymakers might issue and enforce policies preventing their formation. In the United States all three of these approaches have been taken, represented by the activities of the Occupational Safety and Health Administration, the Environmental Protection Agency, and the two major antitrust agencies (i.e., the Antitrust Division in the Department of Justice and the Federal Trade Commission) respectively.[44]

Restorative policies take preventive policy standards a step further by seeking to reinstate a desired state of affairs. These policies not only assume the existence of a desirable condition, but go on to assert that (1) those conditions existed once before and (2) steps can be taken to correct for damages already done. Thus, antitrust activities are not limited to preventing undesired mergers and outlawing collusive agreements among industrial giants attempting to monopolize a market. They also include attempts (frequently unsuccessful) at breaking up monopolies and cartels or getting dominant firms such as American Telephone and Telegraph, Xerox, IBM, or Standard Oil to divest themselves of certain subsidiaries or to behave in a fashion that promotes competition.[45] Environmental policies also include restorative treatments by mandating not only an end to current polluting, but also a re-creation of conditions when there was clean water and clean air. The movement that resulted in policies calling for the reclamation of strip-mined lands is a primary example of this policy category.

Table 5.3 offers a summary of purposive policy types. Of course, these are far from exhaustive. However, they do reflect some commonly applied types of economic policy description. It should be evident from the preceding delineation of these categories that there is considerable overlap among them. It is sometimes difficult to draw a clear line between a policy

Table 5.3 Purposive Policy Models

Policy Type	Purpose
1. Stimulative	1. To generate economic activity
2. Stabilizing	2. To provide smoothness to economic activity; to control
3. Protective	3. To create "safe" economic environments for firms or industries
4. Promotional	4. To render an economic activity or enterprise more profitable and valuable
5. Preventative	5. To stop or halt undesirable activity or deterioration of conditions
6. Restorative	6. To recreate desirable state of affairs

action or statement that is stimulative or promotional, protective or preventative, stablizing or restorative, and so on. Once again we must return to our justification for any model or typology—its utility given our analytic purposes. The key to analytic success with these and all tools and techniques discussed in this book is to remain conscious of their limitations as well as their value.

"LEVEL OF ACTIVITY" DESCRIPTIONS

Students of economics frequently distinguish between activity at the macroeconomic and microeconomic levels.[46] The distinction is basic to economics, and it is a fundamental distinction applied in the description of economic public policies. That policies vary according to the *level of activity* being affected should not come as a surprise to anyone familiar to the American federal system. Some policies are local, while others are regional or national in scope. The same applies to economic policies, which are either micro- or macroeconomic.

Microeconomic policies deal with specific entities involved in the economic system. These entities may be individuals, firms, industries, or sectors of the economy. The policies classified under this category deal with the behavior of these entities, their relationship in the marketplace, and the role they play relative to certain products, levels of income, and similar concerns. *Macroeconomic* policies, on the other hand, deal with the "aggregates" of the economic system: levels of employment, the rate of inflation, the balance-of-trade surplus or deficit, the rate of GNP growth, productivity levels, and other characteristics of the system.

Obviously, whether a policy is micro- or macroeconomic depends more on the intended target of the action or statement than on the specific tools or methods used. Policies aimed at increasing employment may directly influence certain individuals or firms, but they are nonetheless macroeconomic due to the intended target of their activities. The creation of public works programs, for example, may result in the employment of specific individuals in a given locale on a project of considerable value to the community, yet the policy may still be termed macroeconomic if the program was formulated to reduce nationwide or regional unemployment.

Similarly, a special trade ageement between the United States and the People's Republic of China for industrial material may enhance the business of American corporations X or Y, but if the goal of the agreement is a favorable balance of trade then we are dealing with macroeconomic public policy. This can work in the opposite direction, of course. An intensive lobbying effort may bring about trade policies aimed at protecting a specific

Table 5.4 "Level of Activity" Policy Models

Policy Type	Focus On:
1. Microeconomic	1. Behavior and market relations among individuals, firms, industries, economic sectors.
2. Macroeconomic	2. Aggregate characteristics of the economy.

industry (e.g., textiles, steel, automobiles) or promoting another (e.g., aerospace, military hardware), and while these may have macroeconomic impacts they would be classified as microeconomic in accordance with policymaker intentions.

Inevitably, however, these categories prove weak. First, there is always the problem of policies at the border between micro- and macroeconomic. For example, was the synfuel policy proposed by the Carter Administration (see Box 5.5.) microeconomic (because it sought to promote activity among firms in a specific industry) or macroeconomic (because its purpose was to decrease American dependence on foreign fuel sources and/or establish a better balance-of-trade situation)? Second is the difficulty a policy analyst will frequently encounter when trying to determine exactly what policymakers intended when they formulated a given policy. This will be especially true when dealing with a policymaking group such as Congress or a state legislature. The coalition responsible for passing any particular piece of legislation may include legislators whose purposes and intentions may be vastly different. To narrow those disparate intentions down to a single one is usually an impossible task. This and related problems can render the micro/macro distinction difficult to apply and perhaps useless for the policy thinker.

From time to time other models based on level of activity categories have been posited. Most of these are variations on the micro division, but others seek to go further. For instance, one economist has proposed the development of micro-microeconomics—an approach concerned with what occurs within a microeconomic entity.[47] If this idea takes hold, it is possible that we might see greater use of that category for public policies that seek to control what goes on within a firm. Policies such as those enforced by the Occupational Safety and Health Administration and the Equal Employment Opportunity Commission might fall under such a classification.[48] Such innovations in the description of economic policy should be considered by an analyst who is dissatisfied with commonly used models.

THE "TOOLS" APPROACH

When reading any in-depth analysis of contemporary economic policies, it is inevitable that one comes across the terms fiscal, monetary, or incomes policy. These are labels reflecting broadly defined categories of economic policies based on the tools used by government. They do not deal with what governments do, but rather what they work with when they do something.

Fiscal policies are those relying on the use of governmental spending and taxation capabilities. The use of expenditures and taxes has become so common in American public policy that many policy analysts use fiscal measures in analyzing and evaluating almost all policies.[49] However, it is in the area of economic policy that fiscal tools are consciously applied to policy goals. Through spending a government can stimulate or promote economic activity, while taxes can do the same as well as prevent some activities or act as an economic stabilizer. In addition, governments can spend or tax with the intention of influencing either microeconomic or macroeconomic variables. In short, the tools available to policymakers through government spending or revenue-raising activities are numerous and applicable to a great variety of purposes.

Monetary policies use the governments' ability to manipulate the amount or cost of money in the economy. The availability of funds is a critical variable in any economy. If the supply of funds is high relative to the amount of goods and services they can buy, the end result is likely to be inflation and economic growth and stability may suffer. Where the supply of money is low, the opposite condition is likely to result. What determines the supply of money in an economy will vary from society to society, but two basic sources are (1) government's capacity to issue currency, and (2) its ability to control the flow of money though banking and related financial institutions. In the United States, monetary policies are centered in the Federal Reserve banking system which acts as a controller and central clearinghouse for America's financial institutions. Through its ability to loosen or tighten the reserve requirement of member banks (i.e., the proportion of deposits they must maintain on hand), its indirect control over the interest rates member banks charge their customers who borrow money, and its capacity to buy and sell large-denomination government securities, the Governing Board of the Federal Reserve System (also known as the Fed) can exercise considerable influence over American economic conditions.

Monetary policies are inherently of more limited value to policymakers than fiscal policy, for while expenditures and taxes can be directly or indirectly aimed at microeconomic as well as macroeconomic targets, reserve requirements and interest rate manipulations generally influence macroeconomic activity and then primarily indirectly.[50] Despite this limited

THE "TOOLS" APPROACH   119

utility, monetary policies can have a great deal to do with stimulating and stabilizing the economy and thus conditioning productive and distributive activity. In fact, many eminent economists (e.g., Milton Friedman) regard monetary policies as more important than fiscal activities. These monetarists are generally associated with capitalist policy strategies and their influence has been increasing over the past decade as Keynesianism (and its strong reliance on fiscal policies) has lost ground. However, when looking beyond the debate between monetarists and Keynesians, one can see that both fiscal and monetary tools play a significant role in contemporary American economic policy.

Incomes policy involves tools that influence earnings or funds received by individuals (e.g., wages) and firms (e.g., prices, profits). The control or manipulation of incomes has been typical of U.S. policies during times of war, but they have been increasingly applied in recent years in a variety of ways to restrain or help offset adverse inflationary tendencies. The Kennedy Administration was the first to strongly advocate the use of incomes policy tools during peacetime. In its 1962 *Annual Report to the President,* the Council of Economic Advisors advocated establishing "wage-price guideposts" as an Administration policy. These guideposts, according to then-Council Chairman Walter W. Heller, demonstrate how "wage and price decisions should be geared to productivity advances if they are to be noninflationary." Aimed at labor, management, and general public audiences and lasting through 1969, these guideposts attempted to hold wage rate increases to an average equivalent to average productivity increases and to promote overall price stability by urging "price reductions in industries with above-average productivity that will roughly offset increases in those with below-average advances."[51] These guideposts were not backed by direct government controls, but rather depended on "moral suasion" and the persuasiveness of the Administration through a general "educational" campaign or, when needed, "jawboning" of specific economic actors.[52]

On August 15, 1971, President Nixon announced a total freeze on wages and prices involving *direct controls* on most actors in the American economic system. Under authority provided in the Economic Stabilization Act, Nixon began a three-phase program of wage-price controls which would last until 1973. It was the first statutorily authorized application of incomes policy tools in U.S. peacetime history.[53] Generally negative assessments of that effort[54] led President Carter to take a less stringent approach when he implemented a voluntary wage-price control policy in 1978. Based on a system that monitored wages and prices (through COWPs, the Council on Wage and Price Stability), Carter's policies depended on a combination of moral suasion, education, jawboning, and the threat of losing government contracts. The Reagan Administration quickly dismantled COWPs and

Table 5.5 Policy Tool Models

Policy Type	"Tools" Involving
1. Fiscal	1. Use of government's spending and taxing authority.
2. Monetary	2. The control and manipulation of money supply and its cost (i.e., interest rates).
3. Incomes	3. The control and manipulation of earnings by individuals (e.g., wages) and firms (e.g., prices, profits)

abandoned all incomes policy approaches upon taking office. Nevertheless, incomes policy remains a significant tool in the government's arsenal.

Table 5.5 summarizes these three types of economic policy categories. Each category offers a general approach to economic public policy. However, we still have not reached a descriptive level that permits us to concentrate on the specific activities involved in economic public policy.

DESCRIBING SPECIFIC ACTIVITIES

We now turn to those specific things governments do when undertaking public policy. To start we must realize that it is impossible to categorize all government actions and statements relevant to the economy. Here we are face-to-face with the fact that the relationship between political and economic systems in the modern world is so close that it is difficult to comprehend any event in which one does not influence the other. Therefore, in constructing a descriptive typology dealing with *specific activities* of government vis-à-vis the economy, we must attempt to be as inclusive as possible but realize that we must draw the line at some point.

As we have seen in our examples to this point, government actions and statements run the range from moral suasion and jawboning to formal controls and regulations. Some of these activities rely on the manipulation of symbols and incentives, while others depend on threats and the use of force. Which method is used seems to depend on a variety of factors: the policymaker or implementor, the target population, past and current relationships between these parties, the expectations of each, the particular situation involved, and so forth. The resulting actions and statements can be categorized according to two qualities: (1) the variable factor focused on by the policy, and (2) the extent to which that factor is influenced by the government action or statement.[55] Figure 5.2 illustrates the resulting frame-

DESCRIBING SPECIFIC ACTIVITIES

	Degree of Government Activity Influence:	
Factors	*Low*	*High*
1. Market size		
2. Market Structure		
3. Market Resources		
4. Risks/Liabilities		
5. Behavior/Norms		

Figure 5.2. Describing specific economic policy actions: a framework.

work, and a brief discussion of these qualities can help us understand this form of descriptive economic policy models.

Every economic policy is focused on a given relevant factor in the economic system. The selection of any particular factor by policymakers reflects a belief that by manipulating that variable they can produce a desired result. For simple problems it may be sufficient for policymakers to deal with one factor; however, for problems perceived as more complex, governments may undertake an approach relying on the adjustment of a variety of those factors. In general, when contending with economic problems policymakers narrow their focus to variables dealing with markets and firms. The vertical axis in Figure 5.2 lists five common categories for these factors.

The variable, *market size*, is crucial in any society. The size of a market for certain goods and services can range from small and insignficant to large and critical for the economy, depending on the proportion of a society's resources devoted to the production and distribution of a given product. To illustrate the importance of market size, consider the automobile industry at the turn of the century and today. Relative to the economy as a whole, the market for the internal combustion engine was miniscule during the first years of this century. The primary means of transport were the railroad and horse, and what impact motorized vehicles were having was limited to urban areas, and particularly an emerging mass transit industry based on electric trollies and buses. The market for automobiles was so insignificant that the creation of a company to manufacture internal combustion engine passenger cars, or (more often) the bankruptcy of one, would hardly be noticed, let alone have any significant repercussions for the American economy.

Obviously the situation has changed considerably in eight decades. Relatively speaking, the automobile market is not only large, it is the single most important sector in the contemporary American economy. Excluding imports, by 1980 the automobile manufacturing industry accounted for over 18 percent of America's gross national product. No other sector in the economy carries so much weight today, and none can match its influence in determining the health of the U.S. economy. It has been suggested that the passenger car is the symbol of twentieth century America, and that when the automobile industry sneezes today, the entire U.S. economy catches cold. Neither image is too far from the true significance of the auto industry in the 1980s. Its market size is truly important to us all.

BOX 5.6

Two points should be stressed about the factor of market size. First, market size must be perceived in relative rather than absolute terms. A market for widgets valued at millions of dollars in the United States may seem immense in absolute terms, but in a trillion dollar economy its influence is trivial at best. However, in a community of 100,000 people, where the major employer is a manufacturer of widgets, the market for that product is extremely important. In short, on the matter of market size the relative significance of a product must be taken into account.

A second point is that government actions and statements can be used to both increase or decrease relative market size. While we may think of government as an agent favoring antitrust and other activities which restrict the size of industries, it also plays a considerable role in promoting the expansion of certain sectors of the economy. In our example of the automobile industry, a number of public policies contributed to its development, not the least important being the development of a highway and secondary road system without which passenger cars would have remained merely a fad. In other markets, however, government actions have been restrictive regarding size.

Perhaps a government's most effective means for controlling market size is its use of *licensing*. Licensing begins when policymakers declare a product or the practice of a service illegal, and then turn around and issue permits or franchises allowing certain individuals or firms to undertake a legally restricted task or provide a given product. Used carefully, licensing is not only a means for guaranteeing a certain quality of performance or product, it can also expand or contract market size. To expand, government increases the number of franshises or licenses issued. To reduce a market's size, it makes licenses and franchises more difficult to get or even attempts to rescind some previously issued permits.

Still another set of tactics for manipulating the relative size of markets is found in attempts to control product advertising. The primary example of this approach is the American tobacco industry, which has been under severe constraints in its use of the mass media and has even been faced with a government-backed antismoking campaign. The aim of these policies has been to reduce the purchase and consumption of cigarettes and related products—an objective that has been difficult to achieve. More successful for U.S. policymakers have been policies promoting the expansion of markets, and this is an approach having roots in Alexander Hamilton's policies during the first years of the republic and extending to the Carter Administration's efforts to expand the size of the synfuel market relative to other energy sources.

In general, however, there seems to be a greater concern in the United States for *market structure* than market size. For many people, the fact that we are increasingly dependent on a large automobile industry for a healthy economy is not as worrisome as the fact that the market for automobiles is increasingly dominated by two corporate giants: General Motors and Ford Motor Company.[56] As of 1978, GM's share of the total U.S. automobile market was approximately 48 percent, with Ford coming up a distant second with just under 24 percent of the passenger car market, imports included. Considering just domestically produced vehicles, GM held a 59 percent share during the 1979 model year, while Ford accounted for 27 percent and other domestic manufacturers (Chrysler, American Motors, Volkswagen of America) controlled the remaining 14 percent.[57] Taking a broader picture of U.S. markets (see Table 5.6) we can see that the situation found in the automobile manufacturing area is far from unique, and that major market structures in the United States are often highly concentrated in the hands of one or several firms.

Table 5.6   Leading U.S. Industrial Dominant Firms as of 1977, and Their Background

Sales Rank 1977	Firm	Principal Markets	Estimated Average Market Share (percent)	Entry Barriers	Present Position Dates Back to about
1	General Motors	Autos, locomotives, buses, trucks	50	High	1927
7	IBM	Computers, typewriters	60	High	1954
18	Western Electric	Telecommunication equipment	95+	High	1880s
9	General Electric	Heavy electrical equipment	50	High	1900
20	Procter & Gamble	Detergents, toiletries	50	Medium	1940s
29	Eastman Kodak	Photographic supplies	55	Medium	1900
34	United Technologies	Aircraft engines	50	High	1950s
39	Xerox	Copying equipment	70	Medium	1961
61	Coca-Cola	Flavoring syrups	50	Medium	1920s
143	Campbell Soup	Canned soups	70	Medium	1920s
157	Gillette	Razors, toiletries	60	Medium	1910
165	Kellogg	Dry cereals	45	High	1940s
219	Times Mirror	Newspaper	60	High	1960
385	New York Times	Newspaper	60	High	1966
	Various drug firms	Drugs	50–70	High	1950

Source: William G. Shepherd and Clair Wilcox, *Public Policies Toward Business*, 6th edition (Homewood, IL: Richard D. Irwin, Inc., 1979), p. 43.

The concentration of economic power is often regarded as undesirable, and there are frequent movements among policymakers to break up such concentrations, or at least to promote competition among the few dominant firms in a market. At other times, however, the concentration of market power can be regarded as beneficial for the economies of scale or other reasons of social convenience. For example, certain industries are regarded as "natural monopolies" due to the technical qualities of their markets. In such industries the production or distribution of additional product units

DESCRIBING SPECIFIC ACTIVITIES

tends to cost less than those produced or distributed earlier. Under this declining costs characteristic, as the number of units involved increases, costs per unit decreases, thus making it easier for larger firms to undercut their smaller competitors. When this situation is inherent to a given product market, large economies of scale result and potential competition from newer, smaller firms is minimized. The end result is a natural monopoly. As an example, consider the high initial cost borne by electric power or telephone companies when they begin to serve a community. Given the needed high investment levels at the start, the cost per unit of the services they provide will be extremely high for the first consumers. However, hooking up additional customers to the first power or telephone lines will be less costly after that initial phase: in fact with each additional customer added to that service line, the overall cost per unit will decrease. It would logically follow that to get even less expensive service, even greater economies of scale should be promoted. Thus, it would seem that there are some circumstances where policies producing an increase in market concentration may be worthwile.[58]

BOX 5.7

Whether the objective is increased or decreased market concentration, it is evident that government can play a role. Antitrust activity is one mechanism of public policy relevant here. Through antitrust actions the government attempts to either prevent concentrated market structure or restore open competition. The formal aspects of antitrust policy in the U.S. is summarized in Table 5.7, where the relevant statutes are noted in parentheses. What is notable about this summary is that it reflects the fact that what is illegal in U.S. antitrust policy is not market dominance per se, but rather the abuses that might accompany concentrated market structures. Thus, it is not illegal to control close to 60 percent of the domestic passenger car market as GM does, but it is illegal to conspire to restrain trade, to monopolize (or attempt to monopolize), to enter into certain trade restraining contracts, and so forth. Where market structure is regarded as the source of unwarranted monopolization and other activities that abuse the competitive potential of the market, government antitrust policies are activated to prevent further abuse or restore more desirable conditions through the manipulation of market structure. The sought-after remedy may be a court injunction to halt a merger or an order for divesting or breaking up a corporate entity judged to be monopolistic due to its current share of a given market.

The antitrust policy activity of the U.S. government has been neither a speedy nor consistently effective approach. Government agencies have a rather mixed record in attempts to work against market concentration. But what is even more interesting are those markets whose concentrated structures are aided by policies that exempt them from antitrust treatment. Some of these exemptions are *de jure*, that is "based in law." These include regulated industries such as electric utilities, telephone and telecommunications, banks, stock and commodity exchanges, labor unions, major league baseball, organized agriculture, and most public enterprises. Other industries find themselves under *de facto* exemptions, including the major professions (medicine, law, etc.), health care delivery facilities, educational institution, certain major government contractors, and some "patent-intensive" industries. *De facto* exemptions, of course, are subject to change, as is the case with recent decisions by government agencies to challenge professional and legal prohibitions on advertising by physicians, lawyers, opticians, and other markets. Nevertheless, exemptions from antitrust policies are invitations for members of a given product market to move toward increased cooperation and perhaps even monopolization.

There are other activities that can be used to influence market structure. Again, *licensing* can be an effective means for giving a market some shape. The use of *public enterprises* is even more direct. The legalized monopoly held by the U.S. Postal Service over certain types of mail and package delivery is one example, and it is repeated on the local level in many jurisdictions where municipally owned and operated utilities are given exclusive rights over a specified market area. Structure can also be influenced through *subsidies* which can be funneled to dominant firms where concentration is favored or nondominant firms where it is not. *Taxes* can be made to have similar impacts. Even *regulatory* activities may be used to affect structure. For example, an environmental regulation mandating costly equipment or manufacturing procedures may be used to further concentrate a market, just as special "loopholes" for smaller firms can have the opposite effect. In summary, the variable factor of market structure is susceptible to change through an almost infinite variety of policy activities.

See William G. Shepherd and Clair Wilcox, *Public Policies Toward Business*, 6th edition (Homewood, IL: Richard D. Irwin, Inc., $1979).

DESCRIBING SPECIFIC ACTIVITIES

Table 5.7 Summary of the Main U.S. Antitrust Laws

A. It is illegal:
   1. To enter into a contract, combination, or conspiracy in restraint of trade (Sherman Act, Section 1);
   2. To monopolize, attempt to monopolize, or combine or conspire to monopolize trade (Sherman Act, Section 2).
B. In cases where the effect may be substantially to lessen competition or tend to create a monopoly, it is illegal:
   3. To acquire the stock or the assets of competing corporations (Clayton Act, Section 7, as amended by Celler-Kefauver Act);
   4. To enter into exclusive and tying contracts (Clayton Act, Section 3);
   5. To discriminate among purchasers to an extent that cannot be justified by a difference in cost; or as an attempt made, in good faith, to meet the price of a competitor (Clayton Act, Section 2, as amended by Robinson-Patman Act, Section 2a).
C. And, in general, it is also illegal:
   6. To serve as a director of competing corporations (Clayton Act, Section 8);
   7. To use unfair methods of competition (Federal Trade Commission Act, Section 5);
   8. To employ unfair or deceptive acts or practices (Federal Trade Commission Act, Section 5, as amended by Wheeler-Lea Act, Section).

Source: William G. Shepherd and Clair Wilcox, *Public Policies Toward Business*, 6th ed (Homewood, IL: Richard D. Irwin, Inc., 1979), p. 88.

Turning to *market resources* we are actually reflecting the basic fact of economic life that any kind of productive or distributive endeavor relies on the presence of at least land, labor, and capital resources. Given the critical role of these resources, their availability is a matter of great concern in any market and for any specific individual or firm engaged in economic pursuits. Through the control or manipulation of such resources, public policy can have considerable influence on any number of markets.

Governments, for example, can directly subsidize an economic sector and thus increase its capital resources. It may do this to help promote activity in certain sectors of the economy that might otherwise be nonexistent or underdeveloped. For example, low-cost housing for the poor or elderly has been federally subsidized through direct payments of more than $1 billion in recent years. No doubt, without such payments, low-cost housing would exist, but the infusion of that kind of capital was intended to increase the number of units. Before deregulation policies went into effect, another kind of direct subsidy was provided to commercial air carriers through the Civil Aeronautics Board policy of paying airlines for maintaining routes to areas that might otherwise not be serviced. Those direct infusions of capital resources amounted to over $70 million in the 1970s.

The sector that has had the most experience with direct payment subsidies has been agriculture. Over the years, farmers have received payments from the federal government based on what they produced (e.g., domestic wool producers were paid a subsidy of 27.2 cents for each pound of wool produced in 1969), what land they used (or didn't use) to produce a commodity (e.g., the federal government paid producers $77 million in FY70 and $49 million in FY75 under a "land retirement" program which kept 4.5 million acres out of production), and how they produced their commodity (e.g., the use of certain conservation practices brought farmers $185 million in direct payments in FY70).[59] While many of these specific programs have been eliminated, replaced, or substantially reduced, the legacy of direct payment subsidies remains for farmers and may arise again as the agricultural economy becomes increasingly precarious.

Not all resource subsidies take the form of direct payments. At times they come indirectly in the form of substantial tax breaks. By providing specific exceptions to the general tax burden, government can provide a source of financial resources that might otherwise be missing. These exceptions currently take so many forms that they are difficult (if not impossible) to specify. Economist Stanley S. Surrey has attempted to provide a measure of these indirect subsidies by developing what he termed a "tax expenditure budget"[60] reflecting what government indirectly "spends" on an activity or sector by not taxing it or providing it with favorable treatment. Recent federal budgets have included the tax expenditure budget, and Table 5.8 provides an example from the FY83 document.

Another form of indirect subsidy comes in the area of low-cost government loans or loan guarantees. A classic example of the former was the creation of the Rural Electrification Administration (REA) during Roosevelt's New Deal Era. Providing encouragement to private cooperatives supplying power in areas where utilities would not invest, the REA offered them loans at a 2 percent interest rate as well as a significant amount of other technical and economic support. These loans and related REA efforts gave impetus to the creation of 1,000 cooperatives which now serve 6 million customers in 46 states, and by the middle 1970s the cost of the program was over $220 million. Other examples abound, of course: home mortgage loans, small business loans, loans to students, and so on.

Loan guarantees are even more indirect, for while they do not always provide for low interest rates, they do underwrite an agreement between lender institutions and qualified borrowers. Some of these loan guarantees have received considerable publicity. For example, in 1971 a crisis involving the financial condition of Lockheed Corporation led to the creation of an Emergency Loan Guarantee Board with authority to commit the United States to underwrite up to $250 million in loans for that company. Similarly,

Table 5.8 Revenue Losses for Tax Expenditures by Function (In millions of dollars)

Description	1981	Fiscal 1982	Years 1983
National defense:			
Exclusion of benefits and allowances to Armed Forces personnel	1,735	1,885	1,940
Exclusion of military disability pensions	155	165	170
International affairs:			
Exclusion of income earned abroad by United States citizens	610	985	1,285
Deferral of income of domestic international sales corporations (DISC)	1,595	1,465	1,490
General science, space, and technology:			
Expensing of research and development expenditures	1,550	380	−810
Credit for increasing research activities	15	405	580
Energy:			
Expensing of exploration and development costs:			
Oil and gas	3,525	4,065	4,530
Other fuels	25	25	30
Excess of percentage over cost depletion:			
Oil and gas	1,865	1,965	1,695
Other fuels	380	380	425
Capital gains treatment of royalties on coal	100	105	95
Exclusion of interest on State and local government industrial development bonds for certain energy facilities	*	5	15
Residential energy credits:			
Supply incentives	150	205	260
Conservation incentives	425	415	410
Alternative, conservation and new technology credits.			
Supply incentives	180	235	290
Conservation incentives	220	285	315
Alternative fuel production credit	25	55	50
Alcohol fuel credit[1]	5	20	35
Energy credit for intercity buses	5	5	5
Natural resources and environment:			
Expensing of exploration and development costs, nonfuel minerals	45	50	55
Excess of percentage over cost depletion, nonfuel minerals	385	405	440
Exclusion of interest on State and local government pollution control bonds	715	835	970

Table 5.8 (Continued)

Description	1981	Fiscal 1982	Years 1983
Natural resources (contd)			
Tax incentives for preservation of historic structures	60	80	75
Capital gains treatment of iron ore	20	20	20
Capital gains treatment of certain timber income	585	600	615
Investment credit and seven-year amortization for reforestation expenditures	5	10	15
Agriculture:			
Expensing of certain capital outlays	525	545	560
Capital gains treatment of certain income	425	460	375
Commerce and housing credit:			
Dividend and interest exclusion	1,335	2,185	475
Exclusion of interest on State and local industrial development bonds	1,200	1,650	2,185
Exemption of credit union income	−25	5	40
Excess bad debt reserves of financial institutions	325	250	515
Exclusion of interest on life insurance savings	4,060	4,535	4,805
Deductibility of interest on consumer credit	8,675	9,285	9,355
Deductibility of mortgage interest on owner-occupied homes	20,145	23,030	25,490
Deductibility of property tax on owner-occupied homes	9,125	10,065	10,635
Exclusion of interest on State and local housing bonds for owner-occupied housing	685	920	1,245
Expensing of construction period interest and taxes	755	745	645
Capital gains (other than agriculture, timber, iron ore and coal)	17,965	18,315	14,390
Exclusion of capital gains on home sales for persons age 55 and over	450	415	465
Carryover basis of capital gains at death	2,070	2,190	2,135
Investment credit, other than ESOP's, rehabilitation of structures, energy property, and reforestation expenditures	19,445	20,035	20,150
Safe harbor leasing rules	a	3,560	3.945
Amortization of start-up costs	20	75	120
Exclusion of interest on certain savings certificates		515	2,820
Reinvestment of dividends in public utility stock	*	130	365
Transportation:			
Deferral of tax on shipping companies	70	65	85
Exclusion of interest on State and local government industrial development bonds for mass transit		*	5
Community and regional development:			
Five-year amortization for housing rehabilitation	30	45	55
Investment credit for rehabilitation of structures	220	255	300

Table 5.8 *(Continued)*

Description	Fiscal 1981	1982	Years 1983
Education, training, employment, and social services:			
Exclusion of interest on State and local student loan bonds	60	100	155
Parental personal exemption for students age 19 or over	1,045	995	900
Exclusion of employee meals and lodging (other than military)	620	655	680
Employer educational assistance	35	40	40
Exclusion of contributions to prepaid legal services plans	20	20	25
Investment credit for ESOP's	975	1,005	1,095
Deductibility of charitable contributions (education)	925	895	925
Deductibility of charitable contributions, other than education and health	8,485	8,345	8,085
Credit for child and dependent care expenses	935	1,120	1,465
Credit for employment of AFDC recipients and public assistance recipients under work incentive programs	70	45	*
General jobs credit	300	65	5
Targeted jobs credit	305	235	75
Health:			
Exclusion of employer contributions for medical insurance premiums and medical care	14,050	15,330	16,380
Deductibility of medical expenses	3,615	3,925	4,175
Exclusion of interest on State and local hospital bonds	560	680	810
Deductibility of charitable contributions (health)	1,390	1,360	1,345
Income security:			
Exclusion of social security benefits:			
Disability insurance benefits	860	915	910
OASI benefits for retired workers	8,845	9,980	10,525
Benefits for dependents and survivors	1,735	1,915	1,970
Exclusion of railroad retirement system benefits	365	380	370
Exclusion of workmen's compensation benefits	2,730	3,100	3,495
Exclusion of special benefits for disabled coal miners	90	95	90
Exclusion of untaxed unemployment insurance benefits	1,985	2,060	2,710
Exclusion of disability pay	170	155	145
Net exclusion of pension contributions and earnings:			
Employer plans	23,390	25,765	27,500
Plans for self-employed and others	2,170	2,560	3,760

Table 5.8 *(Continued)*

Description	1981	Fiscal 1982	Years 1983
Income security *(contd)*			
Exclusion of other employee benefits:			
Premiums on group term life insurance	1,840	1,900	1,895
Premiums on accident and disability insurance	100	100	100
Income of trusts to finance supplementary unemployment benefits	15	20	30
Additional exemption for the blind	30	30	30
Additional exemption for elderly	2,250	2,355	2,370
Tax Credit for the Elderly			
Deductibility of casualty losses	775	800	850
Earned income credit[2]	610	555	495
Exclusion of interest on State and local housing bonds for rental housing	435	485	535
Deduction for motor carrier operating rights	*	140	75
Deduction for certain adoption expenses	10	10	10
Veterans benefits and services:			
Exclusion of veterans disability compensation	1,255	1,360	1,380
Exclusion of veterans pensions	95	85	90
Exclusion of GI bill benefits	200	175	145
General government:			
Credits and deductions for political contributions	100	80	80
General purpose fiscal assistance:			
Exclusion of interest on general purpose State and local debt	5,855	6,685	7,505
Deductibility of nonbusiness State and local taxes other than on owner-occupied homes	19,085	20,395	21,530
Tax credit for corporations receiving income from doing business in United States possessions	1,120	1,200	1,285
Interest:			
Deferral of interest on savings bonds	−270	−80	50

*$5 million or less. All estimates have been rounded to the nearest $5 million.
[1]In addition, the exemption from the excise tax for alcohol fuels results in a reduction in excise tax receipts of $55 million in 1981, $55 million in 1982, and $55 million in 1983.
[2]The figures in the table indicate the effect of the earned income tax credit on receipts. The effect on outlays is: 1981, $1,320 million; 1982, $1,255 million, 1983, $1,180 million.
Source: "Tax Expenditures," *Special Analysis G, The Budget of the United States Government, 1983* (Washington, DC: Office of Management and Budget, 1982), pp. 34–36.

DESCRIBING SPECIFIC ACTIVITIES 133

in the summer of 1979 an even more serious crisis developed at Chrysler Corporation which asked that a $1 billion loan guarantee mechanism be structured to save it from bankruptcy. Despite the great amount of adverse publicity surrounding these incidents, the use of loan guarantees is far more extensive than most Americans think and has grown significantly in recent years.[61] Figure 5.3 illustrates the growing role of guaranteed loans as a portion of total outstanding credit of the U.S. government and related agencies. Obviously, more and more resources are being provided in this way.

Still another form of subsidy involves not direct payments, but the direct provision of resource-generating services (i.e., infrastructure). Highways, postal services, job training, medical care, education, airport construction and operation, sanitation services, research and development, are examples of services the government offers the private economic sector which the private sector cannot (or will not) provide itself, but which contribute to its economic success. Sometimes there is a direct charge for these services (e.g., user fees, tolls), and sometimes these charges actually pay for what is supplied. More often, however, the services are provided free or at a level of fees well below cost, thus passing on the bill to taxpayers in the jurisdiction or some other group.

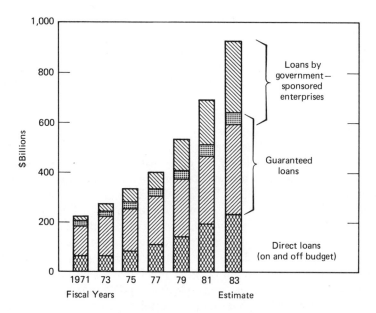

Figure 5.3. Federal and federally assisted credit outstanding. (Source: "Federal Credit Programs," *Special Analysis F, The Budget of the United States Government, 1983*, Washington, DC: Office of Management and Budget, 1982, p. 9.)

The manipulation of market resources is generally used to promote productive and distributive activity in certain economic sectors, but not always. Note how farmers have been subsidized not to plant certain amounts of acerage or to plant them in commodity X rather than commodity Y. In addition, tax expenditures are frequently used to generate certain activities at the expense of others. If you wished to promote the rehabilitation of houses in the center city, what better indirect mechanism than providing a substantial property tax exemption for the family who does that while continuing to burden the suburban household with the full property tax assessment. In other words, resources may not only be given, but may also be given in ways to promote certain types of activity while making other actions less inviting.

The attractiveness or unattractiveness of an economic activity also underlies those government policies focused on the *risks and liabilities* of market activities. Put simply, under any system of law policymakers can provide incentives or disincentives for certain products or services by tightening or loosening the exposure of individuals, firms, or groups to market or legal risks. A common example is the use of *patent* and *copyright* laws. A good deal of the incentive to invent or create in our society comes from the hope that what one invents or creates will bring sufficient financial rewards to warrant the needed investment of money, time, heart, and soul that often goes into such projects. Patent and copyright laws are made for these individuals. By definition, a patent "is an exclusive right conferred on an inventor, for a limited period, by a government."[62] In the United States the life of a patent is 17 years and has been affixed "since 1790 on any useful 'art, manufacture, engine, machine,' since 1793 on a 'composition of matter,' since 1842 on 'ornamental designs,' and since 1930 on botanical plants, and on improvements to any of them."[63] Copyrights, although covering different types of items under different ground rules and for different periods, essentially offer similar protection in giving their holders full and complete rights over the item in question. In other words, patent and related laws reduce the risk that the inventor or creator will not be sufficiently rewarded for his or her work.

Other laws can work in the opposite direction by making an economic actor responsible for a product or what results from its use. *Liability* for a product or service is usually unlimited, with court action being the mechanism through which claims are settled. Thus, if a company produces or distributes poorly constructed widgets, it is liable for its actions in a court of law where someone who was harmed (or even disappointed) by the product can bring a civil suit. Government can take actions to increase or decrease that liability. For example, on certain products the government can choose to bring civil suits of its own as a means for halting or modifying product manufacturing or distribution; or it may bring criminal charges asserting negligence on the part of a company under various product safety acts. Along these lines, there are three federal agencies that now have the power to penalize producers directly for violations of the public safety as reflected in their respective standards or codes: the Food and Drug Administration, the National Highway Traffic Safety Commission, and the Consumer Products Safety Commission.[64]

Liability can also be limited through government policies. A good example is the use of loan guarantees discussed above. Another example is the 1957 Price-Anderson Act limiting the total liability for an accident at a nuclear power plant to $560 million in personal or property damage, with most of that amount to be provided by the federal government.[65] More recently, drug companies asked to produce swine flue vaccine in 1976 would do so only after they were exempted from liability for the drug's use.[66] Obviously, government's ability to manipulate risks and liabilities is proving increasingly important. Activities aimed at affecting this variable can go either way, but the trend seems more in the direction of "socializing risk" and thus spreading the potential liabilities throughout society.

Finally, and perhaps underlying all the factors we've discussed to this point, public policies can deal with the *behavior or behavioral norms* of economic actors. The most direct form of this is government *regulatory activity*.[67] A regulatory policy is one that determines the behavior of an individual, firm, or group, or directs that behavior by providing criteria or standards for it. Regulation, in this sense, goes beyond the manipulation of "secondary" variables (i.e., size, structure, resources, risks and liabilities) and goes right to the factor of how an economic actor behaves. At times regulations are backed up with rewards, but more often they are sustained with the threat of force or some related form of legal punishment.

The most fundamental forms of regulation are *prohibitions,* which forbid certain activities, and *mandates,* which demand that certain actions be taken. Thus, it is illegal to have slaves in the United States today, and commerce in that human commodity is forbidden throughout the world. Other forms of regulation are directly associated with licensing as is the case of making it illegal to practice medicine unless one meets certain standards of behavior and follows certain practices once licensed.

These licensing (and assorted franchising) procedures are applied in a variety of economic fields from broadcasting and aviation to interstate rail service. Once a firm is provided a franchise to partake in these endeavors, it can be held to certain forms of behavior and made to follow a process by which the prices it charges and the services it provides must be reviewed and approved by some administrative unit. For example, commercial broadcasters must demonstrate before the Federal Communications Commission that they can and will serve their respective communities in "the public interest" in order to obtain or maintain their commercial TV or radio licenses. In aviation, at least until deregulation in the late 1970s, air fares and entry into commercially lucrative routes were tightly regulated. Even with so-called deregulation, constraints on prices and flight schedules remained in the early 1980s, but the standards used were much looser and most would eventually disappear. Railroads are under regulations set by the Interstate Commerce Commission (ICC), which mandates service to areas that might be economically unproductive. This was the case, for instance, in the late 1970s when the Chicago, Milwaukee, St. Paul and Pacific Railroad Company fought a continuing battle before the ICC to discontinue its freight service to parts of Montana and other less profitable portions of its line. Under the existing regulatory system, the "Milwaukee Road" could not withdraw without proving its case. In this area as well, however, deregulation is occurring and overall policies are shifting.

Another regulatory approach is the *setting and enforcement of standards*. On the local level, governments have been doing this for years through building and zoning codes which determine what can be built in a community, where, and how. Even more significant today are national and local standards being set for the protection of the environment, the health of workers, and the safety of consumers. The recent proliferation of these "social" regulations (as opposed to "economic" regulations which focus on production and distribution patterns) has created limits on (1) how products are manufactured (e.g., pollution control devices for steel and chemical manufacturing plants, requirements for meeting safety standards for workers); (2) their performance or design (e.g., the amount of emissions from automobiles and their fuel efficiency, the design of toys, the fabric composition of children's pajamas); and (3) whether and how they are used (e.g., required warning labels for cigarettes and detailed instructions for using drugs).

In describing the range of factors public policy may influence, our examples have only hinted at the variety of activities governments can perform. Here is where the second dimension in Figure 5.2 comes into play, for the activity actually involved depends on the degree of government influence over these variables. For example, regarding market size, a low level of government determination would mean policies that generally permit the market to reach its own level. A high level of government involvement, however, might mean a highly controlled licensing system or an outright government monopoly of the industry in question. The same distinction among activities can be developed for policies dealing with market structure, available resources, susceptibility to risks and liabilities, and the behavior or behavioral norms of economic actors. The end result is a descriptive framework allowing us to classify any of the infinite variety of government activities that have been or can be used to influence economic activity.

An interesting characteristic of these government policies, obvious from the many examples discussed above, is that no specific policy activity can be necessarily associated with a specific goal, approach, or set of tactics in economic policy endeavors. Thus, subsidies are useful in changing market size, influencing market structure, or supplying market resources. Regulation, while directly identified with the imposition of behavioral mandates, can also be used to affect market structure by making standards uniformly stringent for all producers or providing exceptions according to market shares. Antitrust policies, jawboning, tax expenditures, patent laws, loan guarantees, liability laws, and so on are all capable of the same flexibility, and they are only a few of the ways actions and statements are expressed by public policymakers.

AN HISTORICAL ALTERNATIVE

Before ending this survey of economic policy description typologies, we should take note of an additional category of descriptive categories often used when analysts reflect on the various strategies, actions, and objectives put to use by government decision makers. Celebrating its fiftieth anniversary in a special 1979 issue, *Business Week* provided its readers with an insightful and critical review of economic policy over that period. In that survey, reference is frequently made to "New Deal policies," "Depression-era legislation." One section in particular illustrates this with the title "Today's Markets—But 1930's Laws." In a similar fashion there are constant references by analysts to "pre-Civil War" economic policies, Progressive-era policies, Great Society policies, and government actions and statements generally associated with specific Presidential administrations (e.g., John F. Kennedy's tax cut, Nixon's incomes policies, Ford's anti-inflation policies).

Although these are familiar and often helpful categories for describing economic public policies, we give them separate status here for two reasons. First, they act as "umbrella" categories under which several types of economic public policies are classified as typical of an era or administration. Thus, to say that a policy is of the "New Deal" period is to provide it with certain characteristics. Generally such policies are Keynesian macroeconomic in focus, make heavy use of fiscal policy tools, emphasize the stimulation of demand, and rely on subsidization and regulation. Therefore, to understand this type of historically based classification, one must first understand the categories described above.

Second, these descriptive categories are probably the least valuable and most distorting of all and deserve to be noted as such. While they may provide easy identification of policies for purposes of an analysis rooted in historical terms (as was the case with the *Business Week* issue), they also lead to stereotypical thinking about policies and associations between policies that may be unwarranted (New Deal policies are liberal, Eisenhower administration policies are conservative, and so on).

If we include this *historical descriptive* scheme, however, we can summarize our categorization models according to the four types of policy description noted and discussed in detail in Chapter 4. "Intentional" models are represented by those classifications focusing on the general strategies and purposes of economic public policies, while categories concentrating on promoting, stabilizing, stimulating, or accomplishing other economic conditions are descriptively "functional." Comparative descriptive models are even more common in the study of economic public policy and are evident in categorizations based on the level of policy activity, the types of tools used, or the specific types of actions involved. Finally, the development approach is found in descriptions similar to those used by *Business Week* and many others who associate policies with historically significant periods.

ENDNOTES

1. This perspective is built into most introductory economic textbooks which deal explicitly with the public sector's role. As a prime example, see Robert H. Haveman, *The Economics of the Public Sector,* 2nd edition (Santa Barbara, CA: John Wiley & Sons, Inc., 1976), especially Part Two.
2. Political scientist Theodore J. Lowi believes this attitude has changed in recent years, and that many Americans now accept government's role in the private sector as a "positive virtue." His presentation of this view and critique of its implications are found in *The End of Liberalism: The Second Republic of the United States,* 2nd edition (New York: W. W. Norton and Co., 1979).
3. The analogy of public policies as "treatments" of unhealthy disorders in the economy is explicitly used by William G. Shepherd in *The Treatment of Market Power: Antitrust, Regulation, and Public Enterprise* (New York: Columbia University Press, 1975).
4. This metaphor can be carried even further with interesting results. For example, among critics of contemporary health care there is a growing concern for what is termed "iatrogenesis," or physician-caused disease [see Ivan Illich, *Medical Nemesis: The Expropriation of Health* (New York: Bantam Books, 1976)]. Extending this to the analogy of government-as-physician treating market-as-patient, one can see a familiar argument very similar to that expressed by Milton Friedman in *Capitalism and Freedom* (Chicago: The University of Chicago Press, 1962).
5. Robert A. Dahl and Charles E. Lindblom, *Politics, Economics and Welfare: Planning and Politico-Economic Systems Resolved into Basic Social Processes*

(New York: Harper Torchbooks, 1953), p. xxi. This contemporary classic is a thorough and systematic presentation of political economy mechanisms and is necessary reading for anyone who wishes some theoretical and conceptual grounding in the subject. A revised elaboration of the Dahl-Lindblom presentation is provided in Charles E. Lindblom, *Politics and Markets: The World's Political-Economic Systems* (New York: Basic Books, 1977).
6. Michael D. Reagan, *The Managed Economy* (New York: Oxford University Press, 1963), p. 4.
7. For a well-written and dramatic presentation based on this attitude, see Susan Love Brown, et al., *The Incredible Bread Machine* (San Diego: World Research, Inc., 1974).
8. This definition can be traced to a number of sources, but it relies most heavily on Robert L. Heilbroner's *The Making of Economic Society*, 5th edition (Englewood Cliffs, NJ: Prentice-Hall, Inc., 1975), Chapter 1.
9. Lindblom, *Politics and Markets*, p. 4.
10. This typology is derived from the overlapping yet distinctive discussions in Dahl and Lindblom, *Politics, Economics, and Welfare;* Heilbroner, *The Making of Economic Society*, pp. 13–20; and Lindblom, *Politics and Markets*, pp. 12–13 and relevant chapters. Dahl and Lindblom posited four mechanisms in their 1953 work (i.e., price system, hierarchy, polyarchy, and bargaining); Heilbroner offered three (i.e., tradition, command and market); while Lindblom's recent work posited three (i.e., exchange, authority, persuasion).
11. Heilbroner, *The Making of Economic Society*, pp. 11–13.
12. See Adam Smith, *An Inquiry Into the Nature and Causes of the Wealth of Nations*, edited by Edwin Cannan (New York: The Modern Library, 1965).
13. Friedman, *Capitalism and Freedom*. For a more controversial explication, see George Gilder, *Wealth and Poverty* (New York: Basic Books, 1981).
14. Derived from Haveman, *The Economics of the Public Sector*, pp. 27–29.
15. Smith, . . . *The Wealth of Nations*, p. 651.
16. Friedman, *Capitalism and Freedom*, p. 34.
17. "Rule of law" is stressed in the work of pre-Adam Smith authors such as John Locke and other "economic liberals." See Daniel R. Fusfeld, *The Age of The Economist*, 3rd edition (Glenview, IL: Scott, Foresman and Co., 1977), pp. 20–22. Contemporary expressions of this assumption are found in F.A. Hayek, *The Road to Serfdom* (Chicago: University of Chicago Press, 1944) and Lowi, *The End of Liberalism*, esp. pp. 300–301.
18. Fusfeld, *The Age of the Economist*, p. 70.
19. Ibid., pp. 66–67.
20. We are using a narrower view of socialism than is typically applied by scholars since we are concentrating on strategies derived from theories rather than empirical examples. Thus, the goal of economic justice is not obvious in some applications of the term "socialist" to public policy. At times socialist-type policies are justified on the basis of expediency or self-interest without any thought of "justice." For example, see Lindblom's discussion of "market socialism" in *Politics and Markets*, pp. 95–97; and James O'Connor's description of "socialism for the rich" in *The Fiscal Crisis of the State* (New York: St. Martin's Press, 1973), pp. 168–169.

21. For a presentation on the logic of the socialist model, see Joseph A. Schumpeter's classic, *Capitalism, Socialism and Democracy,* 3rd edition (New York: Harper Torchbooks, 1947), pp. 172–186.
22. Mercantilism, not capitalism, was the driving force and theoretical rationale behind the colonization of the New World. Thus, settlement of America was undertaken to enhance the monarchial states' wealth and power, not in increase business community profits in the "mother country." See James O'Connor, *The Corporations and the State: Essays in the Theory of Capitalism and Imperialism* (New York: Harper and Row, Publishers, 1974), pp. 156–159.
23. Fusfeld, *The Age of the Economist,* p. 15. The mercantilist approach was also evident in the thinking of the United States' first major economic policymaker, Alexander Hamilton. See his "Report on Manufacturers" in Theodore J. Lowi (ed.), *Private Life and Public Order: The Context of Modern Public Policy* (New York: W. W. Norton and Co., Inc., 1968), pp. 111–122.
24. See the discussion in "Neo-Mercantilism in the '80s: The Worldwide Scramble to Shift Capital," *Business Week* (July 9, 1979), pp. 50–54.
25. Striving for "energy independence" has been an obvious national goal for the United States since the Arab oil embargo and OPEC activity became significant concerns in the early 1970s. On the matter of metal shortages, see "Now the Squeeze on Metals," in the July 2, 1979 issue of *Business Week,* pp. 46–51. On the general implications of such shortages, see "Oil: The Threat of a World Slowdown," in *Business Week* (June 18, 1979), pp. 114–115.
26. "Governments are becoming more and more aware of the importance of knowhow that multinationals possess and how it could help them solve economic and political problems. . . . Governments will therefore demand greater and greater local control. This is not a new problem, but it will increase in the '80s." Carol Peretti of Honeywell Information System in Milan, Italy, quoted in "Neo-Mercantilism in the '80s." *Business Week,* p. 53.
27. "In the new mercantilism, unlike the 17th and 18th century variety, nationals are not relying on tariffs or quotas to protect jobs and profits. Instead, they use new and more subtle market restrictions such as currency manipulation, cartel-like schemes, direct and indirect subsidies to industries, and voluntary export-restraint agreements." See "Neo-Mercantilism in the '80s," *Business Week,* p. 50. On seventeenth and eighteenth century policies, see Fusfeld, *The Age of the Economist,* pp. 16–17.
28. Keynes was a prolific writer, but his theoretical key work is found in one specific volume: *The General Theory of Employment, Interest, and Money* (New York: Harcourt, Brace and World, Inc., 1964; "Harbinger Edition" originally published in 1936).
29. This argument is attributed to one of Keynes' most famous students, Joan Robinson, who calls "contemporary Keynesianism and the conventional view of Keynes' revolution as a 'vulgarized version of Keynes' theory', developed by what she labels as 'bastard Keynesians.' " Cited and expanded upon in Richard X. Chase, "Keynes and U.S. Keynesianism: A Lack of Historical Perspective and the Decline of the New Economics," *Journal of Economic Issues,* IX, no. 3 (September, 1975), pp. 441–470.
30. Fusfeld, *The Age of the Economist,* p. 49.

31. *Ibid.* pp. 47–51; also see John A. Garraty, *Unemployment In History: Economic Thought and Public Policy* (New York: Harper Colophon Books, 1978), p. 73.
32. This assumption is, of course, most often associated with the work of Thomas R. Malthus, although Say's volume pre-dated his *Principles of Political Economy* by seventeen years. Ironically, Malthus' work was severely criticized by David Ricardo, who relied heavily on Say's Law. See Fusfeld, *The Age of the Economist,* p. 50.
33. For a brief yet understandable description of Keynes' theory, see Fusfeld, *The Age of the Economist,* Chapter 9. Also see the excellent discussion in Herbert Stein, *The Fiscal Revolution in America* (Chicago: The University of Chicago Press, 1969), Chapter 7, esp. pp. 156–168.
34. Those who adhere to this "fine tuning" approach were typically termed the "New Economists." For a historical introduction to their work in the 1960s, see Stein, *The Fiscal Revolution in America,* Chapter 16–17; also Robert Eyestone, *Political Economy: Politics and Policy Analysis* (Chicago: Markham Publishing Co., 1972), Chapter 5. For a rationalization of their approach, see Walter W. Heller, *New Dimensions of Political Economy* (New York: W. W. Norton and Co., 1967). Economics, of course, has its fads, and what was new in one era is outmoded in the next. In the early 1980s the label of "new economics" was popularly applied to a group of anti-Keynesians led by Martin Feldstein.
35. That qualification is most evident in the work of Walter W. Heller. He notes, for instance, that goals such as "full employment," "high growth," and "price stability" are merely "proxies, if you will, for such social goals as personal fulfillment, a rising quality of life, and equity between fixed and variable income recipients." (*New Dimensions of Political Economy,* p. 19). In another place (p. 58) he stresses that in "the last analysis, the promise of modern economic policy in a democracy lies in its capacity to serve our ultimate social objectives in a framework of freedom." Still again he states (on p. 107): "I am not unmindful that the economic growth we measure is not everything. There is more to economic life than goods and services, and more to life than economic life. Justice, freedom, valor, lesiure, and wit are not counted in the national product—not because they are unimportant parts of the good life, but because they cannot be measured. . . ."
36. This figure assumed, of course, that some unemployment was inevitable at any particular time. Nevertheless, the exact level of "acceptable" unemployment was debatable. See Garraty, *Unemployment In History . . .,* pp. 242–243.
37. This was advocated by economists Herbert Stein and Arthur F. Burns during their tenure with the Nixon Administration. See Robert Lekachman, *Economists At Bay: Why the Experts Will Never Solve Your Problems* (New York: McGraw-Hill Book Co., 1976), pp. 46–47.
38. See Heller, *New Dimensions of Political Economy,* pp. 194–105.
39. See Heller, *New Dimensions of Political Economy,* p. 76.
40. The 7 percent objective was officially adopted by the Carter administration in the latter part of 1978.
41. See "Thatcher's 'going out of business' sales," *Business Week* (August 6, 1979), p. 37.
42. See Heller, *New Dimensions of Political Economy,* pp. 64–70.

43. In the words of economic policy analysts of the period, what the Carter Administration looked forward to was a downturn characterized as a "soft landing." The imagery speaks for itself.
44. On the concept of preventative policies, see Shepherd, *The Treatment of Market Power*.
45. See Shepherd, *The Treatment of Market Power*, especially Chapter 7.
46. See Kenneth E. Boulding, *Economic Analysis, Volume II: Macroeconomics*, 4th edition (New York: Harper and Row, Publishers, 1966), Chapter 1 for a discussion of the microecononomic and macroeconomic distinction.
47. See Harvey Leibenstein, "A Branch of Economics is Missing: Micro-Micro Theory," *Journal of Economic Literature*, XVII (June, 1979), pp. 477–502.
48. On EEOC activities which might be perceived as "micro-microeconomic" see "Firing Up the Attack on Job Bias," *Business Week* (June 25,, 1979), pp. 64, 68.
49. See, for example, the work of Thomas R. Dye, Ira Sharkansky, and other political scientists.
50. In some instances monetary policies have been used to achieve objectives at the mircroeconomic level. This is exemplified by measures taken in recent years to protect the home construction market during economic downturns. Before these measures were implemented, the housing industry would be among the first to suffer when the Fed make a decision to tighten the money supply. An increase in reserve requirements or interest rates would reduce the supply of money available for home mortgages and thus quickly depress that market. To offset this, banking regulations were modified in the late 1970s to provide savings and loan associations (the primary mortgage bankers) with a source of funds which would give them a buffer against these rapid downturns. By allowing S and Ls to issue high-yield 6-month certificates of deposit for amounts of more than $10,000, policymakers created that buffer. Thus, when the first signs of a recession appeared in 1979 and interest rates began to climb, the impact on the housing market was not as immediate as it was during similar downturns in previous years. Nevertheless, as Fed continued to maintain its tight money policies through 1980 and 1981 that short-term buffer was of little value and the housing market eventually felt the squeeze.
51. Heller, *New Dimensions of Political Economy*, pp. 43–44.
52. "Jawboning" is a technique involving a major actor (such as the President) in an effort to directly talk a "violator" of the guideposts into reversing a decision to raise prices or seek a high wage increase. The first notable example of this was Kennedy's confrontation with U.S. Steel over a 1962 price increase. His ability to "persuade" U.S. Steel to roll back their increases was greatly enhanced by threats to reconsider pending steel purchase contracts from companies choosing to raise their prices. For a summary and assessment of these wage-price guideposts and the use of jawboning, see Eyestone, *Political Economy*, pp. 110–117.
53. For a critical review of Nixon's incomes policy program, see Lekachman, *Economists at Bay*, pp. 25–32. Also see the brief but interesting comments of C. Jackson Grayson, Jr. (the head of Phase II of Nixon's program) in "How to Achieve an American Miracle," *Business Week* (July 16, 1979), p. 9.

54. See James M. Collins, "Price controls: 40 centuries of failure," *Business Week* (December 18, 1979), p. 13. Also see Robert L. Schuettinger and Eamonn F. Butler, *Forty Centuries of Wage and Price Controls* (Washington, D.C.: The Heritage Foundation, 1979). Lekachman, while critical of the way the Nixon wage-price contols were handled, argues for the effectiveness of such incomes policy methods. See his *Economist at Bay*.
55. For a similar approach to classifying public policy activities, see William G. Shepherd and Clair Wilcox, *Public Policies Toward Business*, 6th edition (Homewood, IL: Richard D. Irwin, Inc., 1979), pp. 6–12.
56. In fact, there is concern over the recent trend toward an auto industry monopolized by General Motors alone. Two facts back up this concern: first, since the early 1970s GM has increased its share of the auto market annually; and second, the weakness of Chrysler as a competitor which became evident in 1979. See "GM's Juggernaut: Riding Over the Competition to Push Market Shares Up and Up," *Business Week* (March 26, 1979), pp. 62–77; also "Is Chrysler the Prototype?" *Business Week* (August 20, 1979), pp. 102–110.
57. These figures are cited in "GM's Juggernaut. . . .," *Business Week* (March 26, 1979), pp. 62, 64.
58. Milton Friedman argues in *Capitalism and Freedom* (Chapter VII) that even in the case of a natural monopoly the government should not get involved. He bases this on the assumptions that (1) monopolies are unstable and will ultimately be overtaken in the marketplace through innovation, the use of substitutes, etc., and (2) that once put in place, government intervention is difficult to reverse and many actually aggravate the situation.
59. These figures and others used in this section are derived from Shepherd and Wilcox, *Public Policies Toward Business*, p. 565. Specific agricultural figures for the period 1955 to 1969 are provided in Charles L. Schultz, "U.S. Farm Policy: Who Gets What Benefits," in *The Political Economy of Federal Policy*, edited by Robert H. Haveman and Robert D. Hamrin. (New York: Harper and Row, Publishers, 1973), pp. 182–190.
60. See Stanley S. Surrey, "Tax Expenditure and Tax Reform," in *The Political Economy of Federal Policy*, pp. 82–91.
61. For a critical analysis of this development, see Lowi, *The End of Liberalism*, pp. 281–289.
62. See Shepherd and Wilcox, *Public Policies Toward Business*, Chapter 21, p. 500.
63. Ibid., p. 501. Shepherd and Wilcox note that the 17-year term is a matter of historical accident and that in "most other countries the patent holder is required to put the invention to work." See p. 502.
64. Ibid., pp. 541–544.
65. Under Price-Anderson, the utility that owns and operates the plant needs to have insurance covering only $125 million of damages.
66. See Richard E. Neustadt and Harvey V. Fineberg, *The Swine Flu Affair: Decision-Making On A Slippery Disease* (Washington, D.C.: U.S. Department of Health, Education and Welfare, 1978), especially Chapter 7.
67. Care must be taken to distinguish between this definition of regulation and looser delineations of the term that do not focus on policy actions, but instead are

concerned with what some agency (e.g., Interstate Commerce Commission, Federal Trade Commission) does. We also avoid the broader use of terms which sees all government economic activity as regulatory. Here we are interested in specific actions and statements related to the behavior or behavior norms of targeted populations.

KEY TERMS
Antitrust Activity
Authoritative-command
Automatic Stabilizers
Behavior Variables
Capitalist Policies
Distribution Problems
Exchange
Fiscal Policies
Full Employment
Government Loans
Historically Based Categories
Incomes Policies
Infrastructure
Keynesian Policies
"Level of Activity" Categories
Licensing
Loan Guarantees
Macroeconomic Policies
Mandates
Market Resource Variables
Market Size Variables
Market Structure Variables
Mercantilist Policies
Microeconomic Policies
Monetary Policies
Neo-mercantilist Policies
Persuasion
Political Economy
Preventative Policies
Price Stability
Production Problems
Prohibitions
Promotional Policies
Protective Policies
Public Enterprises
"Purpose" Categories
Regulatory Activities
Risks and Liabilities Variables

KEY TERMS

Say's Law of Markets
Socialist Policies
Stabilization Policies
Standards Setting and Enforcement
Stimulative Policies
Strategic Categories
Subsidies
Supply-side Economics
Tax Breaks
"Tools" Categories
Tradition

CHAPTER 6

Policy Explanations

WHAT IS AN EXPLANATION?

The task of explaining public policy requires identifying the cause of the policy actions and statements. Explanations may deal with questions as diverse as these: Why did the United States escalate its involvement in Vietnam during the 1960s? Why did the budget for social welfare services increase at such a rapid rate during the 1970s? Why has the Social Security Trust Fund approached bankrupcy in the early 1980s? Why do some states annually spend more per capita on highways than on public health? Why did the effort to integrate southern schools succeed while the integration of northern schools failed? Who, if anyone, determines the spending priorities for your city or county government?

Such questions are typically raised by economists, political scientists, legislators, journalists, and citizens concerned with public policy. The search for *policy explanations* may take on various forms, but essentially represents one basic analytic question: why is the policy the way it is?

In this chapter, we review the different forms of explanatory policy thinking and present a number of the most frequently used models for solving problems of explanation. However, first we explore the use and purpose of "explanation" in policy analytic thinking to obtain a better sense of what to expect.

To begin, we need to view policy explanations as attempts to find out what factors determine the form, content, scope, and direction of some government statement or action. In this sense, policy explanations are closely related to the search for theories in the social as well as the natural sciences. One scholar defines the object of this search, *theory*, as: "A set of interrelated constructs (concepts), definitions, and propositions that present a systematic view of phenomena by specifying relations among variables, with the purpose of explaining and predicting the phenomena."[1] From this perspective, explanations are an integral part of a more general goal—the development of valid and reliable theory.

There are several types of explanations used by scientists, the classical and most basic being the *covering law explanation*. Explanations of this type are characterized by the application of some accepted premise to the phenomenon being examined. These premises typically take the form of generalizations or "laws" and represent assumptions that if certain conditions or relationships exist, then specific events or conditions will follow. In the physical world, we assume that the law of gravity and other well-known covering law explanations govern the behavior of animate and inanimate objects. As we will see, no similar covering law explanations for public policy are as widely accepted as these physical laws. However, the need for policy explanations is critical because no policy alternative can be accepted by citizen or decision maker unless a cause for the action is understood.

BOX 6.1

Anyone who has taken a course in basic logic will recognize the covering law explanation and its "if . . . then" form immediately. In the parlance of scientific inquiry, the assumptions made about the world in the form of generalizations or laws are called *explanans,* while the conclusions reached by applying these assumptions are termed *explanandum.* In its most common logical outline, the covering law explanation takes on the following structure:

Explanan	If p, then q
Condition	p
Explanandum	q

Here the logical statement begins with a generalization that if some state of affairs, p, existed, then some other phenomenon, q, will follow. This generalization is the explanan and sets the stage for the explanation by positing a fundamental premise for the analyst to work with.

> We use explanans in our daily routines consciously or unconsciously. To a great extent we live and work according to the guidance they provide. From getting out of bed when the alarm wakes us ("If I don't get up now, then I will be late for class"), to making instant coffee or tea for breakfast ("If I heat this pot of water to 100° C, then it will boil), to determining what is to be done on a given day ("If this is Tuesday, then I have to go to my English class"), we make constant use of explanans to orient and give direction to our lives.
>
> There are two types of covering law generalizations—universal and statistical. If *universal,* then the generalization represents a given and fixed "law" in the strictest sense of that term. The explanan in our formal example would read, "If p then always q." We regard the laws of gravity in this way. *Statistical* generalizations reflect observations of the world which are based, usually, on the laws of probability. An explanan might read, "If p, then probably q." Weather forecasts are good examples of statistical explanations.
>
> See Dickinson McGaw and George Watson, *Political and Social Inquiry*, (New York: John Wiley & Sons, Inc., 1976), pp. 56–69.

Covering law explanations are clearly the most fundamental types of policy explanations. There are also many explanatory models that, while not explicitly based on the covering law form, are dependent on underlying premises and assumptions about policies. First we consider several types of policy explanations that are variations on the covering law type,[2] even though the explanans may not be clearly stated. There are essentially four types of policy explanations that are the variations of the applicable covering law form. These are the rational, genetic, functional, and associational types.

Rational Explanation

The rational explanation assumes that public policies are produced by goal-oriented behavior, and that one can explain a policy by searching out a policymaker's objectives. This view is obviously related to the "intentional" perspective used in descriptive policy thinking when we define a policy statement or action in terms of its objective or purpose. The difference is that in policy explanation, the objective is regarded as the factor that caused or provided the conditions necessary for a specific policy to come into being.

This kind of explanation is often applied in discussions of domestic and foreign policy, typically as a response to questions about the purposes a policymaker is trying to achieve in making a specific statement or undertaking a particular action. With this in mind we can explain a foreign policy move by the People's Republic of China or France by looking for the objective of the policy. The Chinese may improve their relations with the United States in order to improve their ability to import new technologies or to enhance their diplomatic position vis-à-vis the Soviet Union. The French may recognize a new regime in Latin America in order to open new markets for their growing defense industries. In the same way we can explain why a president orders a cutback in government spending or a governor announces plans for a new highway. The objective or purpose in question may or may not be the explicit target of the government action or statement. Thus, as described in Chapter 7, U.S. foreign assistance programs are, at least on the surface, intended to help Third World nations develop economically and to accomplish other humane ends; in point of fact, the underlying objective explaining the policy may be the maintenance of friendly relations with the recipient state or obtaining some leverage in future dealings with that nation.

Genetic or Historicist Explanations

Closely associated with the developmental type of policy description discussed in Chapter 4 are genetic or historicist explanations. These models represent a view of public policy as caused and conditioned by its roots and historical emergence. From this perspective, the explanation of current public policy is found in past government activity or its historical context. Several analysts have attempted, for example, to explain the differences in government social welfare programs among modern capitalist states by looking at the social, cultural, and economic factors influencing the evolution of the policies in each nation.

In the United States, the most rapid growth of the social welfare sector occurred in the late 1960s and 1970s, after the introduction of Johnson's War on Poverty even though that program included no legislation for income maintenance or cash transfers to the poor. In other words, while Johnson's proposals did not involve redistributive programs, some analysts suggest that the War on Poverty did create the conditions for the growth of benefits to the poorest household by focusing the attention of all government agencies on the question, "What does my agency do for the poor?"[3] The result was the rapid addition of policies and benefits for the poor to many established programs. Thus, the genetic explanation for national social welfare programs in the United States sees the War on Poverty and events associated with it as a catalyst for the expansion of redistributive income programs in the 1960s.

Functional Explanations

Like functional descriptions, functional explanations focus on the role played by a policy within a general set of circumstances. Unlike the descriptive counterpart, functional explanations regard that role as the very reason for the existence of the public policy. To a certain extent this type of explanation resembles the rational form, for it looks to the policy's purpose as a determinant. However, there is a difference between the two that, in the abstract, seems quite subtle. While the rational policy is meant to fulfill the policymaker's objective, the functional policy is intended to fulfill a role or condition of the policymaking system or its surroundings.

To make this distinction clearer, let us consider rational and functional explanations for state unemployment insurance programs. Such programs can be explained in terms of the objectives they met for the policymakers involved in their passage. Generally speaking, these "rational" reasons will vary considerably. For legislators in some states the purpose was merely political; that is, unemployment insurance, especially in times of recession, is very popular with voters. The lawmaker may regard his or her vote for it as an investment in the next election campaign. Others may have looked at unemployment compensation as a means for the state to cash-in on federal funds available to states that chose to participate in the nationwide program. And indeed there might have been those who had altruistic motives and based their decisions on the need to protect employees from hardships associated with job loss or temporary layoffs.

Yet despite these objectives and purposes, unemployment compensation plays a significant role in American economic policy, a role that was probably not a primary concern among policymakers when the program was passed on both the federal and state levels. Unemployment insurance functions in our fluctuating economy as what economists call an automatic stabilizer (see Chapter 5). These stabilizers are mechanisms of American domestic policy that react to given economic conditions. When the economy is in a period of expansion and employment is relatively high, unemployment compensation expenditures are relatively low and thus total government spending is held down without any explicit cutbacks by policymakers. On the other hand, were conditions to change and unemployment rates increase substantially, the unemployment compensation program would be more active and the government would be spending more money (without having made an explicit decision to do so) which would, in turn, help stimulate a sluggish economy or at least ameliorate the ultimate effect of a recession. Thus, we can explain the growth and operation of unemployment compensation in terms of its function as an automatic stabilizer just as we can explain it in terms of the objectives policymakers intended to fulfill in its passage. Another automatic stabilizer is the progressive income tax, which can also be explained in functional terms.

Associational Explanations

The logic behind associational explanations is more vague than the previously discussed types. Yet this form of explanation has played such a significant role in contemporary policy thinking that it deserves considerable attention. Many professional analysts have sought explanations for certain public policies not in any specific causal event, role, or historical development, but in those circumstances that seem to demonstrate a high correlation with the existence or nonexistence of a policy statement or action. That is, through observing patterns and events of certain phenomenon and comparing those to the patterns and events associated with a public policy, an analyst can come to conclusions regarding the association between the two.

One might observe, for example, that the occurrence of major social reform policies is associated with the election of members from a certain party; or that there is a reasonably high correlation between tax increases imposed by Congress and the number of federally funded programs; or that their exists a positive relationship between the per capita income of a community and the quality of public education offered to its residents. In one sense, each of these observations represents a comparative description of a public policy, that is, comparing a government statement or event with some other phenomenon. Yet one can begin to speculate about these relationships, particularly if the correlations are reasonably high. *Correlations* can be *positive* (i.e., as one factor increases, so does the other) or *negative* (i.e., as one factor increases, the other decreases) or they can happen by chance, but the more consistent and strong the relationship, the less likely it is that the correlation is merely coincidental. With this in mind, many professional analysts have translated such comparative descriptions into simple explanations by positing that the relationship under examination was in fact causal or conditional. Using our examples once again, the analyst might hypothesize that the election of a particular party results in major social reform policies, that the number of federally funded programs is a cause of increased federal taxes, or that high per capita income is a condition that helps produce high quality education in a community's public schools.

BOX 6.2

With the increased use of social statistics in public policy research, analysts have stepped up their exploration of various public policies based on this simple form of associational explanation. Focusing on comparable units such as cities, states, or even nations, these analysts have developed quite a few explanations inferred from the correlation between public policies and various factors. In studies of police, fire, sanitation, and street maintenance expenditures by American cities, economists and political scientists have discovered that environmental factors explain much of what occurs. Among these factors are per capita income, median family income, property value per capita, population density, and racial composition. Another analyst discovered that similar factors were significant in explanations of urban renewal and educational policies. In addition, many of these same studies found that characteristics of the political system (e.g., degree of party competition, type of chief executive, powers of government) do not explain much, or at least have no independent effects on public policy outside those derived from differences in urban area environments. The same kind of research in regard to various public policies in American states has produced similar conclusions. On the cross-national level of analysis the correlational approach has produced evidence that suggests that environmental factors are more salient than political ones in the determination of public policy, at least in certain areas of expenditure.

The use of associational explanations has generated a great deal of controversy among analysts in recent years. For some, the controversy focused on conclusions reached by the analyses, that is, that political system variables seemed to be less significant than had been previously thought. Still another point of contention has been the methodological assumptions of those who use this approach. That is, there are grounds for questioning this associational approach due to the "leap of faith" an analyst must often take in moving from comparative description to causal explanation. In contrast, some scholars feel that associational explanations can be even more successful if more sophisticated techniques are adopted. This viewpoint is typified by the work of researchers such as Thomas Dye and Harold L. Wilensky.

See Richard I. Hofferbert, *The Study of Public Policy* (Indianapolis, IN: Bobbs-Merrill Co., Inc., 1974), especially chapters IV–VI; also see Thomas R. Dye, *Policy Analysis: What Governments Do, Why They Do It, and What Difference It Makes* (University, AL: University of Alabama Press, 1976), especially Chapters 2–4; and, Harold L. Wilensky, *The Welfare State and Equality: Structural and Ideological Roots of Public Expenditures* (Berkeley, CA: University of California Press, 1975).

Before we consider specific models used in policy explanation, there are a number of points to be made concerning these basic explanatory types. First, each type of policy explanation discussed in this section is an off-shoot of the covering law type. If we were to formally state the explanan underlying each, it would take the "if . . . then" form typical of the covering law form. Thus, for rational explanations the explanan would read "if objective A, then policy B"; in the genetic form, "if sequence of events A through F, then policy G"; for functional explanations, "if role X, then policy Y"; and finally, for associational explanations, "if event A is highly correlated with policy B, then A is a determinant of B."

Second, our discussion to this point has constantly referred to policy explanations as a search for causes and conditions that determine public policies. This statement is perhaps more significant than one would think at first glance. Even professional policy analysts can overlook the fact that explanations do more than seek out causes, that is specific factors that precede and lead to the existence of some conclusions. Phenomena such as public policies are not merely "caused" in the strict sense of the presence of A resulting in the consequent presence of B. Instead, policies are frequently determined by conditions present during a given period or in the general context of policy development. For example, if a person were to take a simple causal approach, then the escalation of American involvement in Vietnam during 1964 and 1965 might be regarded as the alleged attack of North Vietnamese PT boats on U.S. destroyers in the Gulf of Tonkin and the series of discrete events that followed. However, it would be foolish to ignore other factors involved in the escalation decision factors that were not causal events but rather conditioning circumstances. Among these factors were: the Cold War mentality of the 1950s and early 1960s in the United States; the strong anticommunist attitudes of many key policymakers and their belief in the idea that the Soviet Union and mainland China were behind the North Vietnamese effort; the public consensus that supported Lyndon Johnson during the post-Kennedy period and the election of 1964; and the healthy condition of the U.S. economy at the time, which was not regarded as burden on the government and seemed to evoke a feeling that we could afford our Southeast Asia involvement. These and similar factors were as much determinants of the escalation as were the specific events which triggered greater U.S. troop involvement.

Third and finally, it should be stressed that what we have discussed here are major forms of policy explanation, but not the only types. We have not considered *demographic* explanations, which essentially rely on models that explain the growth of populations (e.g., base times rate).[4] Nor have we looked at what social analysts call *dispositional* explanations, which focus on tendencies of an object or person ("He tends to be conservative; therefore he will be predisposed to vote no on this issue.")[5] Dispositional explanation can also be valuable for the student of public policy.

At this point, however, we cannot rest on the knowledge that there are a variety of policy explanation types, for each type represents an even greater variety of models that policy analysts have found extremely helpful in developing explanations of what causes or conditions public policy. In the balance of this chapter we look at a number of those models and discuss their value for policy analysis.

EXPLANATORY MODELS I: THE POLICY SOURCES

Explanations have always meant a great deal to professional policy analysts. It is therefore little wonder that there are a substantial number of extant explanatory models. In fact, the number is so great that a discussion of only a small portion of them could take up an entire textbook. In order to simplify that task we focus on one fundamental distinction which seems to characterize these models: the distinction between models that stress the *sources* of public policy and models that emphasize the *dynamic process* of policymaking. In this and the following section we consider each type and examine several examples of each.

There are many models focusing on what or who generated the public policy being examined. For models in this category, government statements or actions are classified as products of certain roles, institutions, or political interests. Some of these factors are viewed as causal forces directly involved in the policy's formulation, while others are considered more as conditional factors providing the appropriate context for policy development. In either case the focus is the *source* itself. Among the most common of these models are five we discuss in detail: the policy system model; the power structure model; the party or electoral organization model; the institutional/constitutional model; and the individual decision-maker model.

The Policy System Model

In Chapter 3 we discussed the system model as an example of a flexible and useful analytical tool. At that time we noted that among political scientists, the model of the political system was found to be a significant development in the field. As described in detail by David Easton, the political system construct provides a broad and somewhat abstract view of what the political life of a society involves.

Policy analysts have developed a more specific version of the political system model, one that stresses the interplay between the environment and public policy.[6] The *policy system* includes a political system (political process) which converts inputs (environmental factors) into outputs (public policy) which, in turn, add to the inputs through a feedback loop (impact) link.

EXPLANATORY MODELS I: THE POLICY SOURCES   155

By applying this model the analyst is providing an explanation of public policy based on the view that they represent responses to forces brought to bear on political actors and institutions from the general environment. Since the policy system and its outputs are necessary to the continuance of the political system, this model can be considered a functional explanation of policy. That is, policies are the product of a system that functions to translate external pressures into satisfactory responses. Environmental forces involved may be physical (climate, physical characteristics of the surrounding landscape, soil conditions), socioeconomic (per capita income of population, education level, number of cars per family, degree of urbanization), psychological (the ideological climate, public attitudes), or even historical (customs and traditions, past wars). In this model, the policy system acts merely as a mediating mechanism between public policy and environmental factors. The source of government actions and statements is assumed to be the environmental factors.

BOX 6.3

The energy crisis of the 1970s in the United States was a classic example of the impact of environmental forces (in this case, the international environment) on the policy system. The oil embargo of 1973 imposed by the Arab oil-producing nations immediately triggered demands for a national energy plan to reduce dependence on foreign supplies, to insure an adequate supply for heating, industry, and automobiles, and to reduce air pollution standards to conserve scarce energy sources. Some of the demands, such as lowering air quality standards to permit the burning of "dirtier" coal, were met fairly quickly. The demand for a comprehensive energy plan to meet what appeared to be a permanent situation was more complex, involving many components in the political system. More than five years later, the Congress concluded work on a new Energy Act which, although it only partially met most of the demands of constituents and the president, was the first major step toward comprehensive policy. During this five-year period the environment, both domestically and internationally, continued to exert pressure on the policy system through the political upheaval in Iran, OPEC price increases, rampant inflation, and severe winters in the United States. The process and outputs of the policy system (laws and regulations), were unable to keep up with the new demands for action to meet these environmental pressures. The system model, applied to the energy situation in this case, provided a powerful explanation of energy policy as a product of environmental forces influencing political forces and the policy system.

See Walter A. Rosenbaum, *Energy, Politics and Public Policy* (Washington, DC: Congressional Quarterly Press, 1981).

The Power Structure Model

Among the many concepts frequently used but poorly defined by social scientists is power. A useful but elusive term, the idea of power has played a major role in recent attempts to explain public policies, especially at the community level.[7] Models built around this concept share the assumption that the actions and statements of governments are produced by patterns of influence and persuasion. These patterns are regarded as reflections of basic power relationships among individuals or groups. It is on the policies produced by such relationships that power models focus.

To more fully understand such patterns and structures, let us consider one useful definition[8] of power. Power is a relationship between at least two parties, A and B, in which A gets B to do something B would not otherwise do. In short, A has power or influence relative to B. A further delineation of power from this point of view would show that power involves four crucial ingredients:

1. To have power one must have *resources* with which to exercise one's influence. Some power structure models take the view that almost anything A has can be applicable in a power relationship, while other power structure models will tend toward a more narrow definition of useful resources (e.g., legal use of force, the control of society's productive forces, or one's position in society).
2. Since having a resource and being able to use it are two different problems, it is also crucial that one have the *ability* to apply resources in a power relationship. Possessing great wealth or being President of the United States means little or nothing unless one is capable of using those resources to influence others.[9]
3. For power to be consciously exercised and effectively applied, there must be a *willingness* on the part of the power wielder to use his or her resources and ability in a given situation. For example, compare the reluctance of some key (i.e., "powerful") members of the executive and legislative branches to challenge the U.S. policies in Southeast Asia during the Johnson and Nixon administrations with the willingness of thousands of students to protest the war.

4. To have power one must have an *"other"* individual who is susceptible to the willing and able application of resources. This ingredient is perhaps the most significant of the four, for it is at the very core of the idea that power is a relationship with some second party. In everyday use of the term, we often hear that this or that person is "powerful." Yet such use of the term is incorrect from the analyst's point of view, for it implies that power is something a person has or possesses. On the contrary, power is not an inherent characteristic of an individual person; rather, it is only obtained through a social interaction with another person and endures only within that relationship.

This explanation of power and its major components helps us to understand the assumptions of power structure models of public policy. Generally, such models focus on social institutions that have acquired power or influence and use it to determine public policy. Most of the power or influence models, therefore, belong to the broad class of rational explanations, since the exercise of power is intentional and purposive. That is, those who wield power use it to achieve their goals and objectives through public policies.

Among the may variations of power structure models that have been applied to the recent study of public policy, two stand out as archetypes of significantly different views. One is a model derived from the writings of sociologist C. Wright Mills, who wrote in the early 1950s about a "power elite" which (he felt) governed the United States.[16] The other version was developed by political scientist Robert A. Dahl in works published during the late 1950s and early 1960s.[11] His "pluralism" model considers the power structure to be more broadly dispersed. Both models regarded the power structure as a crucial determinant in the formation of public policy, but each perceived that structure in a different way. Mills' model is representative of a long established view of society as being governed by a *single elite*, while in Dahl's view a *plural elite* construct best captures policymaking in American politics.

BOX 6.4

The single elite model regards the power structure as highly concentrated with a few key decision makers on top and a mass of followers below. The plural elite model, on the other hand, sees the power as highly decentralized, with many different elites on top and individuals below who do not necessarily fit the role of followers. In fact, from the plural elite perspective members of the masses are potential elites or power resources that different elites can use to influence each other or the public in general. This contrasts with the single elite picture of the masses as manipulated and noninfluential groups who have little if any chance of moving into the ranks of the elite. In the single elite view, the governing few are not typical of the masses they rule. This runs counter to the plural elite assumption that there are substantial similarities in composition and attitudes between elites and masses.

The single and plural elite power structure models also differ on their respective views of relevant resources. For example, Mills regards the military, industrial, and political sectors of American society as most important and sees the leaders of each institution as part of a single power elite. In his model it is assumed that in each society at different times in history there are certain strategic sectors essential to the social system and that control of these strategic sectors is the key to power. The plural elite model is more open in its interpretation of what is or is not a relevant resource. Power for Dahl and other pluralists derives from a number of resources, some of them reflecting strategic sectors of society, but others rooted in resources as varied as personality, time, community history, and so on.

The models also differ on the question of elite consensus and the policy goals of society. The single elite perspective finds a basic consensus on the fundamental social values and the desire to preserve the present power structure. The public policies endorsed by the ruling elite therefore tend to maintain the status quo in society. Policy change is endorsed only to ameliorate the conditions of the masses or to stave off drastic change. For the plural elitists, there is consensus only on the rules of the game and policy choices result from competition and among the various elites. Public policies are seen as the reflection of the demands of the masses filtered through their respective leaders.

See Thomas R. Dye and Harmon Ziegler, *The Irony of Democracy*, 3rd edition (Belmont, CA: Wadsworth Publishing, 1975); also G. David Garson, *Power and Politics In The United States: A Political Economy Approach* (Lexington, MA: D.C. Heath and Co., 1977).

A major variant of the plural elite model, the *group model* of politics, deserves special attention here. In the American tradition, this model has had its formal expression in the work of statesmen such as James Madison and John C. Calhoun and in the scholarly works of Arthur Bentley and David Truman.[12] In very general terms, the model views the political arena as a place where groups representing all the legitimate political interests of society interact. The interaction takes the form of a struggle among these groups whereby each tries to influence the political system in general and governmental policymakers in particular to adopt their policy priorities. From this struggle, and through mechanisms such as compromise, bargaining, and coalition building, a policy position is reached that will supposedly reflect an equilibrium point among the demands of the groups involved. That equilibrium position is, according to Truman's version of this model, the action taken by public policymakers in their role as respondents to the pull and push of group pressures.

The group model of politics has much in common with the plural elite model. First, it views policymaking as the product of conflict among those involved in the political process. On the basis of what has been called the "iron law of oligarchy" (which essentially states that in any group there will be leaders and followers, or elites and masses), this means that the group model, like the plural elite model views the policymaking process as interaction among leaders of different groups. Secondly, from David Truman's perspective, the group struggle (like the elite struggle of the plural elite model) occurs within the context of rules of the game accepted by the participants. No matter how intense the disagreement among those involved, there will be a fundamental consensus about the system for resolving conflict. Third, both the plural elite and group models share a common view of the role of power and influence in this struggle. For these and other reasons, we consider the group model as a variant of the more generally defined plural elite perspective.

The Party/Electoral Organization Model

In the political system there are many who have differing goals and objectives. Some are politically active because they believe that their policy preferences can be obtained through the governmental process. For these actors, politics is a means toward achieving desired public policies and their activities are generally included in the power models of politics.

Other actors in the political system participate in the governmental process not for the sake of a given policy objective or orientation, but to obtain control of political officers. That is, some people seek election or appointment to office for its own sake. They are more interested in becoming a governor, congressperson, senator, or county sheriff than they are in lowering taxes, ending discrimination, or increasing aid to higher education. For these individuals public policy is a means toward attaining the objective of elective or appointive office. It is this desire for office that is at the heart of the party/electoral organization model.

The assumption underlying this model is that political parties (and similar types of organizations) are formed and operated for the primary purpose of capturing or maintaining an office such as the Presidency or a proportion of legislative seats sufficient enough to give the party voting control of the body. This premise is, of course, rooted in an Anglo-American conception of political parties as brokerage units bringing together a winning margin of electoral votes for a candidate. In this sense it excludes the many political party systems in the world that are more interested in proselytizing their ideologically based programs than in winning office. Although careful analysis of American political parties has shown that to some extent they too have been ideologically motivated,[13] the primary objective sustaining party behavior has been victory at the polls. Therefore, parties shape issues and propose policies to persuade voters, promising they will take action after the election. It is this adapting to voters that makes the party/electoral organization model a potentially meaningful tool in explaining public policy.[14]

This model has taken several forms, some based on the empirical behavior of political parties over the years,[15] others derived from basic assumptions about political behavior.[16] In either case, the situation posited by the model seems to be the same: Where there are competing, nonideological parties, public policies will ultimately reflect a package of programs put together by the victorious organization as part of its strategy toward electoral victory. In the United States these policy packages are formally written up in party platforms, but they are also informally recorded by the mass media's election campaign coverage. The content of each package is supposedly determined by the demands made of the party organization by groups of voters who make up a significant portion of the total needed for victory on election day. All other things being equal, the policy package will contain just enough in the way of promised government actions and statements to induce a sufficient proportion of the electorate to vote for the party candidate while avoiding the alienation of those already committed to the party's cause. Having achieved their goal of electoral victory, party officials are likely to implement these policy promises because (according to the model) they will be held accountable for their program promises at the next election.

The degree to which platform promises are kept is a subject of political controversy and empirical research. Some scholars have found that a majority of promises are eventually kept, particularly if more than one party proposes similar solutions.[17] Other research suggests that policy change reflects long-term shifts in the politcal agenda, while many commentators regard parties and candidates as becoming even less concerned with issues than with image.[18] On its face, the party/organizational model can be classified as one of the family of rational explanations. However, as platform promises and ideological differences become less important than image campaigns and media influence, the model becomes more genetic in character. Parties and candidates are replaced and policies shaped in response to historical forces rather than through attempts to keep campaign promises.

The Institutional/Constitutional Model

If a public policy is perceived as a "product," then the machinery that produces it is bound to be regarded as an important factor in explaining its form, scope, and direction. The basic assumption underlying the institutional/constitutional model is that the formal and informal structures and procedures of government—as well as the many rules of the game of government—have an impact on public policymaking. Thus, institutional models imply an associational perspective; certain types of institutions likely to produce or be associated with certain policy outputs.

For some analysts the institutional/constitutional model is the classical one among the various types available. It is so regarded because it is the model that influenced the work of early students of American politics, as well as the writers of the U.S. Constitution. What the men who gathered in 1787 in Philadelphia sought was not merely a mechanism through which public problems could be solved, but an institutional framework that would develop solutions representative of a broad consensus among the many factions within U.S. society. They perceived the design of governmental institutions as an exercise in political engineering,[19] their purpose being to organize policymaking structures in a way that would result in such consensually based public policies. "Each public policy was to be like a puzzle," states Peter Woll, "the pieces of which were dispersed in the hands of the legislative and executive branches. Public policy would not be put together unless each branch contributed its piece."[20]

Those formal institutional arrangements created the foundation for the current structures of American government which, at best, can only be termed fragmented. In addition to the separation of powers at the national level of U.S. government, the writers of the Constitution vaguely divided jurisdiction between state and federal officials. This federalism and the multilevel intergovernmental structure emerging from it has become increasingly complex over the years, as has the relationships among the President, the two houses of Congress, the federal courts, and the "fourth branch" of government—the bureaucracy. The resulting institutional fragmentation has been useful in explaining why American government generates the kind of public policies it produces.[21]

Of course, there are also informal institutional arrangements that may have an impact on public policy. Morris P. Fiorina argues that such an informal arrangement is playing an increasingly important role in the United States. Calling this arrangement the "Washington establishment," he defines it as "unconsciously evolved and evolving networks of congressmen, bureaucrats, and organized subgroups of the citizenry all seeking to achieve their own goals." According to Fiorina, Congress is the "keystone" of the Washington establishment and he provides empirical evidence to support his argument. For our purposes, however, the importance of his thesis is the use he makes of a model based on informal institutional relationships to explain U.S. public policy.[22]

BOX 6.5

Any history of government reform movements in America will indicate that those who wrote the Constitution were not the only ones to apply an institutional model to public policymaking. Similar views regarding how government works have influenced many advocates of structural and procedural change in our system. On the national level this view has been reflected in the reports of Presidential commissions that have looked into the organization of the executive branch. The Brownlow Committee of the Roosevelt Administration stressed the need to separate the President's personal staff from the Executive Office of the President to improve efficiency in policymaking, while the Ash Council study commissioned by the Nixon Administration sought reorganization of the executive departments to improve policies affecting major sectors of society. Both reports suggested that reorganization of government (based on the premises of the institutional/constitutional model) would improve policy output. The use of the model is even more evident in the work of municipal and metropolitan government reformers who have urged structural and procedural changes in local government (such as the adoption of a city manager plan or a specific budgeting system) as a means of improving public policies and delivery of services at that level.

The rationale behind reliance on these models seem logical and easily justified. It is, after all, quite reasonable to expect differences in public policy among cities or countries where there are significant differences in decision-making structures or the procedures used. Thus, we may expect differences between systems that have centralized policymaking procedures and those characterized by a fragmentation of decision-making powers. Similarly a city manager government will be expected to perform as differently from a strong mayor government, as the unitary system of the United Kingdom or the confederacy of Switzerland performs differently when compared to the federalist structure of the United States. Whether this is what actually occurs is, of course, an empirical question. But the institutional/constitutional model assumes that the empirical evidence will back up such a contention.

On reform through reorganization, see Peter Szanton (ed.), *Federal Reorganization: What Have We Learned?* (Chatham, NJ: Chatham House Publishers, Inc., 1981); on the history of municipal reform, see Martin J. Schiesl, *The Politics of Efficiency: Municipal Administration and Reform in American 1880–1920* (Berkeley, CA: University of California Press, 1977).

The Individual Decision-Maker Model

When all is said and done, the significant actor in any decision-making situation is usually an individual. Even where policies are ultimately made by organizational leaders, whole groups, or even states, it is the individual member or official involved in the process who seems to make the difference in the kind of public policy that results. This model and its several variants provides us with frameworks highlighting the individual actor's role.

There are at least three common types of individual decision-maker models, each useful in its own way for helping analysts explain public policy. The first perceives the decision maker as a *mediator* through which many relevant factors are converted into some policy action or statement. A second approach perceives of the decision maker as an *ideal type* who has certain behavioral characteristics and acts strictly in accord with these in any and all circumstances. The third type also views the decision-making actor in terms of behavioral patterns, but it is more concerned with *empirically observed patterns* that with the consistency of some logically derived idealization. Let us look at each of these and consider at least one example of a variant developed from each approach.

For some analysts the decision maker is a mediating unit that shapes and gives intensity to policy choices while "filtering" various messages and pressures received from the environment. To a certain extent this version of the individual decision-maker model is closely related to the system perspective, but with the distinction that here the stress is on the functional role played by the mediating unit.

A general framework using this mediating perspective was developed for use in the study of foreign policy decisions by political scientists Richard C. Snyder, H. W. Bruck, and Burton Sapin.[23] As illustrated in Figure 6.1, the decision makers provide an essential link between various external variables and the actions that ultimately become the foreign policy of a given nation-state. But in this framework those decision makers are more than merely open channels through which the external variables pass to become actions. As mediating units they translate inputs and have a significant impact on the output of the total system. Their individual "orientations," their perceptions, expectations, and choices, are seen to have considerable influence on the form and substance of the foreign policy actions and statements. In the words of Synder, Bruck, and Sapin, the framework attempts to establish a useful picture of the decision maker's orientation by asking:

> what did the decision-makers think was relevant in a particular situation? how did they determine this? how were the relevant factors related to each other— what connections did the decision-makers see between diverse elements in the situation? how did they establish the connections? what wants and needs were deemed involved in or affected by the situation? what were the sources of these wants and needs? how were they related to the situation? what specific or general goals were considered and selected? what courses of action were deemed fitting and effective? how were fitness and effectiveness decided?[24]

Answers to these and related questions aid in the explanation of policy actions by stressing the substantive consequences an individual actor's point of view is likely to have.

A more formalistic version of the decision-maker model seeks policy explanation in the purposive, goal-oriented activity of individuals. Such an explanation is frequently used in formal policy analysis and reflects the application of a model not derived from empirical generalizations, but rather from established ideal types that have proved quite useful. Typically this version of the individual decision maker model focuses on the activities of a "rational actor" whose behavior is not only purposive, but also consciously calculated and extremely consistent relative to given situations. It is a model that has taken several forms in the social sciences, particularly in the areas of economics, game theory, statistical decision theory, and the analysis of foreign policies.

The classical explication of the rational actor model is found in the work of Thomas Hobbes, a seventeenth century political philosopher who had an enormous influence on modern political thought. From the Hobbesian model there emerged several versions which, despite their use in different fields, have a common conceptual base. Graham Allison summarized these common conceptions in his study of public policy actions taken during the 1962 Cuban missile crisis. Basic to the rational actor model is the role of the decision maker as a "rational, unitary" agent who "has *one* set of specified goals . . ., *one* set of perceived options, . . . a *single* estimate of the consequences that follow from each alternative . . ." and the task of making a "value-maximizing" choice among those alternatives.[25] Applying this to various situations, policy analysts have been able to explain many policy acts that might otherwise make little or no sense.

EXPLANATORY MODELS I: THE POLICY SOURCES

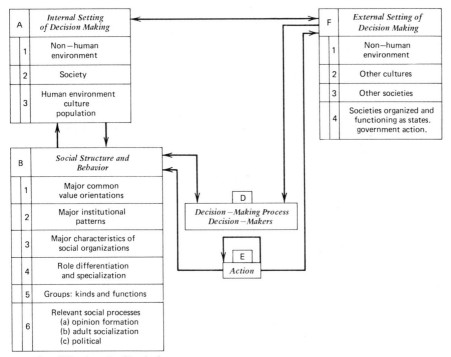

State "X" as Actor in a Situation*
(Situation is comprised of a combination of selectively relevant factors in the external and internal setting as interpreted by the decision—makers.)

*This diagram is designed only to be crudely suggestive. Detailed explanation must be deferred. The term non—human environment is construed to mean all physical factors (including those which result from human behavior) but not relationships between human beings or relationships between human beings and these physical factors. The latter relationships belong under society and culture.

Figure 6.1. Decision-maker as mediator. (Source: Richard C. Snyder, H.W. Bruck, and Burton Sapin (eds.), *Foreign Policy Decision-Making,* New York: The Free Press, 1962, p. 64.)

The third type of decision-maker model is rooted in the observation of individual behavior patterns that might have an impact on public policy. Many of these observations lead analysts to construct models that reflect such regularities in human behavior rather than some idealized activity as those assumed in the rational actor model.

One such model is applied by Morton H. Halperin to help explain certain aspects of U.S. foreign policy. According to Halperin's model, what specific bureaucrats do has a significant impact on the content, form, and direction of American foreign policy. The activities of these bureaucrats are such that one can explain their behavior in terms of three basic variables: personal experiences, individual career patterns, and their respective positions within the bureaucracy and relative to the problems at hand. Given empirical data on these three factors, one can gain useful insights into the bases for particular policies—an accomplishment achieved by Halperin in his analysis of decisions regarding the debate over deployment of an antiballistic missile (ABM) system during the late 1960s.[26] And when taking into account the observed behavior patterns of numerous other decision makers, one can at least partially explain an even more complex event such as the Cuban missile crisis.[27] This focus on individual personal experiences and the historical context of policy decision suggests a reliance on the genetic type of explanation.

While these three types of individual decision-maker models do not exhaust the number of potential variants, they do indicate several ways by which analysts can develop policy explanations based on the assumption that the single policymaking actor is important. Each has its limits, of course, and each must withstand the test of usefulness that governs all policy analysis models.

EXPLANATORY MODELS II: THE DYNAMICS AND PROCESS FACTORS

As important as policy sources are, it is evident that their impact is qualified by the dynamics of policy formulation and program implementation. The multifaceted relationships and interactions of decision making have an impact on policy outputs apart from the institutions and actors themselves. Explanatory models that focus on these dynamic processes therefore are crucial elements in the public policy analyst's arsenal of useful models.

These dynamics take place in two arenas, one involving making of policy and the other dealing with policy implementation. The distinction is an important one in policy thinking, for it brings out an often ignored fact that public policies are not only what governments intend to do or say, but also what they actually do or say. In a now classic discussion of public policy, Jeffrey L. Pressman and Aaron Wildavsky note that, at least initially, a policy is "a hypothesis containing initial conditions and predicted consequences." That is, a policy reflects an assumption that if government does X then at time t, then Y will result at time $t + 1$.[28] What a policy actually turns out to be is quite another matter (see Chapter 8). The crucial point here is that there are two processes at work: that of *policymaking*, which establishes the policy-as-hypothesis, and that of *policy implementation*, which results in policy-in-fact.

The study of policymaking is a well-developed field in policy analysis, and most of the established models discussed in this section emerged from that tradition. The study of policy implementation, however, is a relatively recent development and therefore there are few clearly defined models unique to examining that process.

BOX 6.6

Pressman and Wildavsky stressed the complexity of implementation in their 1973 study of how a federally funded economic development program in Oakland failed despite good intentions and strong financial support. Their text was appropriately illustrated with Rube Goldberg cartoons to emphasize their theme. Two significant elements that emerged from their study were "decision points" (points in the process which indicate the need for an agreement to continue the program) and "clearances" (points at which individual participants are required to give their consent for the implementing process to continue). In short, they put a great deal of stress on the implications of formal and informal institutional hurdles in the implementation process.

Eugene Bardach took a different approach to the implementation process by viewing it as a series of games. For him it is "a process of strategic interaction among numerous special interests all pursuing their own goals, which might or might not be compatible with the goals of the policy mandate." In one sense, this model is an extension of the group model (discussed above) to post-policymaking activity.

George C. Edwards III provided still another framework for understanding public policy implementation. Four basic factors were central to his model: the *communication* of orders and directions to policy implementors by decision makers; the availability of *resources* to effectively implement policies; the *dispositions* or attitudes of the implementors; and the design of *bureaucratic structures* through which the implementation process occurs. Here too, we find many of the policy source factors discussed earlier playing a primary role.

In fact, that is a major characteristic of these and other policy implementation models: they stress the role of policy sources rather than policy dynamics and processes. The four process-focus models discussed below are developed as means to explain public policymaking, but they (and related models) seem just as relevant in the policy implementation arena. Thus, because the uniqueness of implementation dynamics has yet to be captured in a clearly explicated model, we focus on the more traditional policymaking constructs.

See Jeffrey L. Pressman and Aaron Wildavsky, *Implementation*, 2nd edition (Berkeley, CA: University of California Press, 1979); Eugene Bardach, *The Implementation Game: What Happens After a Bill Becomes a Law* (Cambridge, MA: The MIT Press, 1977); George C. Edwards III, *Implementing Public Policy* (Washington, DC: Congressional Quarterly Press, 1980); and, for a more prescriptive analysis, see Walter Williams, *The Implementation Perspective: A Guide for Managing Social Service Delivery Programs* (Berkeley, CA: University of California Press, 1980).

There are, of course, many different models of the policy process and decision making in general; here we look at a few of the more common types. We begin by looking at the formal model of decision making and some of the common perceptions we have about the social processes that underlie public policymaking models.

The Basic Model of Rational Decision Processes

In its most fundamental form, decision-making processes involve the selection of a preferred course of action from among several possible alternatives. In this sense it is very similar to the general problem-solving approach discussed earlier. If asked to construct a model of decision making that reflects the steps which ought to be included in problem-solving, our list would probably include:

- Defining the problem
- Analyzing the problem
- Establishing a goal or objective
- Developing alternative solutions
- Analyzing the alternatives
- Selecting the "best" alternative, i.e., that which wll maximize the goal objective
- Evaluating the chosen alternative once it was implemented

In its various forms, the model we have developed has been identified by various authors as pure rationality,[29] synoptic policymaking,[36] the analytical approach,[31] or the computational strategy[32] in decision making. Although the names vary, there is general agreement that the model is normative; that is, it is more often a reflection of what we believe ought to be the process of decision making than it is a model of the actual policymaking process.

There are many factors working against truly rational decision making. Among other things, the rational process model does not coincide with the actual capabilities of human decision makers. As we indicated earlier in our discussion of human problem solving, the physiological and neurological constraints humans face make completely rational decisions highly improbable. Furthermore, to achieve true rationality in decision making there needs to be a great deal more certainty about all relevant factors and substantially more information than is normally available to policymakers. Thus, the rational process can prove very costly. With these limitations in mind, you have some idea of why this idealistic model lacks credibility.

But low credibility does not render the model completely useless. To a certain extent this model of decision-making processes can generate an explanation of public policy. Analysts find it most useful to explain those situations in which (1) the problem involves relatively minor or small changes in the present situation; (2) there is certainty about the relationships that make up the situation; and (3) there is certainty about the goals or objectives to be obtained. Put differently, the rational-synoptic-analytical-computational process model is more likely to be useful in explaining highly technical administrative decisions. Government actions and statements based on such decisions are to be found everywhere, but they are usually relatively unimportant and rarely become the basis for major analytic investigations. Nevertheless, the formal idealistic model of the decision-making process can prove useful when the appropriate situation is under investigation.

For example, suppose we want to explain why the National Aeronautics and Space Administration (NASA) chose July 1969 as the month for launching the first manned lunar landing flight. Applying this model one would be able to define the problem in terms of NASA decision makers having to select the appropriate time for the launch, and their objectives as wanting to time the voyage so as to meet specific yet critical technical and political time constraints. The technical constraints involved the matter of placing the flight in orbit at the right time so as to avoid wasting efforts or precious fuel resources. Politically, President John F. Kennedy's promise to land an American on the moon before the end of the decade posed a symbolic time constraint that NASA officials assumed to be binding. Given the problem and objectives, the decision regarding appropriate launch dates became an administrative and technical matter which was solved by experts in mathematics, physics, and engineering. It is thus possible to explain some public policy decisions using the traditional rational model.

This model of the decision-making process has other uses as well. We will see in Chapter 8 how the idealistic and formalized version of this rational process model can and has been used to evaluate public policymaking and the policies that result. Our current focus, however, is on its utility in policy explanation. Given its limitations in this regard, we must look at other models that can prove more useful.

The Incremental Process Model

While we may go so far as to claim that the rational policymaking process is not that significant for most analytic explanations, we cannot hold that the decision-making process will therefore always be irrational or arational. On the contrary, there are many instances in which decisions are rendered in as rational a process as is possible, given the limitations of the situation and the policymakers involved. For various reasons already noted, rationality may be severely limited. However, within those limits rationality can be applied.

This process is called incrementalism and it has been used to explain, among other things, the year to year changes in the U.S. budget as an American public policy.[33] Here we have a rational explanation closely related to historical or genetic approaches.

The incremental process model sees policies being changed in a series of steps, or increments. The significance of the change, or the size of the incremental step, is related to three basic variables: the degree of satisfaction with past policy decisions; changes in the problematic situation the policy addresses; and the availability of new or innovative means for attacking the problem.[34] If satisfaction is high, the problem basically the same as before, and the available means limited to old approaches, then the process is likely to produce only minor changes; but if satisfaction is low, the problem different, and promising new methods abound, then incrementalism will tend to produce more substantial changes.

Incrementalism as a policy process has been criticized for its lack of innovation and inherent conservatism and praised for insuring stability and the atmosphere of compromise needed in a political system that produces conflict. The Social Security system provides an example of a public policy that expanded by incremental steps to include far more of the population than ever envisioned by its initiators. The decisions to provide benefits to segments of the population that may have never contributed to the system, from orphans to the blind and disabled, were made incrementally, one at a time. In almost every case, the conditions for slow change were met; high satisfaction with the program, acceptable methods, and predictable changes which could be absorbed by the system. The addition of Medicaid, a program to provide federal aid to states for the health needs of the poor in a manner similar to Medicare for the aged, was not accomplished in the incremental tradition. This innovation was added to the program as a least-minute amendment, partly in response to the War on Poverty's pervading question (what has this program done for the poor?) and partly in reaction to the overwhelming problems of low-income families in obtaining access to medical care in a period of rising health care costs.[35] In this instance, satisfaction was low, a new approach was seen as feasible, and the problem, it turns out, was quite different from providing medical insurance for the aging population. Medicaid, therefore, was a substantial change in policy.

The Satisfying Approach

In 1978 the Nobel Prize in Economics was awarded to organizational theorist Herbert A. Simon for his work on a model of decision making in organizations. According to this model, administrative behavior is something quite different from rational behavior in its pure and formalistically economic forms. Simon claimed that there was rationality in the organizational decision-making process, but that such rationality was constrained; it was, in his terms, "bounded rationality." Years before he began his intensive examinations of the problem-solving capabilities of humans, Simon was making a distinction between types of rationalities. He held that a process was objectively rational if it involved behavior that maximized given values or objectives in a specific situation. On the other hand, there is also a subjective rationality, which involved a process wherein behavior was patterned to maximize the achievement of an objective relative to the *actual* knowledge and capabilities of the decision maker. In a further description of this process he noted that,

> Rationality . . . does not determine behavior. Within the area of rationality behavior is perfectly flexible and adaptable to abilities, goals, and knowledge. Instead, behavior is determined by the irrational and nonrational elements that bound the area of rationality. The area of rationality is the area of adaptability to these nonrational elements.[36]

The significance of this perspective for policy explanation comes in the form of a model developed from Simon's premises. A decision maker behaving under conditions of bounded rationality will not seek to achieve a *maximization* of given goals and objectives (i.e., what is called the optimal solution), but rather will select that course of action which will be *satisfactory* in its attainment of that goal or objective. According to this view, public policies are chosen not because they will best achieve a goal, but because they will at least satisfy the decision maker or those to whom the policymaker is accountable. For obvious reasons this is termed the satisficing model of decision making.[37]

Bargaining as a Policy Process

There are many situations in public policymaking in which two or more parties debate decisions dealing with limited resources, and in such situations the processes of decision-making take on qualities closely resembling competitive market bargaining. Several quite interesting models have been developed to represent this process. Most are simple reflections of human interaction in situations where bargaining is taking place.

The most basic models of bargaining view it as a process involving reciprocal relationships between at least two individuals. Each has an objective, each controls some resources, and each will negotiate with the other for a means to use those resources to obtain his or her objective. This is at the heart of reciprocity, and bargaining is the process that carries the reciprocal relationships forward. The give and take of the process usually results in a compromise giving form and content to the public policy thus derived. Therefore, knowing about the bargaining process can help explain a public policy.[38]

One need not go far to find examples of bargaining in the American policymaking system.[39] It is a common process within legislative bodies as well as between institutions of government. Bargaining provides the basis for a majority coalition in support of policy initiation or change. The passage of the Energy Act in 1978 was a classic example of bargaining both within Congress and between the legislative and executive branches. Virtually all of the detailed provisions of the legislation were the result of compromises. The deregulation of "new" natural gas provides both incentives for exploration (for the producing states such as Louisiana and Texas) and assured growth in supplies to the consuming states (Illinois, Ohio, and the New England states). The Carter Administration, which originally opposed any deregulation of that fuel, compromised its position to get the badly needed legislation out of Congress at all. Thus, the reasons for striking bargains will vary from actor to actor. Some bargains are made on the basis of immediate exchanges (e.g., I'll vote for a deregulation of natural gas if you vote for a program to help the poor pay for increase fuel costs). Bargains can also be made in anticipation of future repayment rather than for immediate rewards (e.g., I'll back deregulation if you agree to support some future legislation I feel strongly about). In addition, the bargaining process may be characterized as a clear two-person relationship or it may, as in the case of Congress, be institutionalized among several hundred persons. On that scale, the process has an effect on the overall thrust of policymaking as well as on specific details and decisions.

Other Process Models

We have focused on four types of explanatory models which regard the policy process as a critical factor. Each has the potential to generate a distinctive picture of government actions or statements. For example, through the rational model we would expect public policies that were carefully designed to optimize the objectives being sought. That is, they would be "calculated" in the purest sense. Incremental processes, on the other hand, are likely to produce policies that are marginally different from past government actions and statements. Those developed under conditions of satisficing are intended to be enough to satisfy relevant parties, but not enough to achieve the optimal solution to a problem. Finally, we took a brief look at bargaining as a policymaking process and saw how this model speaks to policies as compromises among those involved in the decision-making endeavor. In short, processes differ and each process model provides a different insight and possible explanation for public policies.

Many other explanatory models focus on process. For example, there is an entire genre of *game theory models*, which can prove useful in examining process.[40] They give us a picture of the policymaking process as a game between at least two conflicting parties who are attempting to maximize their respective "utilities" (goals, objectives, etc.) while minimizing their "disutilities" (costs, penalties, etc.). The processes involved in playing the game of policymaking will combine bargaining, rational calculation, and other forms of behavior to produce distinctive public policies. Each game is unique, differing in terms of the number of players involved, the rules, possible strategies for each player, and the potential outcomes. Despite the variety of possible games, analysts have developed several specific models that can prove useful. Many of these have been applied to help make sense out of certain policies, especially the interaction among nation-states.[41]

CONCLUSION

In this chapter we introduced the covering law form of explanation as fundamental to the explanation of public policy. Whether the final shape of a public statement or action can be traced to a rational goal, or to historical developments, the attempt to explain such origins is dependent on certain assumptions or premises we make, or some covering law. Several variations on this form (rational, genetic/historicist, functional, and associational) were reviewed and their close relationship to certain descriptive types of policy analysis was established.

Several important points about explanatory models remain to be made. As was stressed in our discussion on policy implementation (Box 6.6), source and dynamic process models are closely related, since certain sources may be characterized by certain processes. Studies of public policy that follow the group model frequently find bargaining to be the major process at work; similarly, rationality is generally expected of the individual decision maker. There is no reason, however, not to find incrementalism at work even among the single elite, particularly if stability is the aim of the power structure.

The interaction between policy source and policy process underscores another point about policy explanation: no simple explanatory model will completely account for policy actions. Policy decision makers have multiple motives, political systems have many goals, and most public policies are the result of many forces. Any attempt to explain such a complex policy as, for example, the federal personal income tax, will immediately need to account for rational goals, historical developments, the activities of the economic elite and the demands of special interest groups, and the role of incremental, bargaining, and satisficing processes. The models of policy explanation help us focus on specific facets of public policies and to explore patterns of policymaking. They are useful in confronting the complexities of government activity.

After the goals and direction of a policy are identified and explained we need to find out if the goals are met and how they were achieved. In Chapter 8 we discuss methods of evaluating the goals and means of policy and, looking beyond those goals, measuring the impact of the policy on society in general. In the next chapter, however, we will consider how policy analysts who focus on American foreign policy use some of the explanatory models discussed here.

ENDNOTES

1. Fred N. Kerlinger, *Foundations of Behavioral Research,* 2nd edition, (New York: Holt, Rinehart and Winston, 1973), p. 9.
2. On discussions of various types of explanation, see Dickinson McGaw and George Watson, *Political and Social Inquiry* (New York: John Wiley & Sons, Inc., 1976), pp. 70–78; Arthur L. Stinchcombe, *Constructing Social Theories* (New York: Harcourt, Brace and World, Inc., 1968), especially Chapter Three; and David C. Leege and Wayne L. Francis, *Political Research: Design, Measurement and Analysis* (New York: Basic Books, Inc., 1974), especially Chapter 2.
3. Sar A. Leviatan, *The Great Society's Poor Law* (Baltimore: Johns Hopkins Press, 1969); and Lawrence M. Friedman, "The Social and Political Context of the War on Poverty: An Overview," in Robert Haveman, editor, *A Decade of Federal Antipoverty Programs* (New York: Academic Press, 1977).
4. See Stinchombe, pp. 60–79.
5. See McGaw and Watson, pp. 74–75.
6. Among other attempts to redraw the political system model for the analysis of public policy, see Ira Sharkansky and Donald Van Meter, *Policy and Politics in American Governments* (New York: McGraw-Hill Book Co., 1975), p. 8.
7. For a brief discussion of the problems of defining power and related terms, see Robert A. Dahl, *Modern Political Analysis,* 3rd edition (Englewood Cliffs, NJ: Prentice-Hall, Inc., 1976), especially Chapter Three; also David V.J. Bell, *Power, Influence, and Authority: An Essay in Political Linguistics* (New York: Oxford University Press, 1975).
8. Much of this is adapted from the approach taken by Dahl, Chapters Three and Four.
9. Richard E. Neustadt, *Presidential Power: The Politics of Leadership.* rev. ed. (New York: John Wiley & Sons, 1976).
10. C. Wright Mills, *The Power Elite* (New York: Oxford University Press, 1959).

11. The classic exposition of Dahl's view is found in his study of New Haven: *Who Governs? Democracy and Power in an American City* (New Haven, CT: Yale University Press, 1961).
12. For a historical summary and critique of group theories, see G. David Garson, *Group Theories of Politics* (Beverly Hills, CA: Sage Publications, 1978).
13. For example, evidence has been gathered which indicates that among party activists there is a more substantial ideological perspective than among party identifiers in general. See Herbert McClosky, Paul J. Hoffman, and Rosemary O'Hara, "Issue Conflict and Consensus Among Party Leaders and Followers," *American Political Science Review* 54 (June, 1960), pp. 406-427.
14. Peter Woll, *Public Policy* (Cambridge, MA: Winthrop Publishers, Inc., 1974), p. 89.
15. See Everett Carll Ladd, Jr. with Charles D. Hadley, *Transformations of the American Party System*, 2nd edition (New York: W. W. Norton and Co., Inc., 1978).
16. See Anthony Downs, *An Economic Theory of Democracy* (New York: Harper and Row, Publishers, 1957); also William H. Riker, *The Theory of Political Coalitions* (New Haven, CT: Yale University Press, 1962).
17. Gerald Pomper, *Elections in America* (New York: Dodd, Mead, 1970). See especially Chapters 7 and 8.
18. Gerald Pomper and Associates, *The Election of 1976* (New York: David McKay, 1977).
19. Austin Ranney, " 'The Divine Science': Political Engineering in American Culture," *American Political Science Review*, LXX (March, 1976), pp. 140-148.
20. Woll, p. 32.
21. The fragmentation of America's governing institutions is central to many critiques of our government. For example, see Harold Seidman, *Politics, Position, and Power: The Dynamics of Federal Organizations*, 3rd edition (New York: Oxford University Press, 1980). On federalism and intergovernmental relations, see Parris N. Glendening and Mavis Mann Reeves, *Pragmatic Federalism: An Intergovernmental View of American Government* (Pacific Palisades, CA: Palisades Publishers, 1977).
22. Morris P. Fiorina, *Congress: Keystone of the Washington Establishment* (New Haven, CT: Yale University Press, 1977), especially pp. 2-3 and Chapter 5.
23. Richard Snyder, H. W. Bruck, and Burton Sapin, "The Decision-Making Approach to the Study of International Politics," in James Rosenau (ed.), *International Politics and Foreign Policy*, revised edition (New York: The Free Press, 1969), pp. 199-206.
24. Synder, Bruck and Sapin, p. 203.
25. Graham T. Allison, *Essence of Decision: Explaining the Cuban Missile Crisis* (Boston: Little, Brown and Co., 1971), pp. 32-33.
26. Morton H. Halperin, *Bureaucratic Politics and Foreign Policy* (Washington, D.C.: The Brookings Institution, 1974), especially Chapter Five.
27. See, for example, Allison's use of what he terms the "bureaucratic politics" model, in Allison, Chapter 5.
28. Jeffrey L. Pressman and Aaron Wildavsky, *Implementation*, 2nd ed. (Berkeley, CA: University of California Press, 1979), p. 44.

29. Yehezkel Dror, *Public Policymaking Reexamined* (Scranton, PA.: Chandler Publishing Co., 1968), pp. 132–141.
30. David Braybrooke and Charles E. Lindblom, *A Strategy of Decision: Policy Evaluation as a Social Process* (New York: The Free Press, 1970), especially Chapter 3.
31. See John D. Steinbruner, *The Cybernetic Theory of Decision: New Dimensions of Political Analysis* (Princeton, NJ: Princeton University Press, 1974), Chapter 2.
32. See the classification developed by James D. Thompson in his classic, *Organizations in Action: Social Science Bases of Administrative Theory* (New York: McGraw-Hill Book Co., 1967), p. 134.
33. A classic examination of incrementalism at work is found in Aaron Wildavsky, *The Politics of the Budgetary Process*, 2nd edition (Boston: Little, Brown and Co., 1974). A more theoretical introduction to the incremental decision process is offered in Braybrooke and Lindblom and in other works by Lindblom, e.g., *The Intelligence of Democracy: Decision Making Through Mutual Adjustment* (New York: The Free Press, 1965), and *The Policy-Making Process* (Englewood Cliffs, NJ: Prentice-Hall, Inc., 1968).
34. See Dror, pp. 145–146 for a summary and critique of incrementalism as a decision process.
35. For a discussion of the expansion of welfare programs, see Barry Friedman and Leonard Hausman, "Welfare in Retreat: A Dilemma for the Federal System," in *Public Policy*, 25 (Winter, 1977), pp. 27–47.
36. Herbert A. Simon, *Administrative Behavior: A Study of Decision-Making Processes in Administrative Organization*, 2nd edition (New York: The Free Press, 1957), p. 241.
37. See James G. March and Herbert A. Simon, *Organizations* (New York: John Wiley & Sons, Inc., 1958), pp. 140–141.
38. The focus on bargaining as a policy process was brought into analysis by Robert A. Dahl and Charles E. Lindblom in their *Politics, Economics, and Welfare: Planning and Politico-Economic Systems Resolved into Basic Social Processes* (New York: Harper Torchbooks, 1953), especially Chapter 17. As a more formalized model it has taken the form of exchange theories; for an introduction to these, see Thomas A. Reilly and Michael W. Sigall, *Political Bargaining: An Introduction to Modern Politics* (San Francisco: W. H. Freeman and Co., 1976).
39. For a classic study exemplifying bargaining as a policymaking process, see Eric Redman, *The Dance of Legislation* (New York: Simon and Schuster, 1973).
40. For an introduction to game theory, see Morton D. Davis, *Game Theory: A Nontechnical Introduction* (New York: Basic Books, Inc., 1973). For its relevance to political analysis see T. C. Schelling, "What Is Game Theory?" and Martin Shubik, "The Uses of Game Theory," in James C. Charlesworth (ed.), *Contemporary Political Analysis* (New York: The Free Press, 1967).
41. For an interesting recent application of game theory to policy analysis, see Arun Bose, *Political Paradoxes and Puzzles* (Oxford/Clarendon Press, 1977).

KEY TERMS

Associational Explanations
Bargaining Models
Bounded Rationality
Clearance
Correlations (positive and negative)
Covering Law Explanation
Decision Points
Demographic Explanations
Dispositional Explanations
Explanan-Explanandum
Functional Explanations
Game Theory Models
Genetic or Historicist Explanations
Group Model
Incremental Process Model
Individual Decision-maker Models
Institutional/Constitutional Models
Party/Electoral Organization Models
Plural Elite Model
Policy Explanation
Policy Implementation
Policymaking Arena
Policy Process/Dynamics Models
Policy Source Models
Policy System Models
Power Structure Models
Rational Decision Process Model
Rational Explanation
Satisficing Model
Single Elite Model
Statistical Generalizations
Universal Generalizations

CHAPTER 7
Explaining Foreign Policy

FOREIGN POLICY AS PUBLIC POLICY

All national governments create policies and institute actions directed primarily outside of their own societies. These public actions are foreign policies. The Iranian hostage agreements, the Panama Canal Treaties, the Camp David accords, and the Strategic Arms Limitation Treaties (SALT I and SALT II) negotiated with the Soviet Union are all examples of policy actions. Problems with foreign policy issues are rooted, in part, in their dual nature. Because such policies are directed toward other nations, they seem intrinsically "foreign" and perhaps even "mystical." Understanding these policies requires a great deal of information, some of which may even be secret; an understanding of foreign languages and customs; and often a special expertise only a few specialists might possess. However, these foreign policy actions and many others may directly impinge on the lives of American citizens by affecting the price of gasoline at the pump, the ability to travel abroad, the economic state of the nation, the number of jobs in American communities, or, in the ultimate case, by engaging the country in war.

The question facing the policy thinker is whether foreign policy is so different from the domestic activities of the government that the tools and models which can be applied to domestic policies are not applicable to foreign policy studies. Most analyses of foreign policy are written by specialists in diplomatic history or international relations who rarely relate foreign policy actions to domestic issues. Among the exceptions to this pattern are the few studies that examine the linkages between foreign policy and the attitudes of the American people[1] and the eternal debate over whether Congress influences the foreign policy prerogatives of the American President.[2]

By our definition of public policy, however, foreign policy is not a different species from domestic policy. We can examine the form and goals of these policies, the sources from which they spring, and the outcomes of foreign policy actions. The purpose of this chapter is, in fact, to demonstrate how the analytic techniques for explanation described in this book can be applied to this class of activities so that we can understand foreign policies as well as we can understand other types of policies. Specifically we will use a number of the explanatory models discussed in Chapter 6 to show why certain foreign policies are adopted. Before beginning our exploration of these policies, it will be useful to review those characteristics of foreign policymaking that cause some analysts to set it apart and that do influence the context in which foreign policy decisions are made and implemented.

Foreign policy differs from other policies in terms of its domestic political ramifications. Unlike housing or income tax policies, most foreign policy questions do not usually involve the extended interplay of major interest groups in American society. Because foreign policy issues rarely involve the redistribution of wealth or benefits from one class to another or the regulation of individual or group behavior, most foreign policy decisions do not arouse significant political conflict in Congress or the public media. In fact, some analysts attribute the strength of the presidency in the foreign policy arena to the relative lack of claims by special economic or social interests in most foreign policy questions. Aaron Wildavsky, for example, has suggested that there are really two presidencies—one for domestic affairs in which the president is severely limited by the power of domestic interests, and one for foreign affairs in which the president is able to exercise decisive leadership because of the absence of domestic political problems.[3] Without doubt, certain foreign policy questions do agitate specific domestic political forces, but the claims of these groups are usually for protection of their special trade interests or respective homelands rather than for benefits to larger segments of American society. The classic example of this type of pressure is the lobbying by pro-Israeli segments of the American Jewish community which is joined frequently by leading fundamentalist Christian churches in support of the special relationship between the United States and the State of Israel. The power of pro-Israeli Jewish interests in the United States is expressed through political pressure on congresspersons with large numbers of pro-Israel constituents as well as through campaign support and votes for presidential candidates. However, even this vocal lobby for a certain foreign policy stance does not claim any special status or privileges within the U.S. government itself.

The view of the President as more powerful in foreign affairs is also related to the Constitutional balance of power in this domain. With the Constitution's designation of the President as the negotiator of treaties and leader in foreign affairs, and with the concurrence of the Supreme Court in numerous cases, the Chief Executive has the preeminent position in foreign policy decision making. Unlike domestic issues, where Congress has every right to initiate new policies to deal with maternal health or the regulation of airfares, the negotiation of agreements with foreign nations or the opening of diplomatic relations with China are within the prerogatives of the President. Through the use of funding legislation, hearings, and amendments the Congress may have some influence over actual foreign policy implementation, but the position is clearly one of reacting to presidential initiatives.[4]

Not only is the president acting on a strong Constitutional foundation in the foreign affairs arena, but the institutions of government that carry out these policies are under his close direction and reflect the specialization of these issues. The President is normally advised by a National Security Advisor who is supported by the staff of the National Security Council (NSC) in fact-finding and making recommendations. The State Department is structured to carry out the policies of the United States in its foreign missions. Having almost no domestic clientele, the State Department is free to serve the President with little pressure from economic or social organizations at home. All of these institutional features are conducive to expert, efficient, and secretive policymaking by the executive branch. The burden of developing domestic opposition to foreign policy initiatives (such as opposition to the U.S. military presence in Vietnam during the 1960s and El Salvador in the 1980s) falls heavily on individual members of Congress and political leaders who do not have the same sources of information and media access as the President. Given the American citizenry's general lack of interest in other nations and their low level of information, it is very difficult to rouse public opinion against presidential actions in foreign policy. Even after extended Congressional debate and media attention in late 1980 and early 1981 over the degree of U.S. involvement in El Salvador, only a tiny percentage of Americans knew where the country was located, let alone what the U.S. role was in that Central American state.

There is also a substantive difference between foreign policy actions and those aimed at domestic problems. The difference, however, is not as clearcut as it might first appear. Much of foreign policy is directed at other nations rather than domestic target populations or economic sectors. In some ways, foreign policy is similar to federal government policies directed at influencing the behavior of individual states by convincing them to adopt certain policies or join certain federal cooperative programs. However, other nations, no matter how small, must be treated in principle as peers of the United States, while domestically the states can be cajoled through financial incentives or effectively sued in federal courts. No matter how new or tiny a nation is, its Chief of State is greeted by the President on his or her state visit to Washington and no outward attempt to influence that nation's domestic affairs can be admitted. Other foreign policies are aimed at even more amorphous entities—international organizations—which rarely possess much power. The United States Ambassador to the United Nations plays an important symbolic role in world politics since he or she must often deal directly with Communist countries, the third world and its leaders, neutral nations and even such entities as the Palestine Liberation Organization, which the U.S. may not recognize officially. It is clear that the U.N., for example, cannot stop the Soviet Union from invading Afghanistan or the United States from flying spy planes over Mainland China; but the participation of the United States in the international organization has enormous symbolic importance.

Although some of the objects of foreign policy are quite different from those of domestic action, other goals are closely related to life at home. Many of the relationships among nations are attempts to implement domestic policies with the assistance of other nations. In other words, the goals of many foreign policies are domestic in nature, but must be achieved through actions in the international sphere. Few governmental officials, either in Congress or the executive branch, would argue that our sale of military equipment such as the sophisticated AWACS planes to Saudi Arabia in 1981 was intended to keep Saudi military infuence paramount among Arab countries of the Middle East. The Saudi regime has helped to keep U.S. gasoline prices down through maintaining high levels of oil supplies on the world market, by supporting peace efforts in that region of the world, and by acting as a moderate force within the Organization of Petroleum Exporting Countries (OPEC). Although the pro-Israeli American Jewish community supported Israel's objections to that sale, the domestic benefits of Saudi friendship seemed clear. Many other relationships which are developed in the context of foreign policy are also aimed at providing real benefits to American citizens; a few would include Japanese agreements on steel exporting practices, sales of grain to Soviet Union, or trade agreements with the Chinese.

PERSPECTIVES ON FOREIGN POLICY

For most policy thinkers, the principal actors in foreign relations are nations rather than politicians, groups, or domestic institutions. This assumption encourages us to view our own country and others in holistic terms; we tend to anthropomorphize nations (e.g., the American eagle and the Russian bear), and we often analyze their actions as if the nation has motivations apart from its citizens. Many of the models analysts use to describe, explain, and assess foreign policies directly reflect this emphasis on the sovereign state. Starting from this view of a world of separate entities practicing individual foreign policies in the same planet, we can classify most analytic models into three types: internal, external, or scientific.[5]

Internal Perspectives

Many analysts examine foreign policies from the view of factors internal to each nation-state. These factors range from the concrete and quantifiable such as the nation's GNP and size of population to such intangible qualities as national character and moral purpose. *Internal* views stress the importance of particular governmental institutions like the State Department as well as the belief systems and political culture of the citizenry. For example, taking such an internal perspective many scholars have suggested that Americans alternate between support for isolationism and a missionary zeal for spreading democratic forms of government.[6] This ambivalence toward other nations results in a great deal of inconsistency in American policies. According to some analysts, this "moodiness" is part of our national character and is due to our self image as a unique and special political system. This ethnocentric image emerged from a history of isolation and an abundance of domestic resources. Seeing U.S. foreign policy from this vantage will obviously have implications for how one describes, explains, and evaluates those government actions and statements being analyzed.

External Perspectives

Another class of models views the United States as one state within a world community. Most of the foreign policy actions of any state are seen within the context of the world situation. These analytic frameworks focus on such factors as the degree of stability in international relationships, the geographic location of nations, and the nation's need for resources, such as oil. The old phrase, "he who controls the heartland [of Central Europe] controls the world," typifies the external viewpoint. Contemporary analysts of the power and influence of multinational corporations also represent this perspective. For example, such studies describe the oil crisis of the 1970s to which the United States and other oil-dependent states reacted, as caused by OPEC's oil cartel in concert with the major multinational petroleum companies.

Scientific Perspectives

The scientific view of foreign policy does not assume either an external or internal position. Proponents of this approach see foreign policy as patterns of action that can be compared and contrasted cross-nationally and historically. Scientific studies are likely to consider the economic trade patterns of many nations simultaneously, or the escalation of threats exchanged between nations prior to the outbreak of war. It is hoped that these studies will eventually lead to the development of theories of international relations.

Since World War II the relationships between the rich and the poor nations have been studied a great deal. We can easily find examples of internal, external, and scientific analyses of the policies of the United States toward poor nations. During the 1960s the United States initiated a number of policies, such as the Alliance for Progress, that used aid to underdeveloped nations as a technique to encourage growth of democratic and capitalistic systems. Some analysts holding an internal viewpoint saw these policies as reflections of the ideological biases of American policymakers while others perceived it as helping our domestic economy in the long run. An external analysis would point to the instability of these developing nations and their candidacy for takeover by Soviet-backed governments as a real cause for alarm. U.S. economic assistance policies can then be described and motivated by strategic concerns. Instead of positing cultural-ideological or strategic purposes, the scientific approach would focus on associational factors such as the policy preferences of United States and third world elites, economic tradeflows between nations, or the internal political conditions within developing societies that might lead to instability.

Scientific analysts may focus on internal or external factors but they do not presume one to be prior. Internal or externally oriented models may use empirical or quantitative methods to support their respective positions. Although we will look only at explanatory models, the three perspectives on foreign policy provide very different orientations for describing or assessing the consequences of those government actions and statements (see Table 7.1 on page 186). Their relative differences, however, are most evident when one is attempting to explain foreign policies.

BOX 7.1

A number of ideological-historical perspectives for analyzing U.S. foreign policies deserve note. The three best-known perspectives—realist, nationalist, and radical—not only focus on certain factors in foreign policy but act as perceptual screens for the analyst in describing, explaining, or evaluating foreign policy actions.

The *realist* school of thought describes the history of American foreign policy as greatly influenced by the international situation. The United States was able to remain aloof from foreign entanglements and to concentrate on its own political integration because the nation was isolated geographically. While the European countries engaged in "balance of power" politics through the nineteenth and early twentieth century to maintain peace and protect their overseas empires, the United States adopted an isolationist position except for its immediate neighbors. Realist analysts such as E.H. Carr and Hans J. Morgenthau see the United States' foreign policy as dictated by the actual situation in the world. Although they disagree as to whether the United States was simply "lucky" during its growth years by being isolated or whether the leaders of the nation intentionally used the European system for protection, they all agree that American policy underwent great change after World War II. At that time, the foreign policy of the United States had to be restructured to fill the vacuum in the balance of power system left by the defeat and collapse of most of the European countries. Most historians of this persuasion approve of U.S. policy since the World War II and support military strength, alliance building, and occasional involvement as necessary strategies to protect the U.S. position as well as aiding stability in the world system. To summarize the realist perspective, foreign policy is described primarily as a pragmatic national response to international conditions which is intended to preserve the nation itself and a certain order among nations; the key variables are external to the nation.

In contrast to the realists, the *nationalist* perspective focuses on the unique characteristics of the United States as important determinants of foreign policy. Where the realists are more concerned with historical conditions between the nations of the world, nationalists such as Dexter Perkins describe U.S. foreign policy in terms of its linkages to the domestic political system. The scholars who follow the nationalist tradition discuss the influence of public opinion on foreign policy, the tendency of the United States to spread democratic regimes to other nations, and the impact of American beliefs in equality and liberty on foreign policy decisions. Since American concern for these political values has been a long tradition, this school of thought sees the post-World War II period, which saw the Marshall Plan, the Berlin airlift, and the Korean War, as the natural expression of a mature and powerful America. As you might expect, this emphasis on the traditions and political values of democracy leads these scholars to describe the history of American foreign policy very positively; the United States is seen as a force for good in the world.

Both nationalist and realist analysts tend to have favorable views of American policies and strategies, although some members of each group began to revise their interpretations of history in recent years. Out of these revisionist efforts and the involvement in Vietnam has come the *radical* approach to American diplomatic history. Where the realists and nationalists describe foreign policy in a good light, radicals such as William Appleman Williams emphasize the negative aspects of U.S. policies. The radical perspective places a heavy emphasis on economic factors in describing both domestic and foreign policies throughout U.S. history. The exploitation of American Indians and the inability to end slavery both are related by radicals to the need for economic growth. All of the foreign policies adopted by the United States over the years are described as strategies to support the capitalist economic system through the exploitation of other peoples and societies. The radical scholars are akin to the nationalists in seeing foreign policies as linked intrinsically to domestic factors, although the two schools hold diametrically opposed views on the consequences and goals of American policies. For radicals, the period since World War II has seen a continuity in American foreign policy, although the increased economic and military power of the United States has made it possible for the nation to make even larger mistakes in policy. The Marshall Plan in Europe is described by the radicals as an attempt to reinstate capitalism and fight off attempts to revolutionize Europe; the Cold War of the 1950s and 1960s and the Vietnam War are described as creatures born of the military-industrial complex in the United States, and even foreign aid efforts with the most honorable of (announced) intentions (e.g., the Alliance for Progress) are described as further tools of capitalist imperialism. For radical interpreters of U.S. foreign policy the only real solution is a revolution to overturn the capitalist system in te United States itself.

See Edward Hallett Carr, *The Twenty Years Crisis, 1919–1939* (New York: St. Martin's, 1939); Hans J. Morgenthau, *Politics Among Nations* (New York: Knopf, 1948); Dexter Perkins, *The American Approach to Foreign Policy* (Cambridge, MA: Harvard University Press, 1962); William Appleman Williams, *The Tragedy of American Foreign Policy* (New York: World Publishing, 1959).

MODELS EXPLAINING FOREIGN POLICY

Policy analysts who concentrate on foreign policy often pay a great deal of attention to describing relevant actions and statements, but far more effort

Table 7.1 Perspectives on Foreign Policy

Perspective	Policy Reflects	Important Variables
Internal	National needs, national character, institutions, political processes	Power resources, goals, institutions, leaders, elites, culture/beliefs
External	International conditions, conditions between nations, other nations	Balance of power, crises, international alliances, other nations' goals
Scientific	Either internal or external or combination	Patterns of relations, behavior of leaders, acts of violence, communications, trading patterns, transfers of capital or weapons

has been made to "explain" foreign policies. The stakes in this area are so high—war and peace, victory or defeat, the survival of a government—that it seems imperative to find models that satisfactorily explain why nations behave as they do. Those who analyze U.S. foreign policy are concerned with explaining the intentions and actions of other nations, both friendly and hostile, as well as understanding the policy choices of their own leaders. Many of these explanations belong to one of the two major classes of models discussed in Chapter 6: source models and process models. The first group, source models, includes theories and frameworks that suggest that the behavior of nations can be explained by a particular quality, institution, or set of circumstances. Process models, however, are not as concerned with identifiable sources of foreign policy decisions as with the ramifications of the process used to make such decisions. These models state that particular kinds of political processes, decision-making processes or international actions cause particular foreign policy outputs.

Source Models

The common expectation of source models is that some person, institution, situation, or characteristic can be found to explain foreign policy actions and intentions. However, not all source models find their respective explanations in the same place. We can divide the source models usefully into external and internal classifications, reflecting two major perspectives discussed above. The external theories posit the cause of the foreign policies as outside of the national system, while the internal models look to institutions or characteristics within the nation for the causal factors. We note that "scientific" analyses also can use these factors as variables associated with specific policy actions.

External Models. The external model with the longest and most distinguished history is the *balance of power* model or, in more modern terms, the international system model.[7] This viewpoint sees national foreign policies, actions, and plans as responses to the configuration of power between all the nations of the world. According to this model, the world community is composed of weak nations and strong nations, each intent on its own survival. In this sense, it is related as well to the realist viewpoint. The strong nations attempt to balance their own military might and positions against each other so that neither will attempt to conquer the other. The late nineteenth and early twentieth century saw the balance of power concept elevated to the most preferred foreign policy strategy and many nations scrambled to make alliances so that forces would reach a balance. Each nation would assess the current alliances and relative strengths of the other nations and then plan a foreign policy to improve its own position, probably by choosing to join an alliance.

The concept of balance between major nations continues to play an important part in explaining the behavior and outlook of nations. Since World War II many analysts have described the world situation as bipolar, meaning that there are two main poles of power, the United States and the Soviet Union. Both powers act to protect the balance between them, and acts that upset the balance (e.g., the Russians placing missiles in Cuba) are regarded as cause for alarm. Others suggest that the balance of power is becoming three-way or tripolar, with the development of China as significant industrial and military power. Still another, more complicated perspective suggests that we live in a bipolycentric world.[8] The United States and the Soviet Union are still the two dominant forces for war or peace but other, smaller centers of power are developing and may influence relations between the two superpowers. For example, the OPEC nations form one center of power, and the Western European allies act as a group to influence both superpowers. These analyses of the world situation make intuitive sense to the citizens and are often used by leaders to explain foreign policy actions.

BOX 7.2

The traditional balance of power model of international relationships has made an interesting transition into a scientific model of the behavior of nations through the device of systems analysis. Many of the

> fundamental characteristics of systems models have easy analogies in the international political system: equilibrium translates into the balance of power between nations; the system is naturally cybernetic because it is self-correcting; and feedback is provided to all components through their own information-gathering institutions.
>
> The most complete adaptation of the system model to international politics was proposed by Morton Kaplan who offers six different systems that could occur in world politics: balance of power, the loose bipolar system, tight bipolar system, the universal system, the hierarchical system, and the unit veto system. Only the first two of these models have actual historical examples, but Kaplan feels that theoretically the others could occur. The purpose for developing these hypothetical models is to be able to predict conditions of stability or change within the world system.
>
> See: Morton Kaplan, *System and Process In International Politics* (New York: John Wiley & Sons, 1957).

The *political economy* of the world is also considered an external source for explaining foreign policy. Although this model is not as often used as the balance of power explanation, it is a powerful explanation for national actions.[9] Political economy models emphasize one or all of many global economic conditions as predominant. For example, many of the foreign policy actions of industrialized nations are seen as caused by the international monetary situation. While the United States managed the world economy for two decades after World War II, the strength of German, Japanese, and other European currencies in recent years has made the monetary situation much more fluid. U.S. actions to discourage imports of cars, steel, or electronic goods from other nations are perceived as attempts to improve the balance-of-payments situation of the United States. Other nations have acted similarly, curbing imports of American goods or placing heavy taxes on their import to strengthen their individual economic situations.

Another focus of the political economy approach is on the exchange of raw materials and finished goods. The United States and Western Europe as well as Japan are heavily dependent on lesser-developed countries for imports of petroleum for fuel and raw materials for manufacturing. This dependency has resulted in soaring energy costs for all of the industrialized nations causing an inflationary spiral. The oil cartel states, mostly Middle Eastern, have raised the price of petroleum in part to discourage the use of the resource as well as to raise their own incomes. The United States is not only dependent on foreign suppliers for oil; many other minerals must be imported to meet our manufacturing and security needs. Figure 7.1 shows

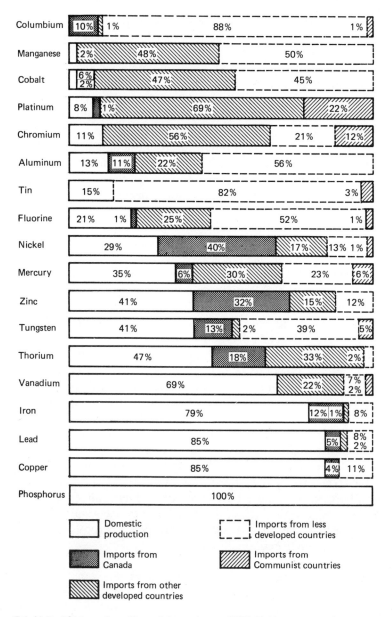

Figure 7.1. United States mineral import dependence, 1976. Net imports are shown as a percent of consumption. Figures are based on metal and metal content of ores and scrap. (Source: *International Economic Report of the President,* 1977, p. 12.)

graphically the proportions of minerals we produce domestically as compared to the amount imported. This raw material dependence has had an important effect on U.S. foreign policy; suppliers of these materials can bargain for weapons (Saudi Arabia), for economic assistance (Venezuela), or for diplomatic recognition (South Africa).

The United States is also the major trading partner for many of the world's lesser-developed nations. The economy of this country so dwarfs the economies of many of our trading partners that U.S. policies in international trade are of utmost important to these nations. For this reason many of our trading partners have full-time lobbyists for economic matters stationed in Washington, D.C., in addition to their normal diplomatic representation. The lesser developed nations, particularly those dependent on sales of a single crop, such as coffee, tea, bananas, and sugar, constantly lobby the United States for treaties that guarantee price stability or for increasing their share of U.S. imports. The major weapon the U.S. used against the Cuban regime of Fidel Castro was outlawing any sugar imports from that country. Since the production of sugar is Cuba's main industry, this action has forced the Soviets and Eastern European bloc to absorb Cuba's production of sugar at a higher economic cost. In other cases, the United States has capitalized on its dominant position in trading and as supplier of industrial goods by demanding, for example, that economic assistance funds given to some nations be spent only in the United States and that the purchased goods be shipped in U.S.-owned freighters. Finally, we note that one of the long-range problems of the global political economy is the production of enough food to support the world population. Here the United States has a great advantage with its highly productive land and advanced farming techniques; American farmers always produce more crops than the domestic population needs. Crop failures in the Soviet Union and China have allowed the United States to use wheat sales as a diplomatic tool to gain other concessions from these major powers.[10] Poor natons who have nothing to bargain with must borrow funds to buy grain from the United States and Canada. In the future, the possibility of mass starvation in many nations will make the food resources of the superpowers even more important in planning foreign policy actions.

Internal Models. The largest class of explanatory models is that which focuses on institutions or characteristics unique to a specific nation. Sometimes these are "great persons" who come to dominate a nation's foreign policy. For instance, many analysts credit Henry Kissinger with the development and implementation of U.S. foreign policy during the Nixon and Ford Administrations. There are other factors as well. The British are often characterized as being tenacious and brave. In exploring international relations this "national personality" is an internal explanation. Although we cannot discuss all the varieties of internal explanatory models, we will look at three major examples: national capabilities, national beliefs, and the executive branch.

The *national capabilities* model considers each nation's natural resources, geographic location and terrain, military capacities, and economic strength as sources of foreign policy.[11] Analysis of a nation's geopolitical situation has a long tradition. Geographically isolated countries, such as island nations like Britain and Japan, are expected to develop naval power and trading relationships rather than concentrate on land-oriented foreign policies. Countries that have extensive and complicated borders are subject to frequent international problems and must spend a great deal of effort developing a foreign policy that makes border protection possible. As an example of the influence of boundaries, we can compare the 5000 mile unarmed border between the United States and Canada with China's millenial concern with its frontier, symbolized in The Great Wall.

National capabilities analyses also can consider economic strengths as a source for national behavior. Powerful nations can demand certain concessions from other states because of their economic position. As noted above, the United States was able to control the world economy after World War II because the dollar was the strongest currency. The United States has also used its economic trading position to try to influence other nations behavior as in the Carter Administration's use of economic sanctions against the Soviet Union after the invasion of Afghanistan and Mr. Reagan's sanctions against Poland in 1981 after martial law was declared. It is likely that the United States cannot really injure the Soviet Union and its allies with such sanctions, but such punishments maybe more effective in smaller or more dependent nations.

Military power is also a source for foreign policy decisions. It appears that the great majority of nations accept the axiom, "if you want to have peace, you must prepare for war." Military preparedness is a high priority even in states where there is little economic base, a situation which allows the United States, France, and the Soviets to compete as arms sellers. The results of scientific studies of the relationship between military power and the likelihood of going to war have been mixed. Some studies show that possessing military might makes war more likely; others show that most wars are begun by less-powerful nations. Military might does not seem to guarantee victory, nor to alter the long-term balance of power.[12]

Today military power has the greatest potential for influencing foreign policy decisions when that power includes the use of nuclear weapons, particularly among the smaller nations. Although Israel does not advertise its own capacity for nuclear power, the attempt by the Iraqi government to complete a nuclear power plant that might have produced fuel for weapons was ended by a surprise Israeli attack in 1981. Other nations that have the capacity to develop nuclear weapons are watched carefully by their neighbors for signs that their military capacity has changed. Among the superpowers who possess this capacity in unimaginable amounts, the very threat of nuclear war is supposed to act as a deterrent to rash actions. The delicacy of U.S.–U.S.S.R. relationships was symbolized by the installation of a hotline between the White House and the Kremlin in 1963, so that both sides would know whether nuclear explosions are deliberate or accidental.

It is easy to assume that certain foreign policy actions are simply congruous with a particular national character: the United States' generosity to its enemies after World War II; the harshness of Soviet repression in Hungary and Czechoslovakia during uprisings of the 1950s and 1960s; the perennial industriousness and competitiveness of the Germans and Japanese. However, we must treat explanations based on estimates of *national character and beliefs* with great caution since we are dealing with a nation composed of individual citizens, not an organic entity. Historically, the concept of national character has been used to account for long-term foreign policy tendencies of nations. America and Great Britain have been characterized as antimilitaristic, opposed to standing armies, and antidraft; Russians have been seen as tough and domineering; and India as deeply pacifistic. It is, of course, impossible for a nation to be any of those things; nations are only aggregates of the people within them, and possess no character traits apart from their people.

We can, however, investigate two sources within the population that might account for such generalizations about ourselves, our allies and our enemies. First, some scientific studies have attributed national tendencies which occur widely within a society to common personality traits. These traits are, in turn, due to practices in child-rearing, peer relationships, and attitudes toward authority inculcated in the citizens.[13] Psychologists have suggested that authoritarian family practices have produced the aggressive German citizen, equalitarian family values are passed on to American children, and that the Japanese emphasis on duty to the family or peer group produces conformity and loyalty. Other studies have examined how different societies regard conflict and compromise to settle differences: Greeks tend to view compromise as defeat, as do Arabs; Africans are more at ease with conflict because it leads to settlement of differences; and many cultures, unlike the American and English, prefer bargaining or conversation.

It is very difficult to differentiate between personality traits caused by child-rearing practices and the attitudes and beliefs that may be transmitted as part of the political culture. The concept of political culture may be defined as the set of beliefs and values with regard to the political system that are taught to all members of a society.[14] The political culture provides support for the system and teaches each citizen what general role to play in the system. If the political culture includes a set of tightly organized beliefs about the world, the nature of humanity, or the direction of history, it may even be termed an explicit ideology. The United States, with its pluralistic culture and emphasis on individualistic goals, may be considered an example of a nation with cultural beliefs but not with an ideology. Conversely, the Russian system officially supports an ideological view of both domestic and international affairs although we do not know to what extent the citizens have internalized the Marxist viewpoint.

The national character traits and culture of a specific country probably have little or no effect on specific foreign policy outputs, but public opinion may have a direct influence on policy decisions. Citizens may share some generalized beliefs with regard to the historic role of the nation in world affairs, such as the American preference for avoiding entanglements overseas or our generally warm feelings toward England and other "mother" countries of the population. Studies also show that Americans generally believe that democracy and free enterprise are the best systems and that we should promote these concepts in other nations. In general, Americans can be described as fairly nationalistic and proud of their own system but permissive toward their leadership. Since most American citizens do not really have much information about international relations or feel it necessary to be concerned about these things, they are willing to follow the President and other national leaders and support their decisions.

Public opinion about specific issues and events can also act as a limiting factor on policymaking. Although Americans generally support the President, memories of the Vietnam experience have left a reservoir of suspicion toward the use of troops overseas. Many Americans felt so strongly about the proposed Panama Canal Treaties that they voted against Representatives and Senators who approved the documents or implementating legislation. Finally, we might note how the failure of President Carter to maintain an image of a strong America in the face of the Iranian situation and the Soviet moves in Afghanistan played an important part in his defeat in 1980.

National belief models include a number of different classes of explanation. Foreign policy actions over the long term may be explained either by reference to commonly held personality traits in a nation or to the overall political culture that supports the governmental system. We may also be able to trace specific policy choices in democratic states (e.g., the decision to intervene in a situation, or to join an alliance) to the expressed opinions of the citizens. Political leaders who must seek reelection keep a close watch on the public for signs that general permissiveness on foreign policy issues is changing to pronounced preferences for action.

> **BOX 7.3**
>
> Some of the most intriguing explanations of foreign policy are based on analyses of the psychological attributes of leaders. Although these factors are idiosyncratic to specific individuals who hold important positions, considerations of the psychological make-up of leaders have important implications for foreign policy analysis.
>
> Some of the factors considered include: the degree of interest leaders have for foreign policy; the amount of biological drive or aggression within individuals; the relationship between a leader's need for power and his or her psychological needs for affiliation and achievement; the degree of authoritarian predispositions or rigidity; high or low self-esteem; and the ability to fit new information into existing cognitive schemes. One study of 36 decision makers in American foreign policy suggests that those who scored higher on dominance in interpersonal relations were more likely to propose use of threats or military force. Those with low scores on interpersonal dominance were more conciliatory.
>
> For a review of this literature, see Lloyd Jensen, *Explaining Foreign Policy* (Englewood Cliffs, NJ: Prentice-Hall, 1981), pp. 13–42.

The third class of internal models focuses on the *executive branch* of government as the principal source of foreign policy goals and actions. In the American political system, a number of offices and institutions within the executive branch can be identified as important actors in foreign policy: the President; the National Security Council, Advisor, and Staff; the Department of State; the Department of Defense; the Joint Chiefs of Staff; and the Central Intelligence Agency and other intelligence bureaus. We can also consider the executive branch as a whole. Because foreign policy decisions often demand speed, secrecy, and considerable amounts of information, the executive branch in almost all states bears the authority for foreign policy decision making. The more urgent the situation, the more power that flows to the executive decision makers. Even though the U.S. President cannot declare war without the approval of Congress, modern weapons technology and the vast scope of U.S. military activities have made much of Congress' power superfluous in emergency situations. Some scholars criticize democratic systems for being too slow and inefficient in decision making because there is a need for national debate and the building of support for a decision.

These critics feel that the granting of authority to the executive branch, while it may not satisfy the requirements of popular consent, is a more effective way of safeguarding the interests of the whole nation. In recent years, examples of executive branch decision making in foreign policy abound: Mr. Reagan's announced sanctions against Poland (1982) and the shooting down of Libyan planes (1981); Mr. Carter's attempted Iranian hostage rescue mission (1980); the Ford-directed rescue of the Mayaguez (1976); and Mr. Nixon's opening of relations with Communist China (1972).

Foreign policies may also be traced to the President and his advisors, the Department of State, or the Department of Defense. The U. S. Constitution clearly designates the President as the chief diplomat of the political system, and it grants the President the power to negotiate agreements with foreign governments as well as the power to recognize governments and authorize official relations. As the President came to be the commander-in-chief of the world's most powerful military force and caretaker of our nuclear weapons, presidential power in foreign affairs continued to grow.[15] Obviously the official who could start a nuclear war needed to control the events that might trigger such a catastrophe. The need for secrecy and efficiency and their personal need to consider the political ramifications of foreign policy decisions led presidents to rely more on personal advisors and less on the official government agencies concerned with such policy, the State and Defense departments. Congress created the National Security Council (NSC) in 1947 to give the president specialized and coordinated advice on international affairs. Formally, the NSC is composed of the Secretaries of State and Defense and heads of other relevant agencies. By the early 1960s the NSC acquired a chief officer, the Advisor to the President for National Security Affairs. Since that time, the advisor, usually an individual of scholarly reputation and/or trusted by the president, has become the president's premier advisor and deputy in international affairs. The holders of the office have included McGeorge Bundy, W.W. Rostow, Henry Kissinger, and Zbigniew Brzezinski. With each increase in the size and prestige of the advisor's role has come an increase in the NSC advisor's staff and a down-grading of the Council itself. Crucial decisions tend to be made by the president together with the advisor and a few trusted aides. Public policy then becomes more idiosyncratic to the advisor currently in place. The best example of this explanation comes from the years of the Nixon presidency. Mr. Kissinger was able to chair the NSC in the president's absence, to negotiate secretly with the Chinese about a new relationship, and to make commitments to the Israelis for weapons and support without ever consulting with the State Department or the Congress. As we have noted, the foreign policy of the Nixon Administration can be considered the Kissinger policy in historical perspective, and the power of this man became a political issue in later presidential campaigns.

One of the reasons that presidents have turned to their NSC advisory staff for assistance is that the Department of State has not been responsive to presidential needs. State's responsibilities include far more than advising the president, and it has recruited and trained its officers with this in mind.[16] The State Department is the primary information gatherer on foreign affairs, an agency for protecting American citizens and businesses abroad, the processor of immigrants, the clerk for passports and other records, and formal representative of the U.S. government within other countries. The Department of State instituted the Foreign Service as a branch of government recruitment and service totally separate from other personnel agencies. Foreign Service officers are recruited from top colleges, examined rigorously before entry, trained in languages, diplomacy, and other skills, and then posted throughout the world. Although these officers are among the brightest college graduates when entering the service, they are trained to be loyal to its rules and, some suggest, to be inherently conservative in policymaking. In many ways, the Department of State can be regarded as a service agency for the President, providing advice, information, and diplomatic representation in every nation. However, the department's own self-study acknowledged that the bureaucratic mechanisms of the department tend "to stifle creativity, discourage risk-taking, and reward conformity."[17] We might expect, then, to find that the State Department is the cause of conservative foreign polices and the indirect cause of the assumption of power by the National Security Advisor.

One more branch of government must be briefly considered as providing input in the foreign policy area—the Defense Department. To a great extent, every function of the State Department is duplicated by the Defense Department, although this agency is far more aggressive in defending its program jurisdictions.[18] The branches of the military service compete with each other as well as with other agencies to increase their personnel and to acquire new techniques. Furthermore, the Defense Department has close alliances with the Congress; their bases and military contracts bring funds and jobs to many constituencies within the United States. Hence the Department of Defense is likely to counsel the adoption of foreign policies that enhance its own role rather than providing objective advice to the president. Although opposition to the President's decisions is rare, members of the Joint Chiefs have been known to voice personal disagreement with presidential decisions in Congressional hearings. For example, after President Reagan announced his 1981 decision to put MX missiles in existing missile silos, thus limiting the cost of the program and its strategic goal, members of the Joint Chiefs publicly expressed their reservations about the new plan.

The extensive documentation available for the 1962 Cuban missile crisis provides us with an example of the interplay of forces within the executive branch of government and how these institutional actors can help explain foreign policy. Because he had felt betrayed by the military and CIA in the 1961 Bay of Pigs affair, President Kennedy was determined to overcome the limitations of foreign policy machinery in this crisis situation. He used his personal advisors for considering the alternatives; he allowed both the State Department and representatives from the military services to contribute to the deliberations, and he even asked the opinions of Senator J. William Fulbright and U.N. Ambassador Adlai Stevenson as the options narrowed. In the end, Kennedy kept complete control of the policy machinery for himself, since he felt that the consequences would be his alone to bear. The direction and operations of the ships in the subsequent quarantine of Cuba were under his direct control and all messages sent to or received from Soviet Premier Nikita Khrushchev were expedited through the State Department to President Kennedy. In one sense, the Cuban Missile Crisis illustrated how well the system could work in concert; in another, it seemed regrettable that Kennedy could not depend on the system working without having to give personal attention to every detail.

Process Models

In contrast to the source models, *process models* find explanations for foreign policy choices in the dynamics of the processes at work. To recall the Cuban missile crisis situation, process models may help explain the policy outputs as the result of the decision-making procedures chosen by President Kennedy; his determination to hear all of the alternatives, to encourage advocacy of all solutions, and to broaden the process but keep it under control led to the correct choice of policy options. Source models look to the characteristics of the presidency and executive branch departments to explain the ultimate outcome in such a situation; process models look to the interrelationships of those institutional actors.

Decision-Making Models. Some of the most important types of process models focus on the actual process of decision making as the explanation for the choice of one policy over another. Decision theory became a more useful tool for policy analysts after the claims of rational decision making were set aside. As we noted in Chapter 6, a number of theorists have examined the premises of rational decision making and suggested that, in fact, most policymakers actually make decisions with far less information and in less time than would be required to make a truly rational decision. Once it became acceptable to consider policy decisions as other than perfectly rational, some analysts suggested that all decisions must be considered to be a function of the organizational constraints of the decision makers, of the information available, and of the motivations of those involved in the decision.[19]

Once we turn our attention to the context within which decisions are made, we can see how bureaucratic organizations and intragovernmental politics can affect policy outcomes. To reiterate the descriptions of the State Department already given, each agency concerned with foreign affairs tends to parochialism, to seeing itself as the one agency of the government with true expertise in the area. This parochialism coupled with the need to justify continued existence and funding leads to intense hidden competitiveness. Bureaucratic agencies tend to seek larger and larger tasks to insure their continued power so each branch of the military services has found it necessary to have their own intelligence capacity. In order to best protect its own position, agencies try to guard their information with great secrecy, thus making themselves indispensable to the President. The inculcation of these traits of loyalty to the department, of parochialism, and secrecy leads to the reward of conformity and a tendency to reaffirm the status quo. There are few incentives for creative thinking since new ideas or position may jeopordize their current status.

What are the policy consequences of these characteristics of bureaucratic decision making? Sometimes the departments and bureaus tend to inaction at best and insubordination at worst. As foreign policy crises arise such as the ascension to power of the Ayatollah Khomeini in Iran or the food shortages in Poland, commentators are heard to ask, "didn't anybody in government know this was happening?" With the size of the American defense and diplomatic establishment in Iran before the fall of the Shah, it is hard to believe that contingency plans for the change of government were never made. These seemingly inexplicable failures of policy planning may in fact be due to the reluctance of bureaucratic agencies to go out on a limb in predictions or planning. Another result of bureaucratic organization is compartmentalized decision making in which one agency is working at cross-purposes with another. In Laos during 1960, the State Department found itself aiding a different army from that supported by the CIA. Finally, to make peace between warring departments and to satisfy the representatives of competing interests, the President must suggest a compromise policy. This is characteristic of pluralistic decision making in the American system and often conducive to conflict resolution on the domestic side. In foreign policy matters such compromises between the wishes of various bureaucratic agencies may turn out to be a non-policy, and cast the President in a weak light.

Another type of decision-making theory looks at the psychology of small group dynamics.[20] A group must opt for one of a number of strategies when faced with a difficult decision. One technique is to decide to deal with today's problems today and to wait until later to deal with any larger policy. In foreign policy, this technique can work quite successfully in the short term, particularly since long-term strategies seem impossible to implement. Another technique is the non-decision or refusal to take any action to solve a particular problem. By refusing to act, the group or individual decision maker can shift the consequences of the situation onto fate, thus avoiding responsibility. Until the Carter Administration began the Camp David peace negotiations, American policy in the Middle East seemed to be a series of event-to-event decisions calculated to keep our oil supplies open but making no progress toward solving the long-term problem, the coexistence of Israel and the Arab states. The Israeli government seems to have made a similar non-decision with regard to the Palestinians who are spending their second generation in refugee camps.

One other phenomenon of group decision making should be mentioned within the class of process variables—the possibility of groupthink.[21] As documented in the 1961 Bay of Pigs case, government officials or presidential advisors working in small policymaking groups can come to share the same perceptions of the world and preference for policy options. Due to the influence of peer pressure and the individual's dislike for being the "outsider" in any group, individuals who feel uncomfortable with the direction a group is taking will hesitate to suggest any alternative. Reinforced by close contact and consensus on the issues, groups can even come to feel invincible and self-righteous about their chosen position.

Reviewing these varieties of decision-making theory, we can see that foreign policy goals and actions may be caused by any one of three kinds of decision-making processes. Some policy outcomes may be the result of the compartmentalized decision-making and conservative biases characteristic of most large bureaucratic organizations. Other decisions may be the direct product of bureaucratic politics in which one agency competes with another for attention, status in the White House, or for funding. Still other decisions are the result of intragroup pressures and reflect the psychological relationships of the participants.

International Process. Analysts of the scientific perspective have also expended considerable effort looking at the patterns of communications and events in the international system.[22] Regardless of the intentions of individual actors, some foreign policy choices seem to be inevitable or uncontrollable. By investigating large numbers of events or communications, scientific analysts hope to find out whether particular patterns lead to outbreaks of violence in the world system. Some analysts have concluded from these collections of data that most interactions between hostile nations can be classified as reciprocal behavior. If one side makes a hostile move, the other nation will reciprocate in similar fashion. For example, studies of the Cuban missile crisis found that for every hostile action of the United States, the Soviets responded in like manner. Studies that apply the same hypotheses to arms races have also shown that a build-up of armaments by one side triggers similar build-ups by enemy states, although one side may place more emphasis on qualitative or technological improvements rather than quantitative ones. There is conflicting evidence as to the likelihood of arms races leading to the outbreak of war, although several studies of great power arms races have found a high incidence of hostilities following the build-up. These models suggest that there are processes of negotiation, hostility, arms acquisition, and recovery which are so likely to occur that the processes themselves may be the explanatory factor rather than the policy choices of individual nation-states.

CONCLUSION

We conclude our review of explanatory models by noting that there are far more models, both of the source and process modes, than we have surveyed here. Explanatory models for foreign policy are readily available and often seem to be quite convincing. One reason why such models are so abundant is that foreign policy, more than decisions on such complicated issues as social welfare or control of the economy, seem to emanate from a single source (e.g., the President, Secretary of State) or from an identifiable group (e.g., the National Security Council). Thus, source models that identify the decision maker or agency correspond with our perception of efficient, rational policymaking. In reality, most decisions on foreign policy questions are fragmented, discontinuous, and result from compromises among many agencies and officials. The most powerful explanatory model would probably be one that incorporates sources and processes throughout the political and international system.

ENDNOTES

1. The principal theoretical work on the linkage between public opinion and foreign policy is that of Gabriel Almond, *The American People and Foreign Policy* (New York: Praeger, 1960). Other sources include Barry Hughes, *The Domestic Context of Foreign Policy* (San Francisco: Freeman, 1968); and Michael K. O'Leary, *The Politics of American Foreign Aid* (New York: Atherton, 1967).
2. For varying perspectives on which branch is more effective, see James Robinson, *Congress and Foreign Policy Making* (Homewood, IL: Dorsey Press, 1967); Thomas M. Franck and Edward Weisband, *Foreign Policy by Congress* (New York: Oxford University Press, 1979); and Randall Ripley, *Congress: Process and Policy* (New York: W. W. Norton, 1975).

3. Aaron Wildavsky, "The Two Presidencies," *trans-action Society*, Vol. 4 (December, 1966), pp. 7–17.
4. See the conclusions of Robinson, *Congress and Foreign Policymaking*.
5. This classification is based in part on the scheme proposed by William C. Vocke, "The Analysis of American Foreign Policy—An Overview," in William C. Vocke, ed., *American Foreign Policy: An Analytical Approach* (New York: The Free Press, 1976), pp. 5–15.
6. See Almond, *The American People and Foreign Policy* for the first statement of tions," in Charles Kegley and Patrick McGowan, eds., *Challenges to America: U. S. Foreign Policy in the 1980's* (Beverly Hills, CA: Sage Publications, 1979). *Political Science Review*, 64 (1970), pp. 536–547; and Frank L. Klingberg, "Cyclical Trends in American Foreign Policy Moods and Their Policy Implications," in Charles Kegley and Patrick McGowan, ed., *Challenges to America: U. S. Foreign Policy in the 1980's* (Beverly Hills, CA: Sage, 1979).
7. For an excellent discussion of the concept and its many meanings, see Ernest B. Haas, "The Balance of Power: Prescription, Concept or Propaganda," in James Rosenau ed., *International Politics and Foreign Policy* (New York: The Free Press, 1967), pp. 318–329.
8. John Spanier, *Games Nations Play* (New York: Praeger, 1975).
9. For more information on the international political economy, see such works as Joan Spero, *The Politics of International Economic Relations* (New York: St. Martin's, 1977); David Blake and Robert Walters, *The Politics of Global Economic Relations* (Englewood Cliffs, NJ: Prentice-Hall, 1976); and W.W. Rostow, *The World Economy: History and Prospect* (Austin: University of Texas Press, 1977). See Richard J. Barnet and Ronald E. Müller, *Global Reach: The Power of the Multinational Corporations* (New York: Simon and Schuster, 1974), for a variation on the political economy model that stresses the role of international corporations in foreign cnd domestic policies.
10. On the use of food as a foreign policy tool, see Dan Morgan, *Merchants of Grain* (New York: Penguin Books, 1980), Chapter 11.
11. These approaches range from the traditional geopolitical study of Alfred T. Mahan, *The Influence of Sea Power in History, 1660–1783* (Boston: Little, Brown, 1918) to the quantitative study of Wayne Ferris, *The Power Capabilities of Nation States* (Lexington, MA: D.C. Heath, 1973).
12. For a review of these studies, see Lloyd Jensen, *Explaining Foreign Policy* (Englewood Cliffs, NJ: Prentice-Hall, 1981), pp. 210–218.
13. For examples of this type of study see Douglas Haring, "Japanese National Character: Cultural Anthropology, Psychoanalysis, and History," *Yale Review*, 42 (March, 1953), and Alex Inkeles, Eugenia Harfmann, and Helen Beier, "Modal Personality and Adjustment to the Soviet Socio-Political System," *Human Relations*, 11 (February, 1958).
14. For a cross-cultural study of national beliefs, see Gabriel Almond and Sidney Verba, *The Civic Culture* (Princeton, NJ: Princeton University Press, 1963).
15. See Arthur Schlesinger, *The Imperial Presidency* (Boston: Houghton Mifflin, 1973); I.M. Destler, *Presidents, Bureaucrats and Foreign Policy* (Princeton, NJ: Princeton University Press, 1974), Roger Hilsman, *The Politics of Policy Making*

in *Defense and Foreign Affairs* (New York: Harper and Row, Publishers, 1971); Louis Henkin, *Foreign Affairs and the Constitution* (New York: W.W. Norton, 1972).
16. See Donald P. Warwick, *A Theory of Public Bureaucracy: Politics, Personality and Organization in the State Department* (Cambridge, MA: Harvard University Press, 1975).
17. Charles Kegley and Michael Wittkopf, *American Foreign Policy: Pattern and Process* (New York: St. Martin's Press, 1979), p. 272.
18. Adam Yarmolinsky, *The Military Establishment: Its Impact on American Society* (New York: Harper and Row, Publishers, 1971).
19. The most thorough attempt to outline the components of decision-making analysis is that of Richard Synder, H.W. Bruck and Burton Sapin, *Decision-making as an Approach to the Study of International Politics* (Princeton, NJ: Princeton University Press, 1954). For a comparison of several decision-making models, see Graham Allison, *Essence of Decision* (Boston: Little, Brown, 1971).
20. For examples of bureaucratic politics and group decision making, see Morton H. Halperin, *Bureaucratic Politics and Foreign Policy* (Washington, DC: The Brookings Institution, 1974).
21. Irving L. Janis, *Victims of Groupthink: A Psychological Study of Foreign Policy Decisions and Fiascoes* (Boston: Houghton Mifflin, 1972).
22. A number of communications and interaction studies are reviewed in Jensen, *Explaining Foreign Policy* pp. 231–242.

KEY TERMS
Balance of Power Models
Decision-Making Models
Executive Branch Models
External Perspectives
Ideological-Historical Perspectives
Internal Perspectives
International Processes Models
National Capabilities Models
National Character and Belief Models
Nationalist School
Political Culture
Political Economy Models
Radical School
Realist School
Scientific Perspectives

CHAPTER 8

Evaluating Public Policy

STUDYING POLICY CONSEQUENCES

Public policies have consequences. The personal consequences of these policies (e.g., the need to pay taxes and Social Security, or obtain licenses, or personal concerns about political issues of national significance) are perhaps the most salient element of public policy for most of us. Although policy description and policy explanation are important analytic tasks for the understanding of public policy, the study of policy consequences is even more essential, because future changes and new policies depend on judgments about current policy impacts.

Policy evaluation is the broad title given to judging the consequences of what governments do and say. There are, however, two distinctive tasks involved in evaluation. One is to determine what the consequences of a policy are by describing its impact, the other task is to judge whether the policy is successful according to a set of standards or value criteria. However, there is a common link between the two which sets them apart from the tasks of description and explanation. Like description and explanation, evaluation studies attempt to answer specific questions related to public policy, and each applies a variety of models and related problem-solving techniques to the analytic task at hand. What differentiates policy impact and evaluation studies from descriptive and explanatory analysis is the focus on policy results or consequences as opposed to policy characteristics or causes.[1]

Obviously, there is an enormous range of policy consequences to consider. We may be interested in the impact of government actions on a very small segment of the population, say, children who need kidney dialysis treatments, or even an endangered species (the last 120 sandhill cranes). At the other end of the scale, the study of policy consequences could focus on the medical and financial well-being of the millions of Americans over 65 years of age. The consequences of the Medicare and Social Security programs affect this population directly, and indirectly affect the entire federal budget and national economy. An increase in FICA (Social Security withholding) taxes, for example, reduces take-home pay of all wage-earning Americans while reducing the drain on the federal budget from Social Security payments. Such an increase can be discussed in terms of its impact on inflation and the international value of the dollar. To evaluate the impact of these vastly different types of policy consequences, we need to use a number of models, scales, and other analytical tools. There are, in other words, different ways to analyze policy consequences. Many of these differences can be attributed to three factors: the purpose of the analysis; what is being studied; and the standards being applied.

THE ANALYTIC PURPOSE

Although many dimensions of policy results can be studied, there are essentially two closely related goals for the evaluation of policy consequences: *impact description* and *judgment*. The first of these goals, impact description, is grounded in the need to find out what the actual consequences of a policy are. The second, judgment, is based in the need to assess some policy result in the light of certain standards. Although both of these goals are considered to be part of policy evaluation, it is important to keep impact description and judgment separate in analysis.

When dealing with policy consequences, it should be necessary to describe their impacts before proceeding to further study. It is always tempting to pass judgment first and ask descriptive questions later. But the systematic policy analyst will begin with a description of policy impacts and resist the attraction of passing judgment—at least temporarily.

It would, of course, be an oversimplification to state that the distinction between descriptive and judgmental analyses of impact is clear and firmly drawn. A better picture is one that admits that the two types of study often overlap. As we noted in Chapter 4 "describing" is neither a mechanical nor objective act. The analyst who sets out to describe policy consequences chooses tools and techniques containing some bias. Certain models or methods of inquiry may be biased toward a particular view of political power (e.g., pluralism, elitism) or preference for one economic system (e.g., socialism, capitalism). Other sources of bias may be institutional (e.g., the organization sponsoring the analysis prefers certain methods or hopes for a particular outcome to ensure institutional survival).

For example, an analyst who is investigating the results of foreign assistance funds granted to an underdeveloped country might report that certain health, welfare, and development goals were achieved, at least in part. If, however, that analyst were more concerned with the goals of American national security, the report may concentrate on the degree to which development funds discouraged the formation of leftist opposition groups that might threaten relations with the United States. On the other hand, critics of foreign aid sitting on appropriations committees of the Congress may focus on the waste of foreign aid funds even though certain projects appear to have succeeded. In this example, various analysts may use the same methods of calculating the funds spent, but the standards related to their specific value preferences probably differ radically.

At the heart of the overlap between descriptive and judgmental impact studies is the fact that both types of analysis apply measures or standards to policy consequences. In a later section we examine these measurement tools as they are used in analytic models. The point to be stressed here is that while there are some similarities between the standards and methods used for impact description and judgmental analyses of policy consequences, the two analytic purposes are distinct and the measures used for each should be chosen with that distinction clearly in mind.

To clarify the difference between describing policy impacts and judging their success, we need to consider why we perform these assessments. One of the primary reasons we employ impact description analysis is to acquire the facts necessary for making a later evaluation. Without sound investigation of policy consequences, the value of such an evaluation would be next to nothing. However, analysts must proceed carefully with the descriptive study if judgment is to follow to avoid prejudicing the outcome of the evaluation.

There is a natural relationship between describing impacts and making judgments about policies. This is so because the impact analysis must gather the information relevant to the evaluation that follows. If we wish to evaluate the impact of the 55-mile-per-hour speed limit on the amount of gasoline consumed by car owners in the United States, the increased cost of goods transported at a slower speed by the trucking industry is irrelevant to the evaluation of the policy. The question of the degree to which the limit was enforced in the various states would be highly relevant to the problem. On the other hand, the impact study should not predetermine the assessment through its methods (reporting only on states where the limit is enforced) or conclusions (comments on the pricing mechanisms for fuel).

The close connection between describing the impact of policy and making judgments becomes more evident when we think about why evaluation analyses are undertaken. The motivation for all such analyses is to find out whether or to what extent a given public policy succeeded or, in contrast, why it failed to achieve its objective. The goal or objective of any public policy is determined originally in the political arena and, therefore, reflects choices between competing notions of the public interest. For example, the objective of establishing a Department of Energy was to provide a coordinated program for relieving on the nation's energy shortage. The Carter Administration charged the new Energy Department to improve production, encourage development of new energy technologies, and to support conservation efforts. President Reagan interpreted his election as a mandate for decreasing federal involvement in the private sector, and, specifically, for dismantling the Department of Energy. To his way of thinking (and view of the public good), the Department of Energy discouraged production and technological advancement through overregulation. Any attempt to describe and judge the impact of the department's activities during its short life will be affected by the standard of measurement applied and the political view of those conducting the evaluative effort. Obviously, members of the Reagan Administration will apply a different set of values to the most unbiased report of the agency's effectiveness and impact than would members of the Carter Administration.

In the sections that follow, we discuss some concepts and methods for identifying the policy consequences to be described. Then we offer several scales that can be used to evaluate policy consequences. Neither set of conceptual tools includes specific measurement devices such as statistical methods, data collection, experimental design, or cost calculations. Instead, we hope to provide the analytical framework for the deliberate and effective application of such specific techniques, keeping separate as much as possible the description and judgment of policy consequences.

WHAT IS BEING STUDIED

It is simple enough to state that the consequences of public policy provide the focus for descriptive and judgmental impact analyses, but it is quite another matter to specify which particular consequences concern us. The choice of which consequence to study determines to a great degree which models and methods will be used and the particular relevance of the analyst's study for students of public policy.[2] Each of the seven dimensions discussed here represents policy consequences, but from a distinct perspective. These include distinctions based on policy sequences, actual or perceived impacts, intended or unintended effects, direct or indirect impacts, temporally ordered effects, tangible vs. intangible results, and specific substantive effects.

Government actions and statements produce consequences in several *sequentially distinctive types*.[3] To start with, they generate *policy outputs* in the form of funds, jobs, material produced, services (e.g., police and fire protection), and so on. These represent public policies as they become manifest in government expenditures or the conversion of public sector resources into activities. In short, outputs reflect the mobilization of government on behalf of a specific policy commitment.

But outputs are only the first in a sequence of policy consequences. Another category of results is the impact on targeted behavior or the state of affairs the policy was intended to influence. Here we can discuss *policy performance* and examine those aspects of the environment specific government actions or statements were meant to change to maintain. Every policy has a target, and every target is supposed to react in a certain fashion according to the rationale of a given policy. Thus, some policies call for compliance to a regulation while others seek to promote types of investment or actions taken by individuals. When analyzing these consequences, we are looking at how the policy performed vis-à-vis its stated intentions.

It goes without saying that public policies have impacts beyond their particular outputs and performance. When a program is implemented or a tax rate increased, the effects spill over beyond the actual mobilization of governmental resources or response of some intended target group. These consequences are analyzed as *policy outcomes* and present both the general and specific influence of a government action or statement beyond the more narrowly defined impact of the policy on an intentionally targeted segment of the environment.

Finally, analysts of policy consequences may be interested in the repercussions of a government action or statement on the policymaking system itself or on given policymakers. Policies produce reactions, and these reactions are likely to include some messages for the officials and institutions that formulate or implement policies. In this sense, we are concerned with *policy feedback* as a type of policy consequence which might prove analytically interesting.

Each of these types of policy consequences can be viewed as analytically distinct from the other, thus providing the analyst with a reasonably clear focal point for study. However, each can also be linked in fact as well as in theory to the others. We can easily see the sequential relationships between these policy consequences: government action produces *outputs* which are then carried out *(performance)* causing *outcomes* which trigger reactions or *feedback*. However, this sequence represents just one that we regard as possible, but not necessary. It is just as possible that a government statement will produce feedback without the mobilization of resources (i.e., outputs), or that outcomes will occur before a policy is sufficiently developed to have an impact on its intended target population (i.e., policy performance).

BOX 8.1

The attempt by the federal government to reduce the automobile emissions contributing to air pollution provides some sterling examples of sequential policy consequences and the complexity of the linkages between them. The first Air Quality Act to specify emissions standards for cars became law in 1965. In 1970, amendments to that law (Clean Air Amendments) were passed requiring all automobiles sold in the United States to meet stringent requirements by 1975. This government action resulted in the establishment of standards, the writing of regulations, and a number of environmental decisions that can be regarded as policy outputs. The primary targeted population was the automobile industry, which responded by designing and manufacturing a number of pollution control devices including the catalytic converter. The adoption of these devices can be considered analytically as an indicator of policy performance.

Identifying the outcome of this emission policy is, however, a much more difficult analytical problem. No two scientists agree on its effect on air quality, although consumers are all well aware of the increase in the cost of automobiles and changed maintenance requirements. A more serious and, for the most part, unanticipated consequence, was the need for unleaded gasoline for cars equipped with catalytic converters. This fuel is more expensive to procure than leaded gasoline and, in a tight energy situation, is increasingly in short supply. Policymakers have been forced to deal with the feedback of inflationary fuel costs and shortages and to continue the dialogue with automakers over future pollution innovations. All of the consequences of the emissions policy proclaimed so boldly in 1970 have been subjected to the influence of external factors such as decisions of the OPEC cartel and the vagaries of public opinion. The interaction between policy action, performance, and outcomes becomes more complex each year making the analytical task even more difficult.

Studying such a sequence of policy consequences is not, however, a sufficient analysis of public results. Policy thinkers might also consider a

number of other characteristics that will make a difference to their studies.
For instance, are they to be concerned with *actual* or *perceived* policy consequences? Many analysts are interested in the objective results of public policies, that is, what actually occurs. Studies abound regarding the costs (e.g., outputs) of a policy, its effectiveness (performance), general effects (outcomes), or the expressed reaction to it (feedback). There is no need to justify our interest in such matters. But why would an analyst be interested in perceived policy consequences? Does it matter to know what an individual or group thought about a policy's costs and effects?

The answer is yes, at least in some instances. Certain analysis deal with the political or social implications of public policies and therefore are interested not only in what policies actually accomplish or how they affect their environment, but also what they are regarded as having done by some relevant group. A state policy thinkers have understood this for years. The fact that recent presidents have enlarged their White House staffs to include special assistants to advise the chief executive on policies affecting women, blacks, Spanish-surnamed Americans, and other minority groups has been perceived by each respective group as symbolizing concern for their problems whether the Administration is able to respond to their demands with policy actions or not. Because it is not necessarily what you do that matters, but what you are perceived as having done that really counts, analysts must be aware of the choice of focusing on either actual or perceived consequences.

As we have mentioned in previous chapters, public policies are actions or statements of government that can be analyzed as types of purposive behavior. Policies have goals and therefore might be described or explained in regard to policymaker objectives. Whether explicit or implicit, these objectives represent the intentions of officials who make or implement the policy. It is therefore reasonable to study policy consequences as either *intended* and *unintended*.

Focusing on intentions, the analyst examines any or all of the goals of a government action or statement. This necessitates a preliminary descriptive analysis indicating just what those goals are. Some of these may be explicated in specific and operational terms, as is the case with policies aimed at cutting the response time of police to emergency calls in half, or when an official of the state public aid department intends to process twice as many applicants per week this month as opposed to last. More often, however, intentions are neither explicit nor clearly articulated in operational terms. Objectives such as reducing unemployment, bringing peace to the Middle East, or setting utility rates in accord with the public interest are not uncommon despite their vagueness. For this reason, a preliminary analysis that describes the objectives of a policy is not only advisable, but crucial where intentions are our focal points.

Unintended consequences may also provide an interesting focus for impact or evaluative studies. Policies more often than not generate results the policymaker either did not consider or hoped to avoid. When proposing higher defense expenditures for the 1980s, few Pentagon officials intended to strengthen the peace movement in Europe. This development makes the acceptance of new armaments politically difficult for our European allies. And when the Department of Health, Education, and Welfare promoted an "access" program for the wheelchair-bound handicapped, which included the elimination of corner street curbs in many cities, it had no intention of offending the blind handicapped who bitterly complained of the problem posed by the elimination of those same curbs. It is thus desirable at times to consider the unintended consequences as well as the intended.

Policies can also be examined for the *direct* and *indirect* consequences they have on their surroundings. Some policies have important direct impacts of interest to an analyst. For example, as a result of increased income tax payroll deductions ("withholding") we would expect individuals to spend less or to maintain spending habits by reducing savings. In the same way, we expect a national speed limit of 55 miles per hour to have a direct impact on the behavior of motorists, on the law enforcement officials of the states, and the money spent on gasoline. But an analysis of these policies for their direct effects alone is not likely to prove sufficient. We are probably going to be as interested in the indirect impacts such as the ultimate influence of increased payroll deductions on inflation and the number of lives not lost through motor vehicle accidents as well as the increase in petroleum available for other uses.

BOX 8.2

One error to be avoided in impact or evaluation analysis is to confuse the intentional/unintentional dimensions of policy consequences with their direct/indirect effects. Policymakers do not necessarily make policies with the idea that they must take action directly aimed at a problematic situation. For instance, in economic policy choices, governments frequently attempt to achieve their objectives by influencing the environment within which a person acts rather than by confronting that individual with specific rules or regulations. So if a government wishes to promote more housing construction, it can do so by manipulating the interest rates banks charge on home building loans. In a similar fashion the government might raise or lower taxes, offer or withdraw subsidies, or take some other indirect step to carry out its objectives. Thus we cannot necessarily link direct policy impacts with the intentions of policymakers. In fact, it might be possible to consider policy consequences in one of four ways represented by the matrix in Figure 8.1.

Returning briefly to the auto emissions policy adopted in 1970, we might consider the direct and intended consequences to be the production of low-emission automobiles; the indirect and intended consequence to be the establishment of local testing programs; the direct but unintended consequence to be the choice of the catalytic converter as the primary control device; and the expense and scarcity of the necessary unleaded gasoline as the indirect and unintended consequence of the Clean Air Act Amendements of 1970.

A related yet quite different view of policy consequences looks at the impact of government actions or statements over time. Policy consequences, like policies themselves, can have repercussions that are not limited to the immediate temporal period. Government activity is analogous to the pebble thrown into a still pond which generates waves of concentric circles, each ripple representing a consequence felt with the passage of time. From this view we obtain a picture of policy impacts having implications during a given time period, followed by further implications in a second time period, followed by a third series of impacts, and so on until the analyst is satisfied with the thoroughness of the study or the effects become so small as to be immeasurable.

In this approach, we are said to be dealing with *temporally ordered effects*. During the initial time period, t_1, we say we are studying first-order effects; during t_2 we are looking at second-order effects; and so on until t_n

Policy Consequences

	Direct	Indirect
Intended	Cars with pollution controls	State and city testing programs
Unintended	Choice of the catalytic coverter	Shortage of unleaded fuel

Figure 8.1. Policy consequences in two dimensions.

where we consider the *n*th-order of impacts. The time period applied will vary with the analyst's interest, and it could range from a day or less up to large temporal periods. Using this perspective on policy consequences, we can examine the intended or unintended and direct or indirect impact of Medicare after its first year in effect, or its second, or third and so on. Professional analysts call this process iteration.[4]

While these views of policy consequences are interesting and fruitful, they cannot be used to draw on our knowledge of the substantive consequences of public policy. For that reason, we turn to other approaches. For instance, we can examine the *tangibility* or *intangibility* of policy impacts. Some policy consequences take material form and can be described or appraised along those lines. Thus we study or evaluate the impact of a new park or recreation center by counting the number of users or by measuring the wear and tear on plant and equipment. The alternative to a concern for tangible results is to focus on an intangible such as the aesthetic pleasure for the community generated by the park or the "civic pride" felt by local residents about the reaction center.

Still another possible substantive distinction regarding policy results is made almost daily by analysts in newspaper editorials or on TV and radio. We frequently hear references to the political implications of a policy or its economic consequences or social repercussions. What these analysts are doing is focusing on specific *substantive impact* dimensions of policy effects in order to describe or assess the impact. Some of these take on considerable importance. A defense spending policy's economic effects—whether intended or not, direct or in direct, immediate or in the future, tangible or intangible—can have great significance for a country, regardless of its implications for national security, the career of legislators who support or opose it, or the President who proposed it. It can influence jobs or inflationary trends or the general business climate of a region. At the same time, an explicit economic policy—one, for instance, which led to a recession period—may have an impact on national defense by stimulating enlistment in military service among the increasing number of unemployed. Following this logic, of course, there is an almost infinite number of substantive possible repercussions of any policy.

In fact there are probably as many dimensions of policy consequences as there are individuals affected by policies. The point that must be stressed is that these dimensions are not mutually exclusive. We have shown in Figure 8.1 how at least two such perspectives overlap, and the same can be accomplished using any two or more of these various dimensions. For example, there have been studies of the unintended, indirect long-term medical effects of a law passed in 1962 regulating the development, testing, and certification of new drugs in the United States.[5] Similarly we have studies of the intended, direct effect of automobile safety regulation and the indirect yet tangible economic and social consequences of the 55-mile-per-hour speed limit after several years.[6] These and many other examples demonstrate how the determination of what policy results are to be studied will make a significant difference in impact and evaluative analyses.

MODELS AND SCALES

After deciding which dimensions of a policy's results are to be investigated, the policy thinker should consider the tools or techniques to use in describing or assessing policy consequences. The key to this analytic problem is the selection and application of appropriate (i.e., useful) models. For descriptive or judgmental impact analyses, the choice of an appropriate model is essentially choosing a *scale of measurement* against which policy consequences can be described or compared.

In this sense, descriptive impact and judgmental analyses are closely related to simple descriptive analysis. As is the case with policy description (see Chapter 4), the basic models appropriate to the analysis of policy consequences are those allowing us to classify, categorize, or compare what we are studying. At this most simple level, in fact, the basic difference between the models and approaches described in Chapter 4 and those we consider in this section is that the former are applied to government actions and statements while the latter are used on policy consequences.

However, the similarity in method between policy description and policy evaluation is overshadowed by the different goals of each type of analysis. The basic policy description summarized in Chapter 4 should be a snapshot of government action while policy evaluations are ultimately pictures of post-action conditions. There is a fundamental difference between classifying a policy according to its objectives and categorizing it in terms of the extent to which those objectives were achieved. There is a substantive difference between an analysis describing how much a government budget document states will be expended on a program and the amount actually allocated. Furthermore, evaluative analysis may go further and apply a set of values declaring whether specific policy consequences are good or bad for the society.

Applying this distinction to a specific program, Head Start's objectives have been described in terms of improving the educational attainment and general welfare of preschool children from "disadvantaged" families.[7] The amount of money appropriated for the program increased each year after its initiation. This kind of descriptive information tells us nothing about the degree to which the objectives were achieved. A descriptive impact analysis of Head Start should ask whether the children enrolled in the program achieved higher reading scores when they entered school, about whether expenditures were primarily for services or equipment, and what proportion of all disadvantaged children were served. In other words, did the program meet measures of educational achievement or budgetary balance or special services? It is this *appraisal* function that distinguishes evaluation analyses from the basic act of policy description.

In this section we consider several of the more common standards and measures used in impact and evaluative models. They can be summmarized in five types: cost-benefit; effectiveness; efficiency; equity; and "social test" models.

Cost-benefit Models

Although conceptually simple and useful, cost-benefit models are difficult to construct and apply. They are common tools for those who advise policymakers regarding the relative value of policy alternatives. In the present context, however, they are also used as a means for dealing with questions such as "what was the impact of policy X?" and "was it good or bad as an action or statement of government?"

For purposes of describing policy consequences, cost-benefit models are extremely useful if well constructed and applied with care. A descriptive impact study stating that a policy cost so many dollars and generated X dollars in benefits is both simple, direct, and easy to comprehend for anyone who understands the value of the dollar as a measuring unit. As a judgmental tool, such a model can provide the analyst with a quick yet meaningful method for passing judgment, for it is merely a matter of seeing that where benefits exceed costs, a policy consequence is good and vice versa; and that the greater the benefit for each dollar spent, the better the policy results.

It would be nice, of course, if cost-benefit analysis was that simple and all we had to do is measure a policy's consequences in monetary terms. As stressed above, however, the key to any application of cost-benefit models is that they be well constructed and applied with care—tasks not easily accomplished.[8]

For one thing, cost-benefit models are built on *scales of valuation* which are themselves subject to debate. By scales of valuation we mean standards and measures that identify favorable (i.e., beneficial) and unfavorable (i.e., costly) policy consequences. Such a scale would be easy to construct if we were able to agree on what constitutes favorable and unfavorable policy results. Such agreement is only rarely achieved in most public policy arenas.

Even if we can define these objectives, we still must agree on a *consistent and reliable* set of measuring units for the policy results. Do we, for example, measure the outcome of Head Start programs as dollars spent per child, or in points of improvement on tests of intellectual ability? Can we agree on measures of health (nutritional content of a daily diet) or on measures of cultural enrichment (Sesame Street)? Sometimes we can use a monetary unit measure such as the dollar or an analytically defined measure of utility (economists, for example, sometimes use a hypothetical measuring unit called a util); or we can agree to use peanuts or peas. In any case, the problems of cost-benefit model construction are immense, thus rendering difficult what seemed at first glance to be a simple task.

If we can construct a potentially useful cost-benefit model, we would next be faced with decisions about *how to apply the measures of value* we have developed. There is always the problem of what to measure, which we discussed earlier in this chapter, but even along these lines cost-benefit models raise added problems. Economists, for example, discuss costs not only in terms of resources used or money spent, but also opportunities foregone. In a world of scarce resources, choices must be made and as one chooses to do X, one has simultaneously chosen not do to Y or A. Funds spent for preschool education could have been allocated to elementary schools for remedial education programs or simply dispersed to poor families as children's allowances, thus elevating the entire family's standard of living. In short, one must deal with "opportunity costs." Adding this extra dimension to the study of policy consequences makes impact and evaluation analysis extremely difficult.

Another problem in applying cost-benefit scales of valuation is that one must contend with the many *intangible consequences* of public policy. Programs that aim at increasing the participation of the poor or any other special class of people in the planning and administration of local programs can produce a heightened sense of political effectiveness for those involved that may carry over into increased political demands for other benefits and services. This certainly intangible consequence is difficult to measure but may affect future policy decisions.[9] The symbolic and intangible results of public policies cannot be ignored in any thorough evaluation analysis, and it is likely these will be assigned a value as favorable or unfavorable, even though they are very difficult to measure.

Despite these problems, cost-benefit models are not useless. In fact, they have considerable potential and are frequently used in analyses that require precision, consistency, and reliability.

Effectiveness Models

Like cost-benefit models, effectiveness models are very basic and simple to deal with, at least on a superficial level. An assessment of policy effectiveness is one that relies mainly on *scales of goal achievement* for the description and judgment of policy consequences.

A number of comments about effectiveness models are in order. First, they are necessarily based on policy intentions. To the extent possible the scale of goal achievement should reflect the explicit objectives of a government action or statement. Second, like cost-benefit and all the other models discussed in this section, a key to success in using this measure is its construction. One major obstacle to this effort might be the lack of an explicit policy objective, thus making the analyst explore for implied goals in an action or statement. In such an exploration one might discover the policy's objective to be something other than is stated. Another problem arises in cases where there is not one goal but several; and this, in turn, is likely to be complicated by the fact that some objectives may be explicit while others are only implied.

The federal Food Stamp program provides an example of a policy possessing multiple and sometimes conflicting goals.[10] The explicit objective of the program is to provide for the basic nutritional needs of poor individuals and families, using a minimum of coercion and administration. The program, which is administered by the Department of Agriculture, also serves to support farm prices. Besides achieving certain goals for the farming sector and lower income groups, regulations that restrict purchases with the stamps (i.e., no soap, cosmetics, liquor, or pet food) enable the government to supervise the consumption habits of the poor, ostensibly to ensure a thrifty although nutritious diet. Which of these goals should be adopted to measure effectiveness?

In addition, we must consider the problems associated with developing the specific scale of measurement once policy objectives are known. At the least we can probably construct a scale of achievement that allows us to classify a policy result as effective or not effective. However, few policies are totally effective or ineffective, and it would probably be best to consider degree of achievement in constructing our scale. But here we run into a number of methodological problems, for we must develop the model carefully so that it is useful and still reflects policy intentions. If the policy objective was numerical to begin with, our job would be simplified. Let us say that the U.S. government embarks on a policy of fuel conservation wherein it establishes a target of reducing foreign oil imports by 3 million barrels per week. Such a goal can be easily scaled. Other policy goals, however, are not as tangible. For example, one objective of recent U.S. economic policy has been to increase the confidence of foreign investors in the American dollar. How does one measure confidence? Of course, indicators of that confidence can be developed (e.g., amount of foreign investment), but no matter how close that indicator is to the policy objective, the fact remains that it is not a precise measure.

Third, as with other models, construction is not the same as application. One must take care that the scale of goal achievement is used appropriately; in this case the scale must relate to policy performance. A policy cannot be regarded as effective merely because government spends money on it; yet some policy thinkers forget this basic fact, and the result is a poor measurement of policy effectiveness. That the government spends a considerable amount of its resources on fighting a war, whether a war in Vietnam or a domestic war on poverty, should not be misread as an indicator of effective policy performance. Although this should be obvious, it is still not uncommon for someone to point to policy *outputs* as an indicator of how effective government policy has been. If one is careful in the application of a well constructed effectiveness model, such mistakes would rarely occur.

Finally, we must note that the use of an effectiveness model for describing policy consequences does not necessarily imply a judgment about the policy's consequences. Because an analyst finds that policy to be effective (i.e, it measures high on the scale of goal achievement) does not mean that the analyst believes the policy consequence to be good or desirable. An effective policy can also be an undesirable one, so the description of impact is clearly distinguishable from that of judgment of policy accomplishments. On the other hand, where the analyst believes a policy objective to be desirable, then the scale of goal achievement can simultaneously provide us with a description and assessment of a policy consequence.

Efficiency Models

The word efficiency can take on several meanings depending on what one is analyzing. For some analysts efficiency means "the best way," while for others it is equivalent to effectiveness and goal achievement. In addition, there are many analysts who use efficiency to examine processes such as policymaking and policy implementation rather than policy results as we do here. The efficiency models described here, therefore, are only several of a number of types.

In using efficiency models, we are concerned not merely with goal achievement (i.e., effectiveness), but also with the quality of the policy result being examined. In achieving an objective, to what extent were policy results the most appropriate that was possible? That is, to what extent was a given level of policy performance accompanied by other desirable qualities of policy consequences?

What are the qualities relative to policy outputs and outcomes which may be assessed as desirable? On a very general level, it is usually assumed that an effective policy consequence achieved at the least cost (relative to other effective policy results) is desirable because it is efficient in its use of resources. Thus we can discuss efficiency relative to *scales of output costliness*.

However, many analysts would perceive this scale as too narrowly defined and would seek to discuss efficiency in regard to outcomes as well. For example, an effective policy consequence that generated either too many undesirable side effects or not enough additional desirable outcomes will be regarded as less efficient than an equally effective policy consequence that produced a minimal amount of undesirable spillover effects or a relatively large number of unintended yet desirable outcomes. This can be called the *scale of outcome desirability*.

Bringing these two scales together in Figure 8.2, we have a matrix with four categories that can be used to describe and assess policy consequences in terms of their respective efficiency. For purposes of a descriptive impact analysis alone, this model and the typology it generates have obvious value because they provide some basis for characterizing a policy consequence in terms of degree of efficiency. On the judgmental analysis side, and assuming the policy thinker believes the objectives of the policy to be worthwhile, this model also facilitates the efficiency assessement of a policy result. Obviously, for example, a policy consequence that falls into category I of the matrix will be less valued than one found in either II or III, and these in turn will be judged less desirable than a policy consequence classified in cell IV.

We can use alternatives proposed for coping with the energy crisis of the 1970s and 1980s as examples for each of the categories. The construction of nuclear generating plants is considered by many to be extremely inefficient; this would be a type I solution due to its high cost and potentially low outcome desirability in terms of potential danger. Cells II and III of he matrix may be exemplified, respectively, by converting most homes to solar energy (desirable but very expensive) and converting most generating plants to coal (cheap but environmentally dirty). Conservation of energy is, obviously, a Category IV solution since it provides for desirable consequences at a low cost if the public can be persuaded to implement it.

There are other efficiency models from which the policy analyst can choose, and this example is not intended to foreclose options for the analyst.

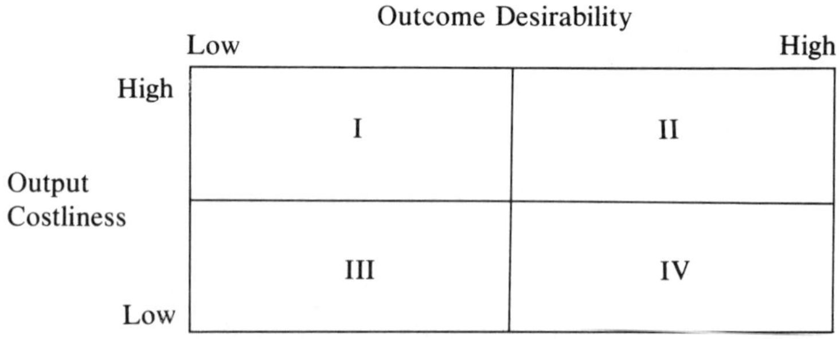

	Outcome Desirability	
	Low	High
High	I	II
Low	III	IV

Output Costliness

Figure 8.2. Types of efficiency.

However, there are certain points to be stressed. First, the description or judgmental assessment of a policy consequence using an efficiency model assumes that policy effectiveness has already been considered or is taken into account during the analysis. One is not limited to studying the efficiency of just those policy results with *high* effectiveness. Instead, one can undertake to study the efficiency of a policy consequence at any level of effectiveness. Recalling the Head Start program as an example, we could measure the efficiency of these educational programs in terms of dollars spent per child or improved scores even if the program was relatively ineffective as judged by the lower percentage of poor children enrolled.

Another point to be stressed is that, as with other models used for descriptive impact and judgmental analyses, careful construction and cautious application are the keys to success. The construction should reflect what the analyst defines efficiency to be. If this means applying only the scale of output costliness, *or* only the scale of outcome desirability, *or* some combination of these or alternate measures, then so be it. But once the model is built, it should be used with care in order to avoid distorted findings and to generate genuinely useful analyses.

Equity Models

Equity models are difficult to describe for several reasons. First, the concept of equity is rarely well defined. Effectiveness and efficiency, despite their broad use, are nevertheless identified with certain characteristics that make them useful concepts. Equity, on the other hand, does not have an equally useful "handle." We often associate equity with the ideas of "fairness" and "justice," but such terms are themselves vaguely defined and thus of little use.

Second, while an ambiguous concept, equity is something everyone desires. Therefore, one cannot ignore it, especially as it relates to policy consequences. The point is to make certain of what we mean by equity when we develop and apply a model based on it.

Third, and perhaps most significant, is that what is regarded as equitable will depend on the policy being investigated and the individual and societal perspectives of the analyst.[11] What is regarded as an equitable policy result in one context by an analyst may be defined as inequitable either in a different context or by a different analyst. The differences involved will go deeper than a mere problem of measurement. What is likely to be involved are distinct value systems and attitudes that may place two analysts at opposing ends of a spectrum.

To clarify the problematic nature of equity models, let us consider some examples. As a first step we note that the equity of policy consequences can be described and assessed in several ways. The questions of equity may relate to the availability of outputs or to how the government is implementing its actions and statements. What is equitable or inequitable in this regard can be measured through the application of a model based on *scales of opportunity*. An opportunity scale would measure or categorize policy consequences according to the access one has to the available policy outputs. In this sense, some policy outputs are more accessible than others. Certain outputs are generated that can be obtained by anyone, others are limited to those who qualify, while still others are further restricted to some narrowly defined special group. Which of these opportunity levels is most equitable for a given policy output will depend on perceptions of what is at stake. For certain policy actions, such as freedom of speech or the dispensation of justice, equal opportunity for all should be the standard of equity. For other policies, opportunities might be equitably limited to those who qualify (i.e., unemployment insurance) or those in need (i.e., aid to families with dependent children).

A second type of equity model focuses on policy performance and relates to treatment received in relation to policy goals. How was the targeted population treated? Here *scales of treatment* might be appropriate. Exactly what constitutes fair or equitable treatment will, of course, depend on the situation under examination. While it may be deemed equitable in the interest of detecting fraud to inquire into alternate sources of income for a welfare applicant, it is not a requirement for the payment of pension funds for a retired worker. Similarly, public laws make clear that it is not fair to deny credit to any person on the basis of sex, although it is equitable to use the prior credit record for such a decision. One must note that standards of equitable treatment change as societal values change. Therefore, if we choose to apply a model based on a scale of treatment, we must consider a number of circumstantial factors and develop our scale with great care.

Finally, equity measures are frequently used to describe and assess policy outcomes, and most often this calls for a model based on what we term *scales of distributional effects*. Any policy outcome will have impacts that vary within a given environment or among members of a certain population. Some of those outcomes will have a greater impact—positive or negative—on one group or area than another. This distributional effect of public policy can be seen in the impact of national defense expenditures. When the Cold War was at its height, the federal government undertook policies leading to the opening or expansion of many military and defense-related installations. In addition, innumerable defense contracts were issued, creating many jobs, particularly in the Sunbelt (i.e., all across the South, but basically in the area from Texas to California). As a result, there were tremendous population gains in certain areas (and losses in others, e.g., the Snowbelt of the Midwest and Northeast) which created pressures on many local communities which were obligated to supply educational and other services without any immediate gain in resources to help meet those needs. In the short run, at least, the distributional effect of the national defense policy was inequitable in the burdens it placed on these "impacted" areas. Congress made adjustments for this through special legislation and appropriations to aid local communities; but the long run effects of population loss and reduced tax base have not been alleviated for states in the Northeast. It is not surprising to find a Snowbelt Senator like New York's Daniel P. Moynihan arguing for aid from the federal government to make amends for those policy outcomes—a claim based on an equity model using a scale of distributional effects.[12]

Whether based on opportunity, treatment, or distributional effects, equity models are often used both to describe policy consequences or to evaluate them or (as in Moynihan's case) to do both. Frequently their use is haphazard or polemical, and little thought is given to the model or scale being applied. The conscientious analyst should try to apply these models in a way which makes clear the measure being used.

Social Test Models

As the last of our policy evaluation model types, *social test models*[13] are both the easiest to understand and most difficult to discuss. On the one hand, they are relatively simple models that have scales that are usually easy to construct. On the other hand, they represent such a diverse number of specific models and scales that it would be difficult if not impossible to summarize their objectives.

A social test model is one developed by reference to some specific social, political, or economic interest. It typically reflects the extent to which a policy consequence is favorable to that interest. For example, we often hear policy thinkers state that a given policy produced results which were pro-labor, pro-railroad, pro-environment, or anti-consumer. To the extent that these models can be associated with a measure they would be based on *scales of interest satisfaction*. Such models can be useful for describing impacts if the scale of measurement is carefully constructed. Since they are really an outgrowth of personal or group interests, however, social test criteria are more frequently judgmental.

CONCLUSION

The scales discussed in this section can be used either to describe the actual consequences of a government policy or to judge the consequences against a set of values or expectations. They are intentionally broad because they represent the fundamental concerns of policy evaluation rather than specific methods, procedures, or measurements. It is extremely important for the policy analyst to first specify the purpose of policy evaluation—impact description or judgment—and then to be explicit about the scale being applied. After these analytic tasks are defined, then the policy thinker can select from a myriad of techniques to carry out the analysis of the details. As we have noted before, public policies are the result of political as well as bureaucratic and technical decisions. The consequences of policies are frequently discussed in the media or the halls of government only in terms of value judgments in order to win political support for the policy and for a particular set of values. Policy analysts also hold individual views about which policies are best for society, but the goal of the analyst is to hold these value judgments separate from the description of policy consequences and from applying specific scales of performance to policy impacts. Following this evaluation procedure will greatly enhance our ability to understand the complex goals, processes, and impact of public policies in our society.

ENDNOTES

1. This special focus is rarely made explicit in the literature of policy analysis. In fact, one often gets the impression that some analysts believe policy study is, by definition, the examination of policy consequences. For example, see the approach to impact and evaluation studies offered in Carol Weiss, *Evaluation Research: Methods of Assessing Program Effectiveness* (Englewood Cliffs, NJ: Prentice-Hall, Inc., 1972); Grover Starling, *The Politics and Economics of Public Policy: An Introductory Analysis with Cases* (Homewood, IL: The Dorsey Press, 1979), pp. 495–513); and David Nachmias, *Public Policy Evaluation: Approaches and Methods* (New York: St. Martin's Press Inc., 1979).
2. For a discussion of the relationships between impact studies and analytic purposes, see Kenneth M. Dolbeare, "The Impacts of Public Policy," in Cornelius P. Cotter (ed.), *Political Science Annual: 5* (New York: Bobbs-Merrill Co., Inc., 1974), pp. 89–130.
3. The sequential distinctions used here are developed from discussions in a variety of sources. See Ira Sharkansky, "Environment, Policy, Output and Impact: Problems of Theory and Method in the Analysis of Public Policy," in Ira Sharkansky (ed.), *Policy Analysis in Political Science* (Chicago: Markham Publishing Co., 1970), pp. 61–79; Thomas B. Smith, "The Policy Implementation Process," *Policy Sciences*, 4 (1973), pp. 197–209; and Paul Sabatier and Daniel Mazmanian, "Toward a More Adequate Conceptualization of the Implementation Process—With Special Reference to Regulatory Policy," mimeograph, July, 1978.
4. On iteration, see Edith Stokey and Richard Zeckhauser, *A Primer for Policy Analysis* (New York: W. W. Norton and Co., Inc., 1978), pp. 52–57.
5. See William M. Wardell and Louis Lasagna, *Regulations and Drug Development*

(Washington, DC: American Enterprise Institute for Public Policy Research, 1975).
6. See Sam Peltzman, *Regulation of Automobile Safety* (Washington, DC: American Enterprise Institute for Public Policy Research, 1975).
7. See Gilbert Steiner, *The State of Welfare,* (Washington, DC: The Brookings Institution, 1971), pp. 63–65. Also see discussion in Chapter 9.
8. On cost-benefit methods, see Stokey and Zeckhauser, *A Primer for Policy Analysis,* Chapter 9; also E.J. Mishan, *Cost-Benefit Analysis: An Informal Introduction,* 3rd edition (New York: Praeger Publishers, 1976). For examples of how cost-benefit methods can be used, see Edward M. Gramlich, *Benefit-Cost Analysis of Government Programs* (Englewood Cliffs, NJ: Prentice-Hall, Inc., 1981).
9. See Daniel Patrick Moynihan, *Maximum Feasible Misunderstanding* (New York: The Free Press, 1969).
10. See Gilbert Y. Steiner, *The State of Welfare* (Washington, D.C.: The Brookings Institution, 1971), Chapter 6. Also see discussion in Chapter 9.
11. For an interesting typology of equity see Aaron Wildavsky, *Speaking Truth to Power: The Art and Craft of Policy Analysis* (Boston: Little, Brown and Co., 1979), pp. 367–370.
12. See Daniel P. Moynihan, "The Politics and Economics of Regional Growth," *The Public Interest,* no. 51 (Spring, 1978), pp. 3–21.
13. On social test and related criteria, see discussion in James D. Thompson, *Organizations in Action: Social Science Bases of Administrative Theory* (New York: McGraw-Hill Book Co., 1967), Chapter 7.

KEY TERMS
Actual-Perceived Consequences
Cost-Benefit Models
Direct-Indirect Consequences
Effectiveness Models
Efficiency Models
Equity Models
Impact Description
Intended-Unintended Consequences
Judgmental Analysis
Policy Evaluation
Policy Feedback
Policy Outcomes
Policy Outputs
Policy Performance
Scales of Distributional Effects
Scales of Goal Achievement
Scales of Interest Satisfaction
Scales of Opportunity
Scales of Outcome Desirability

Scales of Output Costlinesss
Scales of Treatment
Scales of Valuation
Sequentially Distinctive Consequences
Social Test Models
Substantive Impacts
Tangible-Intangible Consequences
Temporally Ordered Consequences

CHAPTER 9

Evaluating Social Welfare Policies

A DEFINITION AND AN OVERVIEW

Governments have been involved in welfare policy longer than many people would suspect. Societies have always made some arrangements for those who were without support or the ability to take care of themselves. For example, early laws in American communities provided a specific list of items to which a window was entitled at her husbands' death, even though all property was inherited by his relatives. The widow's legacy included enough household belongings, and a sufficient stock of pigs, chickens, and cows to enable her and her children to survive. Other ordinances dealt with "poor farms," "potter's fields," and public almshouses.[1]

From these early concerns with the welfare of the poor have come literally hundreds of laws, programs, and regulations labeled *social welfare policy*. Although there is no agreed-upon definition of this policy area, we will define social welfare policies as all governmental activities that transfer benefits or social resources to individuals or groups considered needy in order to enhance their life circumstances or expectations. Underlying this definition is the notion of transferring benefits to special populations. Thus, public institutions such as libraries or state universities that provide equal benefits to all eligible individuals are not social welfare policies, while special reading programs for inner city children or basic education grants to college students from low-income families are transfers from the public sector to individuals on the basis of need.

As an arena of government action, the vast array of government activities that make up American social welfare policy present many opportunities for evaluating public policy. These policies are particularly controversial for a number of reasons. First, they frequently involve explicit costs and benefits to individuals within society. Second, welfare policies tend to reflect society's values and attitudes about achievement and motivation. Furthermore, the "state of welfare" in the United States is an excellent example of how a public policy can expand almost without direction until it seems to have too much momentum to be changed or reformed.

Before demonstrating how evaluation models might be applied to social welfare policy, we need to better understand this complex set of government actions and intentions. U.S. social welfare policy might be described as a multi-ringed, three-story circus. A wide variety of programs ranging from housing allowances to food stamps and public jobs are playing at the federal level while other programs or hybrids of federal programs are creatures of state and local government. Many federal programs are expanded upon and administered by the states while other programs (like Social Security) are organized and administered by the federal government alone. Not only are the various programs instituted and administered by different agencies and levels of the federal system, but the substantive goals and intended targets of these programs often vary so widely as to counteract each other. For example, a job training program that teaches skills to a welfare mother in preparation for finding a job can work against the goal of providing decent housing for that mother's family. When the former welfare recipient begins to earn a certain level of income, her family may be forced from subsidized housing into the private rental market which they may not be able to afford. Other welfare programs also work, if not at cross-purposes, at least without regard for their respective goals.

As we noted in Chapter 8, evaluating the consequences of public policies requires adopting an explicit standard of measurement. In the case of welfare policies and programs, the wide variety of programs, methods, and administrative arrangements reflects an equally broad spectrum of objectives these policies are meant to achieve. Some analysts regard the Aid to Families with Dependent Children (AFDC) program as having certain *punitive* goals. In many states, the monthly benefit is calculated to be less than the minimum survival budget for the family's needs. This practice may be intended to punish people for being poor or, at least, to discourage people from joining the program. Other programs, such as General Assistance which provides a minimum check to almost any needy person, serve to *alleviate* the effects of poverty. The Social Security program includes a number of policies intended to prevent certain classes of people (in this case the elderly, orphans, and widows) from becoming poor by creating a trust fund for their benefit. Still other programs are intended to prevent the spread of poverty conditions. *Preventative* policies such as the Neighborhood Youth Corps (see below) have played an increasingly important role in U.S. social welfare policies in recent years. Finally, a number of social welfare policies have been adopted with the goal of rehabilitating poor people, poor children, or poor communities. Many of the programs subsumed under the War on Poverty were based on belief that the poor could be retrained and thus enter the productive workforce. The Neighborhood Youth Program and the Job Corps are two examples of such *rehabilitative* programs. This brief survey of the different goals of social welfare programs demonstrates the importance of specifying the appropriate standard or scale of values for evaluating the consequences of any of these programs.

THE POLITICS OF EVALUATING WELFARE POLICY

Social welfare policies typify the problem of evaluating programs that provoke fundamental conflicts over societal values. Citizens, professional analysts, and political decision makers hold strong opinions about the programs now in existence, their consequences, and the appropriate strategy for improving welfare policies. In general, liberals, conservatives, and radicals on both the left and right all agree that the present amalgam of policies is unsatisfactory and require reform. However, there are many proposals for reforming these policies, and each is based on a different evaluation of the current policies and their respective consequences. We look briefly at some of these viewpoints on reforming welfare because they demonstrate the hazards of ideologically based policy analysis. Then we will present several examples of applying more explicit standards of evaluation to the consequences of specific social welfare programs.

Perspectives on social welfare policy can be arrayed on an ideological continuum from right to left. *Conservatives* believe that most public welfare activity is unnecessary and that it actually increases dependence on government. Although most conservatives see a need for aid to some groups such as the disabled, elderly, or small children (orphans, etc.), some would argue that all such state aid should be eliminated or minimized.[2] Most *liberals*, believing that it is the purpose of the state to take positive action on behalf of its citizens, support the concept of social welfare, although they may differ on the specific programs and strategies chosen by the policymakers. Of course, corresponding to the extreme conservative position there are those on the left who see the entire system as supportive of a capitalist society and incapable of true change. These critics often call for a major redistribution of wealth so that welfare would be unnecessary. With this range of opinions about the purpose and function of social welfare policy, it is no surprise that two evaluations of the same social welfare policy may bear little resemblance to each other.

Furthermore, social welfare policy analysis is characterized by fundamental disagreements over the administrative problems of the system. Conservatives often attack social programs as the most corrupt, wasteful, and fraudulent of all government actions. Typical of such opinions is that expressed by Senator Russell Long of Louisiana: "It's my judgment that you don't need any more people on welfare!"[3] Liberal commentators often criticize social welfare programs as insufficient, badly administered, unfair, and degrading to individual recipients. When introducing his welfare plan in 1977, President Carter described the current policy as "cruel and unworkable."[4]

These disagreements over the consequences of the social welfare programs necessarily reflect extremely disparate assessments of the welfare system and lead to very different proposals for reforms.[5] Critics who support the goals and methods of current programs or (in the case of conservatives) who acknowledge the necessity for certain policies such as aid to blind or disabled persons, frequently prefer *incremental* or step-by-step reforms. Their descriptions of welfare policies emphasize the correctness of the goals (i.e., rehabilitating the unskilled through job training) but criticize program management. Liberals who feel that welfare programs denigrate the poor through patronizing casework, or conservatives who decry program costs and efficiency, advocate reforms that would completely revamp all social welfare programs into a coherent, well-administered, equitable general transfer policy such as a guaranteed income plan. Not surprisingly, these *radical* reformers of both the right and left describe the faults of the welfare programs in similar ways.

Making sense of these various perspectives is no easy task. However, if we are to understand these common evaluations of social welfare policies, we must also be conscious of the viewpoint of the analyst. Figure 9.1 provides a typology of social welfare policy perspectives that might help us gain such understanding. It reflects the transposition of two dimensions, each representing a major division among analysts. The horizontal continuum represents the ideologically based distinction between liberals who favor government intervention that will enhance the lives and well-being of the needy and conservatives who seek to limit such official public sector activity to that minimal amount which is absolutely necessary. The vertical dimension distinguishes between those favoring incremental and small changes in the social welfare system and those who seek radical and fundamental reforms. Although there is an almost infinite variety of viewpoints represented in Figure 9.1, four major types predominate.

Type I *(liberal-incrementalist)* regards an expanding social welfare pol-

REFORM TYPE	IDEOLOGY	
	Liberal	Conservative
Incremental	I *Evaluates* programs as sound and aimed at the needs of the poor but underfunded. *Prescribes* more funds, federal controls, reorganization, more equitable procedures.	II *Judges* programs to be overambitious, overfunded, corrupt, fraud-ridden but some welfare program is necessary. *Prescribes* less money, better management, serve the real needs.
Radical	III *Assesses* the programs as patronizing, degrading to poor, as serving needs of status quo. *Prescribes* total reform, ending the current bureaucracy, support redistributive programs.	IV *Evaluates* programs as too much intervention, costly, socialistic, disincentive to work. *Prescribes* "negative" income tax as incentive to work, more efficient, less corruption.

Figure 9.1. Social Welfare Policy Perspectives.

icy arena as both necessary and desirable. The policy thinker holding this viewpoint would, however, believe that social welfare programs tend to be underfunded and sometimes arbitrarily or carelessly administered. Thus, the liberal-incrementalist would have a positive and expansive attitude toward welfare policies but remain critical of mismanagement and inequities in its implementation. On the other side of the issue, the Type II *(conservative-incrementalist)* perspective sees social welfare policies and programs as a necessary evil that must be continuously scrutinized and modified in order to minimize the waste, fraud, and corruption that accompanies them. This latter group would suggest minimal aid, efficiently administered programs, and as little expansion of public welfare programs as possible.

Type III analysts would take a *liberal-radicalist* orientation and perceive social welfare policies as desirable, but not in their current form. For this group, current policies do not serve the needs of the poor and needy, but rather those of the governing elite who favor the status quo. From a Type III view, only a radical change in social welfare policies would be acceptable. The same can be said for Type IV *(conservative-radicalist)* analysts, except they regard public sector social welfare as unnecessary as well as undesirable. For them too, the system needs to be completely restructured with emphasis placed on private sector incentives to meet the needs of the impoverished and needy.

It is obvious that a policy analyst's perspective will influence his or her assessment and conclusions on social welfare policies. However, as we stated in the preceding chapter, it is extremely important to distinguish between describing the impact of a policy accurately and applying value criteria to that consequence. Political rhetoric and analysis such as that presented in Figure 9.1 rarely makes that distinction. In the section that follows, we illustrate the consequences of several different programs through the use of analytical models that try to separate descriptive impact analysis from judgment.

MODELS FOR EVALUATING SOCIAL WELFARE POLICIES

There is no overarching social welfare policy in the United States. As policy thinkers we are all faced with a bewildering array of programs, policies, regulations, and agencies, each serving some purpose linked to the economic and social well-being of groups within the society. Because of the overlapping aims, inconsistent purposes, and contradictory methods of these policies, it is virtually impossible to assess social welfare policy as a whole, although politicians and commentators do attempt such evaluations regularly.

Although we cannot reach a conclusion about the impact of welfare policies in the aggregate, it is worthwhile to take a brief look at the range of policies and level of expenditures that make up this national effort. Table 9.1 lists the major components of federal social welfare policy, the level of expenditure, and the number of recipients, all categorized by the type of transfer. These classifications—dollars, recipients, and transfer mechanisms—represent the consequences of social welfare programs, although as yet we have not chosen a scale by which to assess the meaning of these figures. The importance of these programs to the nation is, however, easy to see: the total amount of funds expended equals 40 percent of all government expenditures and 25 percent of the population is involved in one or more of these programs. The table also reveals the great variation in scope and funding of these policies, which contributes to our problem of assessment. The levels of funding range from the over $100 billion distributed through the Social Security System (OASDHI) to the relatively small budget line ($245 million) of the Legal Services Corporation. Some of the programs such as food stamps serve a wide range of clients while others like black lung benefits (for coal miners) are available only to a designated group.

We should also note the different mechanisms for transferring resources from the government to recipients, for variations in the use of these mechanisms will also influence the consequences of social welfare policies. These are described in Box 9.1.

Table 9.1 Major Categories of Social Welfare—1978 Benefits (Selected Federal Expenditures)

Program	Benefits Paid (in millions)	Beneficiaries
1. Cash Assistance		
Social Insurance		
OASDHI	$59,818	22,000,000
Unemployment Insurance	10,016	2,350,000
Black Lung Assistance	281	592,000
Railroad Retirement	594	2,417,000
Public Assistance		
AFDC	10,800	10,800,000
SSI (Aid to Blind, Disabled)	6,400	4,300,000
Veteran's Benefits	10,000	5,000,000
2. In-Kind Assistance		
Food		
Food Stamps	5,165	15,200,000
School Programs	2,300	30,000,000
Meals for the Elderly	38	NA
Education		
Basic grants	1,588	1,864,000
Work Study	458	853,000
Loans	1,959	1,085,000
Housing	4,887	3,000,000
Health		
Medicare (elderly)	29,000	27,000,000
Medicaid (poor)	11,900	21,000,000
3. Indirect Assistance (selected programs)		
Manpower programs	4,200	
Aid to elementary and secondary schools	5,800	
Legal Services Corporation	243	

Source: U.S. Department of Commerce, Bureau of the Census, *Statistical Abstract of the U.S., 1980.*

BOX 9.1

The principal and most obvious way to help the poor is through *cash transfer* programs. Social insurance programs like Social Security and unemployment insurance send benefits in the form of cash to recipients. Payments to the blind and disabled citizens as well as AFDC clients are also cash transfers. These distribution systems are easy to understand, simple to administer, and relatively easy to measure through the totaling up of payments.

A far more difficult technique to understand or to audit is the *in-kind* transfer, involving assistance in commodities or services with some legally determined cash value. Welfare programs involving the direct provision of foods, clothing, or other goods were once the major form of aid in most of the United States. Today, however, in-kind transfers include food stamps exchangeable for groceries, vouchers for housing, provision of public housing, and school breakfast and lunch programs. All of these transfers are given a stated value for the purposes of budgeting; however, this value may be arbitrary, unrealistic, or inflated for political or economic reasons. A prime example of such attempts to set "value" is found in the public housing program's efforts to stimulate new construction of apartments for the poor. Housing authorities may establish a market value of $650 per month rent for units in a building to be constructed by a private developer with a goverment loan at low interest rates although comparable apartments are available in the same neighborhood for $350 per month. The artificially high value of the apartments in the new building serves as an incentive to encourage developers to engage in construction of needed units, since the bulk of the rent for each apartment will be paid by the government itself. The families who live in the units pay only a regulated percentage of their incomes, say $75 per month. Furthermore, "in-kind" transfers allow for almost no client preference, so that the value of the aid is really much lower in the eyes of the recipient who may have been able to make greater use of a cash transfer. Clearly, many public housing projects are not located in the neighborhood tenants would prefer nor are school lunches planned at the request of the students. This "don't look a gift horse in the mouth" attitude reflects, in part, the old punitive philosophy for assistance.

A third type of benefit program closely related to in-kind transfers is based on the provision of *direct services*. The government has provided free legal services to the poor through laywers whose salaries are paid by the government. Frequently these legal service attorneys become advocates for the poor in such areas as tenant rights, usury cases, and unfair contracts. A much larger direct services program was instituted to provide health care for the poor through Medicaid. Although the doctors and hospitals have been paid by the government for their services, the patients have not been required to make any kind of co-payment for medical services or certain appliances (e.g., as eyeglasses) supplied with the program. Like other direct services programs, Medicaid services are difficult to limit since the demand for medical care seems to be constantly increasing due to technological advances as well as the actual needs of the population.

The fourth type of benefits we may call *human capital* or *social investment* programs. Included in these are manpower or job-training programs and educational programs such as Head Start or Basic Educational Opportunity Grants. These programs provide intangible benefits such as skill or level of competence to the recipient, usually through locally established and administered programs. Sometimes the benefits are actually provided through a tuition check or job-with-pay for the recipient.

Finally, we can classify some transfer programs as *community benefits*. The community action programs, which originated during the War on Poverty, were supposed to enhance the political strength of the poor in local communities by funding community organizers and training for the poor. Such "politicizing" efforts generated great opposition from local mayors and have been replaced by categoric and block grants, which pass through the local general government and enable cities to improve neighborhoods, expand mass transit, or build recreational facilities.

See W. Joseph Heffernan, *Introduction to Social Welfare Policy* (Itasca, IL: F.E. Peacock, 1979); Robert H. Haveman (eds.), *A Decade of Federal Anti-Poverty Programs* (New York: Academic Press, 1977); and Robert D. Plotnick and Felicity Skidmore, *Progress Against Poverty* (New York: Academic Press, 1975).

Our analytic problem is to choose which consequences of social welfare policies to study, to specify the most important dimensions of those consequences, and to choose proper scales of measurement (or models) for analyzing policy consequences. Given the broad scope and range of social welfare policies in the United States, we will limit the analytic task by focusing on five specific programs or policies and applying our tools to the consequences of each.

Neighborhood Youth Corps

Aimed primarily at high school age youth, the Neighborhood Youth Corps (NYC) was created as part of President Johnson's War on Poverty Program. Its main purpose was to provide jobs for high school youths after school until graduation.[6] According to this preventative philosophy, these employed young people would learn appropriate job skills and attitudes as well as earn enough money to meet their economic needs. The primary purpose of the program was to incresae the graduation rate of students who might otherwise drop out of school for economic reasons. The federal government shared most of the administrative costs of the program with local government or community sponsors while the actual wages were paid in part by private employers.

With such clearly stated purposes and using a relatively simple strategy, a combined model of *effectiveness* and *efficiency* seems most applicable to see whether the program achieved its goal at an acceptable cost level. (However, as we see below, a *cost-benefit* scale proves much more relevant.) Recalling the characteristics of the effectiveness and efficiency scales of measurement from Chapter 8, we need to define the goal or stated intention of the policy, specify the outcomes we will measure, and keep our focus on policy performance relative to the outputs of government. In the case of the Neighborhood Youth Corps, we know that the stated intention was to increase the graduation rate of disadvantaged youth. We need to investigate the degree to which the program achieved its goals relative to the costs incurred.

One study of the Neighborhood Youth Corps applied such an effectiveness/efficiency model to the consequences of the program as it operated during the years 1965–1967.[7] To measure the degree to which the program achieved its primary and secondary goals (its effectiveness), the study compared the educational achievements and participation in the labor force after high school of two groups of young people, participants in the Neighborhood Youth Corps and a control group of those who did not participate. The study also calculated the relative cost (efficiency) of the program to the federal government, to the private sector, and to the participants themselves in terms of leisure time lost (opportunity costs). In terms of overall effectiveness and efficiency, the results were mixed. Study data show that there was no improvement in the rates of graduation for youth in the program compared to those who did not participate. The probability of graduation for both groups was almost identical.

Nevertheless, the Neighborhood Youth Corps did make a difference in the prospects for employment and earnings after graduation. The comparison between the two groups showed that program participants earned an average of $831 more in the year after graduation than did nonparticipants. Although the difference in taxes paid by the two groups was not significant, the NYC participants had an average of 2.3 months less time out of the labor force. The researchers concluded that, given the cost of the program and the estimated social benefit from labor force participation after graduation, "in monetary-economic terms, the in-school and summer NYC, taken as a composite, has been an efficient social investment." But here "efficiency" was actually defined in *cost-benefit* terms. This is a particularly useful dimension to study because the goals were so clearly stated. In terms of benefits, the program sought to provide a particular education benefit—increasing time in school in order to enhance earnings potential after graduation. The study found that while the goal of improving chances of graduation was not achieved (i.e., the program had low effectiveness relative to its stated goals), participation did confer significant benefits in terms of employment and earnings opportunities. Furthermore, the study noted that program participants' enthusiastic endorsement of the program may have contributed to better work attitudes later on. Finally, there may have been an intangible benefit in keeping youth occupied during the politically volatile summers of the 1960s, although there is no way to measure this aspect of the program.

The application of efficiency measures to the Neighborhood Youth Corps revealed some interesting results. If the consequences of this policy are considered in terms of the primary goal of the program—an increase in the number of students graduating from high school—then the program is probably not an effective nor entirely efficient way to achieve this purpose. However, if we look at a wider range of benefits, including the post-program behavior of participants and certain unmeasurable benefits like attitudes, then the Neighborhood Youth Corps measured well on cost-benefit and, indirectly, on efficiency scales. This analysis illustrates the importance of specifying what achievements are to be considered and how an expansion of the list of goals to include unexpected or intangible benefits can change both the model being used and the final assessment of consequences.

Legal Services Corporation

Like the Neighborhood Youth Corps, the Legal Services Corporation (LSC) provides indirect benefits to the poor in America. Where the NYC attempts to improve the chances of poor youth through an investment in their skills, the LSC provides government-paid legal representation and advice to the poor to help enhance their quality of life. LSC is a government corporation founded in 1975 to replace the Legal Services Program (LSP) and to give that antipoverty program a permanent, less political status for the future. The original program, enacted in 1965, sponsored lawyers who could give legal counsel on such matters as divorce, leases, and personal finances to impoverished individuals.

The roots of the LSP/LSC program were three-fold: (1) the assumed social obligation of the various state bars who had always recognized a need to serve those who could not afford legal help; (2) a tradition of privately supported legal aid offices often founded to help specific immigrant communities; and (3) the services of social reform groups like NAACP to help individuals defend their civil rights. Although the goals of the program were never clearly articulated, it is clear that it was originated to meet the needs of several groups: the poor, social reformers, and the lawyers themselves. To assess the consequences of this program, particularly in relation to the demands and needs of these specific groups, it is appropriate to use a *social test* model. This model examines the extent to which policy consequences satisfy the interests of designated groups in society. Whether the policy is implemented in such a way as to meet the expectations of those social, economic, or political interests is the primary question.

Like many programs created in response to interest group pressures, the original Legal Services Program had multiple objectives. One of its primary goals was to provide legal counsel for those too poor to pay for such services. The members of local bar associations supported this goal because it met their professional obigation to society and tended to increase litigation for the local area, potentially making their own practice more lucrative. If the increase in the number of clients over the first decade is any indication, the program was quite successful in meeting its goal of providing legal services. The number of clients increased from 350,000 in 1967 to over 1.3 million within the first ten years of operation; participating lawyers spent between 75 and 90 percent of their time on casework.[8] Furthermore, Legal Services lawyers spent a substantial amount of their time in court or dealing with government agencies on behalf of their clients. The caseload per laywer was so great that one of the criticisms leveled at the agency was that there were too many unresolved or open cases per lawyer. If we consider the needs of the professional bar, the private practice lawyers, or the clients, it seems that the LSP/LSC met the social test criteria well.

Another group to be considered is the poor population of the United States as a whole. Although the LSP/LSC lawyers may have served a large number of clients, can we say that the needs of the poor population were being met? Unfortunately the program was not large enough nor geographically distributed in such a way as to reach many of the poor. In 1975 the estimated number of people defined as impoverished was about 29 million; however, only 12 million lived in areas where they might have had access to an LSP/LSC agency. The rural poor were not being served, and it was not economically feasible to establish offices in rural areas. If the social test is based on the overall needs of the poor, then legal services did not meet the challenge.

Finally, we might consider the degree to which the legal services programs met the demands of social reform groups. Many early supporters of the program saw the establishment of these offices as providing the impetus for legal reform. The job of the lawyers was to litigate on behalf of classes of people and thereby to bring change in the legal status of the poor. Such litigation and activity on behalf of the poor should have led to reforms in tenant rights, criminal and civil rights, employment discrimination, and a host of other matters in which the poor did not have the same legal advantages of other citizens. Because there was no agreed upon definition of legal reform (nor was it politically acceptable for the national office to decide how much legal reform work should be done by each local office), it is very difficult to measure the performance of the agency in this area. To the reformers who hoped that law reform would actually move classes of people out of poverty, it is clear that the LSP/LSC program was not successful. Some of the more idealistic supporters and employees have been disillusioned by the ability of state legislatures or government agencies to work around legal decisions or to reverse gains through new legislation.

Supporters who sought to improve the availability of legal services to the poor because it was the equitable thing to do would see the attainments of the program as fairly successful although limited by problems of funding and distribution. Finally, those reformers who felt that the provision of quality legal services to the poor with some legal reform as a side benefit was the goal of the agency would see the program as having met the social test. Like other measures and models, we see that the way in which goals are defined is crucial to the outcome of the application of the model.

One of the reasons why it is difficult to draw a conclusion about LSP/LSC using the social test measurement model is because the program evolved without clear direction or stated objectives. We can see why the social test scale is hard to apply if we look at the *sequential consequences* of the program. The actual policy *output* can be measured in the number of lawyers hired, the cases processed, the funds expended for salaries and office staffs, the number of clients served, and precedents established. Considering that there was no federally funded legal program for the poor in the early 1960s and that clients numbered over 1.3 million by 1975, we can say that the outputs of the program added a new dimension to the legal system.

The *performance* of the program is a different kind of consequence. This is where the debate over "casework" versus "law reform work" becomes important. Assessing the actual performance of the poverty lawyers in terms of program objectives is, as we have seen, problematic because different groups adopted widely varying objectives for the program. Assessing the performance of the legal services agencies also includes assessing the administrative services provided by the national office, the degree to which funds were wisely used, and the way in which clients were treated. As noted above, the *outcomes* of the policy can be viewed in many different ways, depending on the goals of the groups involved. It seems clear that the program did not really alleviate poverty for many people, although it did provide a new consciousness of the rights of the poor.

Within the context of the outcomes of the LSP/LSC program, it is also useful to consider another dimension of consquences: *indirect* or *direct effects*. The direct effect of legal services was help with leases, tenant suits, tax appeals, unemployment insurance claims, divorces, child support agreements, and the establishment of certain civil rights. Rarely was there a verdict in a major court case or a law that was the direct result of the program, although many class action suits were filed and won. It may be that the LSP/LSC did not get credit for its work or, more likely, that many other political and legal forces combined to bring about changes in the legal system. This perspective leads us to consider the indirect effects of the policy. The whole judicial system has become more aware of the rights of the poor in recent years and more legislation has been written making class action suits possible. These developments may in part be traced to a consciousness that the poor and other classes (e.g., the handicapped and women) have legal needs as a group. Another effect has been the willingness of governmental agencies, such as housing authorities and welfare departments, to consult legal services staffs before instituting regulations in order to avoid litigation. On the individual level, some commentators suggest that clients with experience in the legal system become more competent on their own behalf and safeguard their own rights. Finally, an indirect effect of the program on the private sector is an awareness on the part of business, landlords, and others that the poor have legal rights and some power to defend their position.

Finally we can consider the *feedback* to the policy as a consequence. Obviously, some of the law reform work of the agency caused heated opposition from private sector lawyers, from local administrators, and from public officials both at the state and national levels. Attempts have been made to regulate or constrain the reform efforts of the agency. When the program became a government corporation, for example, the legislation required permission of the local director for filing class action suits, limited representation of juveniles, and prohibited any cases involving abortions. Since 1975 these restrictions have been tightened and loosened several times in response to the demands of various political and social groups; however the overall benefit of offering legal services is widely accepted. We see, therefore, that the degree to which policy consequences measure up to social test criteria is related to which consequences—output, performance, outcome, or feedback—are being examined as well as whether the emphasis is on direct or indirect effects.

BOX 9.2

The "poverty lawyers" were often described in Congressional debates and conservative rhetoric as a cross between Communist conspirators and misguided social reformers. Often they were compared to muckraking consumer advocates such as "Nader's raiders" or to the civil rights workers of the 1950s for their methods, demographic characteristics, and motivations. This often unflattering portrait of young, white, upper middle class intellectual activists added heat to debates over the purposes and organization of the agency. Recent studies have shown that there was a real gap between the perceived nature of this agency and actual character of its personnel. The poverty lawyers were young but not drawn from elite schools. Rather than serving a missionary year and leaving, most served for at least 4 years, leaving for other public service work. They were also criticized for being "too white" and "too male" to adequately serve the needs of the clientele. Although the data shows that the lawyers were overwhelmingly white male (74%) this proportion is far less than the proportion in the population of all attorneys, which is 96% white male.

Income Maintenance Programs

Both state and federal governments have enacted policies using cash payment transfers to alleviate the circumstances of poor people. The policies of the federal government are the most varied, extending from payments for the blind and disabled and reimbursing the states for Aid to Families with Dependent Children to the Social Security payments "earned" by retired Americans. Cash transfer programs are an excellent example of policies that can be judged by the scale of *effectiveness* as well as illustrating the difficulties of applying this model. Effectiveness scales measure the degree to which a given policy achieves the stated goal of the policy; the principal focus of the model is on the stated intention or goal of the policy. The primary problems of applying such scales are those of identifying the goals of the policy and of actually measuring policy outcomes.

Up until the early 1960s, the goal of most governmental transfer policies was *alleviative*—to improve the quality of life for the poor to the extent that their survival was assured and (with the help of social casework) help them correct the problems that made them poor. The poor were considered to be deserving of charitable efforts, but the responsibility for ending their condition rested with the poor themselves. With the inception of the War on Poverty in the mid-1960s, the federal government adopted the goal of ending poverty in our society in 10 years through a combination of rehabilitative, preventative, alleviative, and redistributive programs proposed by the Johnson Administration. With the adoption of this goal, new notions of effectiveness were adopted; we could measure or count the number of people in this country whose incomes fell below the "poverty line" and then, after transferring income to these families, count the number of people remaining below this imaginary line. As we have seen, some of the programs associated with the War on Poverty were not effective or did not receive enough funding to have much effect on ending poverty. By the mid-1970s many of the antipoverty programs had changed from idealistic crusading agencies to client-oriented service agencies, and the War on Poverty had officially ended. However, the ideal of the War—to end poverty in the United States—seemed to have become a permanent goal of government policy. The expansion of Supplemental Security Income (SSI) programs to include more people, the extension of Social Security benefits to persons who had contributed less than the minimum requirement, the expansion of Medicare and Medicaid programs, and the many proposals to pass some sort of guaranteed income program all symbolize the commitment of the federal government to using cash transfers to lift individuals and families out of poverty.

Literally hundreds of studies have been conducted to measure the effectiveness of these cash transfer programs. Not surprisingly, the conclusions often vary because analysts have defined the scale of goal attainment very differently. To begin our review of these disparate evaluations, we will examine the concept of poverty. Any measurement of the social welfare programs must start with an acceptable definition of the characteristics of poverty so that we know how many poor people there are.

First, a choice must be made between an absolute and a relative poverty line. Some observers argue that in a very materialistic culture such as the United States, only a relative definition of poverty makes sense. For instance, if, at a certain time period, the standard of moderate middle class life includes one car, a single family residence, kitchen appliances, and a television, then those persons who cannot achieve a certain proportion of that quality of life feel "poor" and perceive themselves to be outside of the mainstream of life.[9] Determining the relative level of poverty raises nearly insurmountable problems, since it would vary by the region of the country, degree of urbanization, and, most importantly, by choice of components of being "well-off."

An alternative (and widely accepted) method of measuring poverty is based on a survival index, which recalls old theories of alleviative welfare. The poverty line is fixed at three times the cost of a food budget for a family, with variances for life style (urban or rural), size of family, etc. This index is based on a "market basket" of food products judged to provide a nutritious but low-cost diet for individuals and is adjusted as inflation increases food costs for all shoppers. Obviously, this absolute poverty line emphasizes the obligation of society to help the poor survive, not to raise their income to a level comparable to that of the non-poor. The advantages for this method of computing poverty are its sensitivity to inflation, its comparability over time, and its capability to identify what proportion of persons are "poor" each year and thus show what progress has been made in reducing poverty.

Given a definition of poverty as family income, we can proceed to examine the various analyses of the impact of social welfare programs. The first 10 years of income maintenance programs have been extensively documented.[10] In 1964, 36 million persons, or about 19 percent of the population, had incomes below the poverty line, while by 1973 only 11.1 percent of the population were poor. The cash assistance programs alone have taken 44 percent of the pretransfer poor out of poverty. *In absolute terms,* then, the first decade of social welfare programs reduced the number of poor individuals by a considerable degree. However, if we consider the growth in per capital income and consumption during that period, the relative position of the poor vis-á-vis the rest of the population may not have improved much at all. Another study calculated the value of in-kind assistance such as food stamps and housing aid to poor families. This analysis shows that the impact of in-kind aid, together with cash assistance, reduces the official poverty gap (the amount of dollars estimated to bring all the rest of the post-transfer poor above the poverty line) by half.[11]

BOX 9.3

If we shift the scale of judgment from money income measured against the poverty line to one that examines the distribution of all income in the United States, the effectiveness of the welfare programs is subject to even more controversial findings. In a 1975 article titled "The Stability of Inequality," economist Kenneth Boulding suggests that there has been no real progress toward income quality in the United States since 1950. His calculations suggest that the lowest one-fifth of the population has received about 6−7 percent of the aggregate income of the U.S. over this time period, with virtually no change in its share. There has also been very little change for those persons and households who are in the top fifth of the population. He concludes that it is easier for the rich to save than the poor and that inheritances are the major source of maintaining inequalities.

The same critique of the overall distribution of wealth and income in society has been made by other economists. The redistribution of income on a more equal basis is clearly a topic with enormous implications; however the argument of these analysts does call attention to the fact that income maintenance programs and in-kind transfers do not, and are not intended to, end the existence of poverty. Rather the programs are mostly alleviative strategies that enable the poor to live at a minimally acceptable level.

In direct contrast to the perspective of Boulding is the critique of Edgar K. Browning. In his controversial analysis of the effects of social welfare programs, he finds that the income "distribution has become dramatically more equal in recent years as a result of egalitarian policies." Browning adds up all of the federal outlays for cash assistance and other types of transfers to the poor and finds that the total federal transfer per poor person in 1973 averaged $1139. For a family of four, the total combined transfers would equal about $4500 dollars, a figure above the 1973 poverty line of $4250. He asserts that the reason that we cannot claim more success in the war against poverty is that, by definition, poverty is calculated only on cash income; therefore a certain number of families will always fall below the line. However, between 1964 and 1973, the amount of in-kind transfers per poor person increased from $42 to $657 (by 1464 percent) and these are not counted in deciding the extent of poverty. By adjusting the income figures for sectors of society in terms of income, benefits, minus taxes, etc., Browning finds significant changes in the overall distribution of income since 1952. Although their share of net income has increased very slowly, he attributes an enhanced position of the poorest segments of the population to wider distribution of education and earning potential, to in-kind transfers, and to increases in leisure time for the lower income groups. Browning, like those analysts who find no change in distribution, does not assert that overall wealth is being redistributed in society, although he does see the attainment of education as increasing potential for individuals and families.

See Kenneth Boulding, "The Stability of Inequality," *Review of Social Economy,* 33 (April, 1975), pp. 1–14; Lester Thurow, *Generating Inequality* (New York: Basic Books, 1975); and Edgar K. Browning, "The Trend Toward Equality in the Distribution of Net IIncome," *Southern Economic Journals,* 43 (July, 1976), pp. 912–923.

MODELS FOR EVALUATING SOCIAL WELFARE POLICIES   243

Further problems in determining the impact of the overall set of social welfare programs are introduced if we consider that many in-kind transfers are overvalued in terms of what the recipients might desire. For example, we noted earlier how rents are set at an artifically high rate in public housing projects for various accounting purposes and, therefore, the value assigned to that housing as an in-kind transfer is much higher than either the market value of the housing or the price the tenant family thinks it is worth. Alternatively, most calculations of income exclude not only in-kind transfers but the value of real property or other sources of income. In part, this accounts for the number of elderly poor who may own their own homes but still have poverty level retirement incomes. Even discounting these nagging problems in accounting, we might conclude from the work that uses the official poverty line as its scale that social welfare programs have removed a substantial number of individuals and households from poverty.

We can also look at the subgroups within the population who have received cash transfer payments to see which groups have benefited the most or the least from these policies. The question of who benefits from such welfare policies is one of the most controversial to be considered in the public arena because there is a great difference between the actual and perceived beneficiaries of the programs. Many opponents of welfare or of public spending focus on the perceived consequences of cash transfer programs as the target for their anger. They often suggest that the welfare program is a massive fraud in which cash is paid out to "welfare queens" or able-bodied men who drive new Cadillacs. Most Americans believe that welfare recipients are able-bodied adult citizens and that the population being aided the most is predominantly black.

Many of the problems associated with planning an effective antipoverty program are more easily understood if we look at the actual recipients of cash assistance programs. As Table 9.2 shows, there have been some changes in the demographic characteristics of the poor since 1965 but several facts are outstanding. First, almost 40 percent of the persons who are poor live in households with a white male as its head while 28 percent have white females heading the families. Because whites are the majority population in the United States, it is true that by 1972 only 6 percent of the households headed by a white male were poor but that is still an enormous number of families. On the other hand, while households headed by a nonwhite female account for only 20 percent of the poor families, the incidence of poverty among all such households is 57.4 percent. Other data indicate that 20 percent of all poor households are headed by a person over 65 years of age and that almost 30 percent of all very young households (with the head less than 23) are in poverty. We find, therefore, that the typical poor person is probably very young or very old, lives in the South, and is white. From the perspective of the individual, the person who is most likely to find herself in

Table 9.2 Persons in Absolute Poverty According to Race and Sex of Head of Household (in percentages)

	White Male	Nonwhite Male	White Female	Nonwhite Female	All
Composition of the poor					
1965	48.0	20.1	18.6	13.3	100
1972	39.1	13.5	27.5	19.9	100
Incidence of poverty					
1965	9.5	35.8	31.9	66.2	15.6
1972	6.1	19.5	29.7	57.4	11.0
Composition of total population					
1965	79.0	8.8	9.1	3.2	100
1972	76.6	8.2	11.0	4.1	100

Source: Robert D. Plotnick and Felicity Skidmore, *Progress Against Poverty, A Review of the 1964–1974 Decade* (New York: Academic Press, 1975), p. 89.

poverty is the black female with responsibility for a family, particularly if she is under 30.[12] Given this portrait of the poor, cash transfer programs can effectively move families out of poverty if recipients are older and have fewer needs for housing, clothing, etc. Cash transfers at the alleviative level can do little to move families with young children and a single parent who is responsible for their care to any other status.

BOX 9.4

One of the solutions proposed for the entire social welfare program is a *guaranteed income program* or *negative income tax*. The consequences of such a program include: considerable freedom for the recipient to choose his or her lifestyle, reduced administrative costs and casework interference in the person's life, and enough security to encourage savings and life planning for the poor so that they can eventually change their status. This is only a brief summary of the reasons given to support such a plan. The major ideological objection to a guaranteed income is that it is redistributive in its essence and frankly recognizes an obligation for the wealthier segments of society to provide cash for the poor, whether they contribute to productivity or not. A more bureaucratic objection is that the poor need services and in-kind transfers as well as income and that social services (and a bureaucracy of caseworkers) is absolutely necessary for these people to triumph over disadvantage. However, the guaranteed income plan, which was first introduced by Nixon and defeated in 1973, has been subjected to several studies. The results of the tests confirm some of the hypotheses about the behavior of the poor and also suggest unintended consequences that are unsettling even to the plan's supporters. Some of the studies showed that the poor were encouraged to save for large purchases and to plan for their futures when their income was guaranteed and they had discretion on how to spend the payments. However, even if the income was paid to households with both husband and wife present, and no penalty was assessed for being unemployed, the guaranteed income seemed to encourage the break-up of households and the establishment of more female-headed households. To quote Senator Moynihan, "the experiments seem to indicate that there is a pronounced increase in maritial instability in families that have the more comprehensive guaranteed-income arrangements. . . ." Other unexpected results cited by the Senator included a reduction in hours worked by all adults involved, and a positive change in the attitude of women toward work. What seems to have happened in the experiments was the coinciding of the "independence" effect of a guaranteed income with the movement toward more equality for women, and more acceptance of the working mother. These unintended consequences of the guaranteed income experiments undoubtedly have reduced the probabilities of such a system being adopted in the near future. However, these consequences also call attention to the difficulty of predicting how human behavior will be altered by social policy, and mitigate against any kind of radical reforms.

See U.S. Congress, Joint Economic Committee, "How Income Supplements Can Affect Work Behavior," *Studies in Public Welfare, No. 13,* 1974. Daniel Patrick Moynihan, interviewed in *Fortune* (December 4, 1978), p. 144.

Food Stamps

The Food Stamp program originated in 1964 after urging by Presidents Kennedy and Johnson. Local communities and states could either participate in the new program or a program for the distribution of surplus commodities to the poor. The policy has always been intended to provide a more stable market for farm commodities as well as helping the poor attain a better diet. By 1967, evidence of malnutrition and widespread hunger, particularly in several Southern states, triggered new concern for the poor.

The Food Stamp program was authorized to provide free food stamps for the very poorest households and allowed a family of four to purchase up to $100 in food stamps. The amount that the household was required to pay varied with the income received by the family. The program was made mandatory for all communities in 1973, coverage extended to many new recipients, and eventually the purchase requirement was dropped altogether.[13]

The nutrition policies of the United States have always had two purposes: to improve the nutrition of the recipients and to keep up the price levels for American farm producers. Although these two goals make analysis of the total long-term impact of the program difficult, we can concentrate on the social welfare aspects of the program alone. Because the program is generally supported by the agricultural sector of society, the overall goal of the policy—to feed the poorest members of society—is widely accepted. This goal leads us to adopt a *scale of equity* to measure the consequences of the policy so that we can find out whether food stamps have been available to everyone who really needs them (scale of opportunity) and whether different subgroups in society receive equal benefits from the program (scale of distribution).

One of the most telling criticisms leveled against the Food Stamp program was that the neediest families could not take advantage of the benefits because of the purchase requirement. Of all the poor, those who need the help most are the ones likely not to have any cash to purchase stamps, while the recipients who can afford to buy stamps are probably those who have the least need or may be those engaged in fraudulent activities. In 1975, only 50 percent of those eligible for the program actually participated. To address this problem of equity, the 1977 Food Stamp reform bill dropped the purchase requirement so that even the poorest families would receive the stamps.[14]

The impact of the program can also be examined on a scale of distributional equity. In the early years of the policy, many local communities choose not to participate in the program. These communities, primarily located in Southern states, effectively prevented large numbers of the poor from receiving nutritional help. Other questions of distributional equity lead us back to the original intent of the policy. Were Food Stamps intended to alleviate the conditions of the permanently poor, those who could not escape the conditions of poverty through any effort of their own, or those who were temporarily "down and out"? The program was subjected to serious criticism because some of the groups that did receive benefits (e.g., striking workers, workers who were between jobs, college students, and people who evidently had other assets in private property such as expensive cars) were able to benefit from this help while other, needier persons, were not. These problems of distribution were also attacked by new provisions in the 1977 reforms, which tightened requirements for students, the unemployed, and persons with private property.

The reforms passed by Congress in 1977 present another cycle in the continuing history of the Food Stamp program. To understand why the program is constantly under revision and review, it is useful to look at the *temporal* dimension of consequences. As noted above, the Food Stamp program originated in 1964; Table 9.3 shows that the number of recipients was 633,000 and the cost less than $36 million. By 1977, the program had grown to 17.4 million recipients at a cost of $5.4 billion. The size of the program has varied with the changes enacted in eligibility and the purchase requirement. From a pilot project to use up surplus products, policymakers instituted the purchase requirement, made the program mandatory for all communities, expanded the eligibility requirements, and then, in 1977, eliminated the purchase requirement for all recipients. The increase in recipients and funds expended between 1977 and 1980 clearly demonstrates the impact of changing the purchase requirement. The cost of the program in 1979 and 1980 was so much higher than Congressional estimates that the ceiling on expenditures had to be revised each year.

Looking at the vast increase in the Food Stamp program over the 18 years of its existence suggests that either our notions of equity have changed or that it was politically unpopular to admit how much hunger existed in America in the 1960s. Obviously increases in the demand for Food Stamps do correspond to economic recessions and unemployment, but other increases are due to the expansion of eligibility for the program. Politically, as the program was extended to more and more groups and communities—the elderly, the unemployed, young families, rural areas—it has become more difficult to control because the political constituency is so large that members of Congress felt constrained to vote for it. Finally, the program, which is administered by the Department of Agriculture rather than Health and Human Services, has strong backing from senators and representatives from the farm states; thus, the only real opposition to the program can be based on cost alone.

BOX 9.5

In an effort to reduce the expenditures for the Food Stamp program, the Reagan Administration requested large cuts in the program for FY82. The final measure passed the Congress in 1981 was estimated to eliminate one million recipients from the program and to reduce expenditures by at least $1.7 billion dollars in fiscal 1982. The Reagan proposals included a general raising of the standards for eligibility, eliminating benefits for striking workers unless they were eligible before striking, freezing deductions for housing, postponing increases in benefits related to inflation, and eliminating any federal funding for outreach programs which inform people of their possible eligibility for the benefits.

Other efforts to limit the nutritional programs for the poor included the attempt to change the size of school lunches by reducing the size of a hamburger patty and the number of french fries served, increasing the price for school lunches for most school children, cutting eligibility for free breakfasts, and eliminating federal aid to purchase lunchroom equipment for schools.

Housing Allowances

In 1973 the Department of Housing and Urban Development (HUD) funded one of the largest social experiments ever attempted in the United States—the Housing Allowance Experiment. The goal of this trial (which involved more than 25,000 families in 12 metropolitan areas) was to see if giving housing allowances to poor families to spend on better housing would be more cost-efficient than other ways of providing housing for the disadvantaged. The federal government has a long history of policies aimed at aiding individuals from all economic classes to find adequate housing. Upper and middle income groups benefit from the deduction of mortgage interest which lowered income taxes, while lower income individuals qualified for V.A., FHA, or Farmer's Home Administration mortgages at lower than market rates. Although these subsidies to private housing work well for the majority of Americans, none of the federal programs for the poor can be rated so well. In general, public housing projects were criticized for becoming centers of crime, bad management, and hastening the decline of neighborhoods. Furthermore, like Food Stamp programs, studies found that many federal subsidies ended up helping families who were at the upper end of the eligibility range while poorer families received little or no help.[15]

HUD approached the housing allowance program with a number of objectives. First, they were searching for less expensive yet effective ways to provide decent, safe housing to the disadvantaged. Second, the HUD officials sought to establish a program that could cope with existing housing shortages and the deterioration of inner-city housing. Finally, they sought a program that would have no adverse consequences for the overall quantity or cost of housing in a particular market. Clearly, this trial policy was to be

Table 9.3 Federal Food Stamp Program: 1961 to 1979*

				Value of Stamps Issued			Federal Govt. Contribution	
Year (ending June 30)	Number of Participating Areas	Participants[1] (1,000)	Average Monthly Participation (1,000)	Total Retail Value (mil. dol.)	Cost to Participants (mil. dol.)	Total (mil. dol.)	Percent of Total Retail Value	Average Monthly per Participant
1961	6	50	50	1	(z)	(z)	46.1	$7.68
1965	110	633	425	85	53	33	38.0	6.38
1970	1,747	6,457	4,340	1,090	540	550	50.4	10.55
1971	2,027	10,549	9,368	2,713	1,190	1,523	56.1	13.55
1972	2,126	11,594	11,109	3,309	1,512	1,797	54.3	13.48
1973	2,228	12,107	12,166	3,884	1,753	2,131	54.9	14.80
1974	2,818	13,524	12,662	4,727	2,009	2,718	57.5	17.61
1975	3,035	19,197	17,064	7,266	2,880	4,386	60.4	21.41
1976	3,035	17,982	18,549	8,700	3,373	5,327	61.2	23.93
1977, prel.[2]	3,035	18,050	17,058	8,340	3,262	5,058	80.7	24.71
1978, prel.[2]	3,037	15,120	16,044	8,311	3,146	5,165	62.6	26.83
1979, prel.[2]	2,950	19,265	17,710	7,230	[2]745	6,485	([3])	30.51

*(Beginning 1975, includes Puerto Rico, Guam, and Virgin Islands. Data for U.S. are periodically revised; therefore data will not match U.S. totals in table 216)
Z Less than $500,000.   [1]As of end of fiscal year.   [2]For year ending Sept. 30.
[3]As of Jan. 1, 1979, participants were no longer required to pay for a portion of total value.
Source: U.S. Dept. of Agriculture, Food and Nutrition Service. In *Agricultural Statistics*, annual.
Source: Statistical Abstract of the U.S. 1979.

measured on a *scale of costs and benefits*, for the government, for the participant, and for the communities in which it was tried.

The housing allowance program was implemented in 12 different metropolitan areas and designed to allow several different assumptions about the housing market to be tested. Any family of two or more persons or single elderly or handicapped person was eligible to participate in the program if their income fell below a specified limit. The family would receive a housing allowance equal to the difference between the estimated cost of average housing in the local market and one-fourth of the family's income so that they would have the same proportion of their income to spend in housing as the level generally accepted as economically safe for upper income groups. Families involved in the study could spend more or less than the estimated amount for rent, but they had to live in qualified housing, units that were inspected and met certain requirements of plumbing, wiring, and safety. Recipients could choose to fix up their current homes and not move at all.

On an overall measurement of cost alone, the housing allowance program worked very well. At the end of five years, the data showed that the cost per family in the experiment averaged $1150 per year, broken down into $900 in payments and $250 in administrative costs. Comparable figures for other subsidized housing programs were costs of $1650 per family in public housing or rent supplements of $1310 per year. New or rehabilitated units of housing cost over $4000 per year to the government.

To measure the consequences of this housing experiment with regard to its benefits, we need to look at two dimensions of anticipated benefits. First, the government was concerned with the cost versus substantive impact on the housing market in each community where the program was in effect. In two cities, the research focused on the demand for such housing with particular concern for how many eligible families signed up, what choices they made with the money, and their satisfaction with their choices. In another two areas, the experiment was designed to test the impact of the supply of housing by opening the program to homeowners as well as renters and setting no limit on how many families could enroll, thus increasing the supply of dollars for housing in the community.

The results of the demand experiments indicated that the program reached some of the poorest households, including minority families. Most of the families lowered their housing expenses by staying where they were already living and spending some money on repairing the units. The great bulk of the housing allowance went for other family expenses. In general, the participants in the experimental programs were very satisified with the experience and with the housing itself. In the two cities where the supply experiment took place, there appeared to be no effect on the housing costs of the market; in neither city did housing costs increase any faster than either regional or national averages. This finding can probably be explained by the fact that most of the families chose not to move or spend more for rent so the new dollars were injected into the whole economy, not the housing sector.

Other benefits that concerned the planners of the experiment can be discussed as ranging from *tangible* to *intangible*. The goal of the program was to provide better housing to people at less of a sacrifice and at less public cost. To receive the allowances, all of the participants had to live in inspected, qualified housing so that the goal of putting all of the people in better housing was met. However, as noted already, most of the families fixed up their current houses or cooperated with landlord repairs to meet these requirements. A less tangible consequence to be considered is whether the program increased the integration of the cities or moved more poor families into suburban areas. The evidence showed that of the families that moved, most black households went to neighborhoods with lower minority concentrations than their old area. Some families moved from the cities to the suburbs, but small percentages moved from the suburbs back into the central city. In summary, the housing allowances helped those who did move to find better neighborhoods but made very little change in the composition of neighborhoods or the racial mix of surburban areas. Yet it would be misleading to say that there were few intangible benefits, because the most outstanding change was an increase in disposable income and consumer choices for all participating families.

To summarize the costs and benefits of the housing allowance program, we might say that the benefits obtained in terms of better housing and improving the overall lives of the poor were efficiently obtained at the costs cited above. Interestingly, we also note that the benefits planners thought were desired by the poor were not those the poor families chose to obtain.

CONCLUSION

Rather than attempt to apply one scale of impact measurement to the social welfare policies of the United States in the aggregate, we have focused on five specific programs. We have applied scales of efficiency, effectiveness, cost-benefit, social test and equity to the programs and policies. Of course, more than one scale may be appropriate to a particular policy and dimensions other than the ones presented here may be chosen. What is important to articulate is the scale being used in the analysis. The whole domain of social welfare policies illustrates the problems of confusing scales of efficiency and effectiveness or outcomes with outputs. If we look at the outputs of the federal government to fight poverty, for example, there should not be any poor persons left; however if we look at policy outcomes, this has not become the classless society.

ENDNOTES

1. For the historical antecedents of American welfare policies see: Walter I. Trattner, *From Poor Law to Welfare State* (New York: The Free Press, 1974); Frances Fox Piven and Richard A. Cloward, *Regulating the Poor* (New York: Random House, 1971); and Samuel Mencher, *Poor Law to Poverty Program* (Pittsburgh: Universiity of Pittsburgh Press, 1967).
2. See, for example, George Gilder, *Wealth and Poverty* (New York: Basic Books, 1981).
3. *Congressional Quarterly Weekly Report* (April 29, 1978), p. 1065.
4. *Congressional Quarterly Weekly Report* (May 2, 1977), p. 851.
5. For examples of liberal and conservative, radical and incremental reforms, see Mark D. Worthington and Laurence E. Lynn, Jr., "Incremental Welfare Reform: A Strategy Whose Time Has Passed," *Public Policy*, Vol. 25 (Winter, 1977), p. 49; "Controversy Over Carter Administration Proposals," *Congressional Digest* (May, 1978); and Barry Friedman and Leonard J. Hausman, "Welfare in Retreat: A Dilemma for the Federal System," *Public Policy*, Vol. 25 (Winter, 1977), pp. 25–79.
6. Henry Levin, "A Decade of Policy Developments for Improving Education and Training for Low Income Populations," in Robert H. Haveman (ed.), *A Decade of Federal Anti-Poverty Programs* (New York: Accademic Press, 1977), pp. 123–88.
7. See *ibid.*, and Gerald Somers and Ernest Stromsdorfer, "A Cost Effectiveness Analysis of In-School and Summer Neighborhood Youth Corps: A Nationwide Evaluation," in David Nachmias (ed.), *The Practice of Policy Evaluation* (New York: St. Martin's Press, 1980), pp. 67–79.
8. The statistics on the Legal Services Corporation and views on legal reform are based on Ellen Jane Hollingsworth, "Ten Years of Legal Services for the Poor," in Haveman, *A Decade of Federal Anti-Poverty Programs*, pp. 285–314.
9. For discussion of poverty lines, see Robert D. Plotnick and Felicity Skidmore, *Progress Against Poverty* (New York: Academic Press, 1975); Harrell R. Rodgers, Jr., *Poverty Amid Plenty* (Reading, MA: Addison-Wesley, 1979), pp. 93–103; and Diana Appelbaum, "The Level of the Poverty Line: A Historical Survey," *Social Science Review* (September, 1977), pp. 514–523.
10. Laurence E. Lynn, Jr., "A Decade of Policy Developments in the Income Maintenance System," in Robert H. Haveman (ed.) *A Decade of Federal Anti-Poverty Programs*, p. 89.
11. Cited in ibid., p. 95.
12. These probabilities are calculated by Plotnick and Skidmore, *Progress Against Poverty*, pp. 97–105.
13. Lynn, "A Decade of Policy Developments in the Income Maintenance System," pp. 75–77.
14. Congressional Quarterly Inc., *Congress and the Nation, Vol. 5, 1977–1980*, (Washington, DC: 1981), pp. 681–685.
15. Bernard J. Frieden, "Housing Allowances: An Experiment that Worked," in *Policy Studies Review Annual*, Vol. 5, Irving Louis Horowitz (ed.) (Beverly Hills, CA: Sage Publications, 1981), pp. 476–496.

KEY TERMS
Absolute Poverty Line
Alleviative Programs
Cash Transfer Programs
Community Benefits Programs
Conservative-Incrementalist Views
Conservative-Radicalist Views
Direct Services Programs
Guaranteed Income Programs
Human Capital/Social Investment Programs
Income Maintenance Programs
In-kind Transfer Programs
Liberal-Incrementalist Views
Liberal-Radicalist Views
Negative Income Tax
Preventative Programs
Punitive Programs
Rehabilitative Programs
Relative Poverty Line
Social Welfare Policy

CHAPTER 10

Policy Thinking and Policy Analysis

WHERE TO GO FROM HERE

We began this exploration of policy thinking by noting how pervasive and problematic public policies are. In subsequent chapters we developed a problem-solving approach to policy thinking and introduced you to the basic analytic tasks of policy description, policy explanation, and the study of policy consequences. With this background you should have some understanding of what it takes to comprehend what governments do and say. As an interested and aware citizen, you should now possess the capacity to think clearly about public policies.

For many people, however, being an aware citizen may not be enough. For some, policy thinking of the sort introduced here is just a beginning. For a variety of personal and professional reasons, you or one of your classmates may find it desirable to go beyond a citizen's understanding of public policy toward a career in public policy analysis or in a field where more sophisticated analytic tools and techniques are commonly used.

What are the vocational opportunities open to policy analysts? As we will see in this chapter, there are at least four options. A key factor in knowing these options is to remember that *all* policy thinking is a form of problem solving. What varies among different policy thinkers are the nature of the problems they face, the motivations underlying their efforts, the principal approaches or methods they use in their problem-solving endeavors, and the kind of training they need to develop as "good" policy analysts.

THE ROOTS OF MODERN PUBLIC POLICY ANALYSIS[1]

To get a clear picture of the career options available to policy thinkers, it would help to know about the intellectual development of the policy analysis field. The flurry of scholarly and professional activity termed public policy analysis is a recent development within the social sciences. Its newness is characterized by Dwight Waldo as resembling a situation where a young person has found a first job and is now seeking a career. Yet, in its period of relative youth, the study of public policy has achieved a great deal and continues to demonstrate considerable promise. Shaped by events from the Great Depression to campus rebellions of the late 1960s and early 1970s, public policy analysis recently began to provide form and direction to the very disciplines that created it. In the process it is changing not only university curricula but the methodology and content of certain disciplines and career opportunities for many aspiring policy thinkers.

Among social scientists in general the traditional focus in policy analysis has been on the institutions and processes of public policymaking rather than on public policies themselves. Studies that actually focused on public policies, that is, those that regarded them as the primary subject of concern, evolved slowly within the social sciences as reactions to several major developments over the past fifty years. The most important of these forces were the Keynesian revolution in economics during the 1930s and 1940s, the development of what Harold D. Lasswell labeled "policy sciences" during and immediately after World War II, the adoption of quantitatively sophisticated budgeting techniques by the federal government during the 1960s, and the impact of the campus rebellions of the late 1960s and early 1970s on academic social science.

The Keynesian revolution was instrumental not only in justifying public sector intervention in the economy but also in establishing a foothold in government for the first professional analysts of public policy. In the United States these economic analysts were eventually institutionalized as the Council of Economic Advisors in an attempt to put specialized advice "at the President's elbow."[2]

The creation of the Council in 1946 also drew on the acceptance policy analysts achieved during World War II. Many psychologists, sociologists, and public administrators had been mobilized during the war effort. Some of these research directions in the policy sciences continued after the war and became institutionalized in private "think tanks" such as RAND and, in public sector, research and development agencies established in a number of federal departments.[3]

The work of the policy sciences, together with some innovations in private corporate management techniques, brought new budgeting approaches to the federal government in the 1960s. The programming-planning-budgeting (PPB) process introduced by Robert McNamara to the Department of Defense (and mandated in 1965 for all agencies) shifted the focus of most government organizations from operational and personnel concerns to decisions about agency goals and objectives. Public budgeting, in short, went from the realm of the accountant to that of the policy analyst.[4]

A fourth major force producing the current interest in public policy analysis emerged from the turmoil of American university campuses during the 1960s and 1970s. Cries of "irrelevance" and accusations that scholars were serving only the "establishment" led to a renewed interest in the real impact of government policies, particularly from a critical, if not radical, viewpoint.[5]

All of these influences, plus various improvements in scientific and rational decision-making techniques, led to the adoption of policy analysis in many sectors of public life. As a direct consequence of these developments, the number of individuals calling themselves public policy analysts grew in number, until today we have what can best be described as a diverse and growing corps of social scientists who identify with the field. What is even more significant is that the field developed into a variety of endeavors, each sharing the label, public policy analysis. To understand the different branches of the public policy analysis tree that emerged from unique historical roots we must turn to a discussion of the various reasons for pursuing public policy analysis as a vocation. From these motives we can get a sense of the different options open to policy thinkers who wish to do more than merely satisfy their responsibilities as citizens.

MOTIVES, METHODS, AND TRAINING

Political scientist Austin Ranney provided a partial response to the question of what motivates policy analysts when he took note of three fundamental reasons for studying public policy: scientific, professional, and political.[6] Here we examine those three as motivational perspectives and add an additional motivating viewpoint to round out Ranney's study.[7] From this classification of policy analysis roles we can speak to the question of what makes one policy analyst use one approach while another uses a different methodology.

Scientific Reasons

According to Ranney, there are policy analysts who believe their studies "will add significantly to the breadth, significance, and reliability of . . . a special body of knowledge."[8] From this point of view, the prototypical policy analyst is a scientist, that is, a person involved in "basic research" who is "restrained, dispassionate, conservative, and willing to suspend belief, pending more evidence."[9] Such an individual is a "policy analyst" in Thomas R. Dye's sense of that title: one engaged in a search for the causes and consequences of policies who has a concern for "explanation rather than prescription," who undertakes with "scientific rigor" the analysis of policies, and who makes an "effort to develop and test general propositions . . . and to accumulate reliable research findings of general relevance." Thus, scientific policy analysis is accomplished to discover what policies are and why they are, but *not* what they ought to be. In short, policy analysis for the scientist is not policy advocacy.[10]

What are the implications of this approach? For the policymaker they are significant, since the study of public policy for scientific reasons can prove a frustration to decision makers. In a critique of policy analysis, Dye discusses several basic conflicts between "decision-oriented" policymakers and "theory-oriented" (i.e., scientific) policy analysts. Underlying these differences is the belief that whereas the policymaker seeks "guides for effective government action" the policy analyst (as scientist) "seeks to test and develop theories about the causes and consequences of public policy."[11]

For those who teach policy studies, this scientific approach would mean stressing the importance of social science methodologies and other techniques related to systematic research. The student would learn the logic of empirical inquiry, its capabilities, its limits, and how it is applied. In addition, the scientific study of public policies would mean training in the proficient use of theory-building research methods and the analytic frameworks associated with them. In short, to be a "scientific" policy analyst is to learn the discipline of basic research. It is to seek the accumulation of knowledge for knowledge's sake. For some, the task of scientific investigation also includes critical analysis.[12] In either case the curriculum developed with such purposes in mind would reflect an emphasis on scientific methodology, with practical policy concerns playing a secondary role.

Professional Reasons

Some individuals study public policy in order to improve it. As one author puts it, although the scientific approach represents the study *of* public policy, there are those concerned with studies *in* public policy.[13] Ranney describes this approach as the study of public policy which seeks the application of "scientific knowledge to the solution of practical problems."[14] Policy improvement is the end, and the application of expert "policy knowledge" is the means. In the post-World War II period, Harold D. Lasswell called for development of "policy science," believing that from relevant studies in certain fields there will emerge an approach that "will bring about a series of 'special' sciences within the field of social sciences, much as the desire to cure has developed a science of medicine . . . distinct from, though connected with, the general science of biology."[15]

The need for (and design of) a policy science profession has received a great deal of attention in recent years.[16] Even more significant is the fact that applied policy research has become a major component of government programs at all levels in the United States. This occurred through what economist Alice M. Rivlin terms a "quiet revolution" wherein policy analysis became "part of the decision process" and the policy analyst an accepted "participant at the decision table."[17] The indication of the impact of this revolution is found in a 1974 survey of federal agencies conducted by the General Accounting Office, which uncovered a 500 percent increase in expenditures for professional policy research (specifically program evaluations) between 1969 and 1974.[18] A similar expansion in the use of professional analysts is evident at the state and local levels, where policy analyses are used extensively to assess program effectiveness and improve administrative productivity.[19]

The ever-increasing role of professional policy analysts in government has neither gone unnoticed,[20] nor lacked critics.[21] Nevertheless, one can approach the study of public policies from the professional perspective, and a curriculum structured along these lines would seek to provide students with the background necessary to develop policy science skills. Here, as in the scientific approach to policy analysis, there would be a strong concern for methods of scientific investigation. However, the tools and techniques of "professionals" will differ from the basic research of the "scientists." The stress is increasingly on applied research. Thus, from the professional perspective, policy analysts should be able to specify their goals and the values sought. It is also crucial that they be capable of (1) effectively defining and diagnosing policy problems, (2) proposing policy alternatives, (3) developing models that can aid in the achievement of desired ends and methods for testing those models, (4) establishing intermediate goals, and (5) estimating the feasibility of various policy programs.[22]

The overall objective of the professional policy analyst is to serve the policymaking system with either policy-issue knowledge (i.e., information about a substantive policy matter, such as defense or health care) or policy-making knowledge (i.e., dealing with the organization and operation of the structures and processes for formulating, implementing, and evaluating public policies).[23] In summary, a basic introduction to public policy analysis for the professional would necessarily emphasize the evaluative and instrumental functions of policy studies and focus on how analysis could be used to improve public policies or the policymaking system.[24]

Political Reasons

For others the function of public policy analysis is to provide a basis for advocating a particular policy position perceived as "right" and politically warranted. Ranney and Dye are both critical of this perspective, regarding such political work as unscholarly, since it is seemingly highly subjective and (as they see it) a misapplication of the social scientist's role.[25] There are others, of course, who believe that policy analysts have fulfilled such political functions in the past, and have done it well. This is a point made by Daniel Patrick Moynihan, who points out that until recently the task of social scientists who were asked for advice on policy matters was to justify a given position. Policy analysis was frequently political, not professional. Its task was giving credence to certain policy positions, not challenging them.

> Advocates of social change, especially to the degree that they base their advocacy on normative grounds, are naturally disposed to be impatient, to ask that remedies be as near as possible immediate. So long as social science was essentially asked to certify that the normative grounds were justifiable, its task was relatively simple, and it could be sure to be invited back for the next round of certification. But once it was asked to actually implement—forthwith—the normative imperative, it is up against a very different matter indeed.[26]

Despite controversy over the value of undertaking policy studies for political reasons, an argument can be made that the contemporary study of politics and policies has its roots in the teaching of rhetoric,[27] and that political policy analysis follows in a long tradition of political rhetoric, which develops supportive evidence on behalf of specific policy positions.

Teaching policy analysis for political reasons would involve the development of fundamental research skills and instruction in the rhetorician's methods of rationalization and argumentation. Work and training based on this approach would focus on substantive issues and their effective presentation. And since there is often "no better offense than a good defense," the student of political policy analysis would also be adept at critical thinking and capable of responding to those who oppose a preferred position. At the heart of this approach is the primary objective of neither discovering nor applying policy-relevant knowledge, but rather convincing others of the correctness of one's position on an issue.

Administrative Reasons

In addition to Ranney's original three reasons for studying public policy, a fourth can be added. It is taken for granted that those who are called upon to carry out a policy ought to comprehend it. Ideally, they should try to understand the policy, the intent of those who passed it, and the various means available for implementing it. Their objective should be to administer the policy both efficiently and with the greatest effectiveness. To do so, they should become policy analysts.

Herbert A. Simon has taken this point even further by noting that "administrative processes are decisional processes: they consist in segregating certain elements in the decisions of members of the organization, and establishing regular organizational procedures to select and determine these elements and to communicate them to the members concerned." Following this line of thought, "correct" administrative decision exists when the "appropriate means" are used "to reach designated ends. The rational administrator is concerned with the selection of these effective ends."[28] In other words, the effective implementation of public policy or any other set of goals given to administrators depends on the policy analytic capabilities of the administrator. Understanding a policy, being able to divide it into its component parts, and developing appropriate strategies to achieving the ends as stated are the keys to rationality in administrative decision making and the source of concern among implementors for the task of public policy analysis. In their attempt to achieve higher levels of rationality, many administrators do, in fact, undertake a special form of policy analysis.

By the early 1960s, government agencies throughout the United States were incorporating basic cost-benefit policy analysis into many of their administrative decisions to help the bureaucracy meet is objectives at the lowest possible cost. In the years that followed, systems analysis and PPB came to the foreground as a means for fitting the policy objective to "suit available resources." We entered the period of program budgeting, where the administrative analyst began to determine both the ends and means of policy, that is, the "best" objectives and the appropriate combination of resources to be used in their achievement. Aaron Wildavsky traces this development in an essay highly critical of the administrative analyst. According to Wildavsky, the administrator moved quietly from technician (benefit-cost analysis) to analyst (systems analysis) to policymaker (program budgeting) during this period, and in the process many "political" aspects of policymaking became irrelevant and thus ignored.[29]

Regardless of the implications, administrative policy analysis has become quite sophisticated in recent years, especially as incorporated into budget and management techniques. A course on policy analysis for administrators would focus almost exclusively on the latest tools available for improving the efficiency of policy implementation, from OR (operations research) and PERT (performance evaluation and review techniques) to critical path method and PPB. It would stress the application of microeconomic analysis to questions of policy choice, and promote the use of simulation, gaming, and automatic data processing where possible in the implementation process. In short, administrative policy analysts would be well trained in contemporary management science,[30] and the curriculum written for them would be in that field.

PERSONAL POLICY ANALYSIS

Within the broad range of approaches generated by these four reasons for doing public policy analysis are found the four major career options open to policy thinkers who want to go beyond the basics outlined in this book. However, the fact that there are those who think of public policy as a vocation or with a high level of sophistication should never be permitted to discourage those who think about public policies for purely *personal reasons*.

The *personal policy analysis* endeavor differs from the scientific in seeking available information and clarification rather than new "truths" and in having as its objective the facilitation of personal choices rather than the accumulation of knowledge. Like professional policy analysis, this personal approach makes use of many techniques and whatever knowledge is available; yet however much the end products of both professional and personal types of analysis may resemble each other, the objectives differ substantially. Professionals are technicians who work to solve the problems of their clients. The utility of policy analysis for citizens is found in the capacity it gives them to reach tentative solutions to some of the basic policy related problems. Where the professional seeks to find and apply appropriate knowledge (knowledge that is scientifically credible and technically reliable), citizens seek insight and some comprehension that allows them to understand and reflect upon (and perhaps even participate in) ongoing policy debates.

Nor is the personal approach the same as the political. Politicians study and apply policy analysis to maximize the possibility that the values and priorities they support or represent will be accepted. What they look for are methods by which to rationalize and obtain the adoption of particular policy positions. But, although those undertaking policy analysis for personal reasons may value one policy position over another, their primary objective is to understand the problems policies confront and the value of alternative courses of action being considered. Policy analysis for personal reasons is not policy advocacy; it is not necessarily political, although it may become a factor in personal political acts like voting.

And obviously it is not the same as administrative policy analysis, at least not unless the citizen is specifically concerned with the efficiency of policy implementation and is seeking to understand the policy execution process. The techniques of administrative policy analysis are often very sophisticated, and to apply methods such as benefit-cost analysis is difficult enough for the trained public administrator, let alone the concerned citizen. Nevertheless, individuals who undertake policy analysis for personal reasons ought to familiarize themselves with the concepts underlying the policy analysis of management science, if for no other reason than to know its capabilities and limitations.

The point is that personal policy analysis is an important endeavor. We ignore our education in it only at the risk of becoming less capable citizens—that is, less able to contend with those pervasive and problematic things governments do and say.

THE PROBLEMATIC FOUNDATIONS

We have argued throughout this book that thinking about public policy was similar to problem solving. We can now return to that basic theme to complete this book for it is the differences among policy analysts concerning the nature of public policy problems that distinguishes each approach from the scientific to the personal. It is a fundamental irony that public policies are simultaneously sources of solutions and causes of problems. Public policies are responses to human needs that have become public issues. In that sense they are solutions to problems—reactions to some particular dilemma faced by government officials. Yet public policies are themselves generators of dilemmas, and not only for government decision makers. Put briefly, if one quality pervades all public policy, it is its problematic nature.

This quality has its impact on public policy analysis. For, from each perspective we have discussed thus far, public policy takes on a distinctive problematic character, depending on the way it is approached. Scientists, for example, regard policies as *theoretical problems*. That is, scientists view public policy, its causes and consequences, as a challenge to the accumulation of knowledge and the development of a scientifically credible and empirically warrantable theory of that phenomenon. Their objective is to predict consistent patterns of public policy with some certainty. For scientific analysts it is the unexplained and unpredictable which is at the heart of the problem of public policy. It is a gap in social science knowledge they seek to fill, and the creation of a credible theory is their primary objective.

For professional analysts, those who seek to apply the scientific approach to public problems, policies are *design problems*. They want to apply the credible theoretic knowledge at their disposal to the improvement of current or future policies. Thus, they are often involved in the dissemination of relevant information used to facilitate improved policy choices; but even more crucial are their attempts at helping to recognize the structures and procedures through which public sector decisions are made. For professionals the problems of public policy design are twofold: deciding which policies are "best" (i.e., optimal for the task at hand), and determining which policy-making mechanism will result in the selection of the optimal choice from among several alternatives. In either case the problems they contend with ultimately stress the development and organization of a better policymaking system, one that applies rational and empirically warranted knowledge to the making of public sector decisions.

The political policy analyst considers policy statements and actions as *problems of value maximization*. They seek, for either themselves or others, the adoption and institutionalization of a specific set of priorities. At times this means seeking changes in current policy priorities; at other times it calls for a defense of the status quo. In this view public policies pose problems as either objectives to be achieved or barriers to be overcome. The political analyst fights for a set of values, and the analysis undertaken for this purpose reflects that goal.

Administrative policy analysts face problems of a different sort, for, as policy implementors, their objective is to carry out the designs and priorities given them by legislators or other decision makers. While in practice these analysts deal with design and value maximization problems, their primary focus is on public policies as *problems of application*. Ideally, their objective is to carry out efficiently and effectively the programs of government that have been authorized, to apply them as intended by the policymakers, and to enforce relevant sanctions and incentives where necessary. Developing the right organization and procedures for accomplishing these tasks is at the center of the administrative analyst's concern.

Although all of these perspectives on public policy problems are important, they are the concerns of relatively few individuals. Of greater importance is the fact that public policy statements and their ramifications become a part of every person's life. Thus, public policies are *problems of contention* for the general public, and we all deal with these problems differently. Whatever the course of action we choose, we do live (and must deal) with public policies. Who we are makes a difference. However, public policies are part of our lives whether we are black or white, Christian or Jew, laborer or banker, scientist or administrator, professional or politician.

Table 10.1 summarizes the relationship between these problem orientations and the various approaches to public policy analysis. In each case, the perceived problem follows from the analyst's motivation, and this in turn conditions the approaches taken and the training received. What are the implications of this view? It is evident that the field we call public policy analysis is so diverse that it would be impossible to summarize, let alone

Table 10.1

Type of Policy Analyst	Public Policy Problem	Motivation	Approach	Relevant Training
1. Scientist	Theoretic	Search for theory, regularities, "truth"	Scientific method, objectivity, pure analytics	Basic research methods, canons of social science research
2. Professional	Design	Improvement of policy and policymaking	Utilization of knowledge, strategic	Strategic; benefit-cost analysis; queuing, simulation, decision analysis
3. Political	Value maximization	Advocacy of policy position	Rhetoric	Gathering "useful" evidence; "effective" presentation
4. Administrative	Application	Effective and efficient policy implementation	Strategic, managerial	Strategic; same as profesional with stress on those talents useful in implementation
5. Personal	Contention	Concern for policy impacts on life	Mixed	Use of many models and techniques from other approaches; less sophisticated

learn it in its entirety. What you have learned in this book, however, should provide a foundation for developing your ability as a personal policy analyst or a basis for further study that might someday provide you with the career in public policy analysis.

ENDNOTES

1. Much of the following was first presented in Barbara A. Bardes and Melvin J.Dubnick, "Motives and Methods in Policy Analysis," in *Improving Policy Analysis*, Stuart S. Nagel (ed.) (Beverly Hills, CA: Sage Publications, 1980), pp. 101–127.
2. Walter H. Heller, *New Dimensions of Political Economy* (New York: Norton, 1967), Chapter 1.
3. Harold D. Lasswell, "The Policy Orientation," in Daniel Lerner and Harold D. Lasswell (eds.), *The Policy Sciences* (Stanford, CA: Stanford University Press, 1951), p. 4; also see Irving Louis Horowitz and James Everett Katz, *Social Science and Public Policy in the United States* (New York: Praeger Publishers, 1975), especially Chapter 2.
4. For background, see Leonard Merewitz and Stephen H. Sosnick, *The Budget's New Clothes: A Critique of Planning-Programming-Budgeting and Benefit-Cost Analysis* (Chicago: Rand McNally College Publishing, 1971); Ida R. Hoos, *Systems Analysis in Public Policy: A Critique* (Berkeley, CA: University of California Press, 1972); and Robert H. Haveman and Julius Margolis (eds.), *Public Expenditures and Policy Analysis*. Chicago: Markham, 1970), especially parts four and five; Fred S. Hoffman, "Policy Expenditure Analysis and the Institutions of the Executive Branch," in Haveman and Margolis, p. 242; and Alice M. Rivlin, *Systematic Thinking for Social Action* (Washington, D.C.: Brookings Institution, 1971), especially Chapter 1.
5. For instance, see the work of the Union for Radical Political Economics, which was established in 1968. Specifically, see Richard C. Edwards, Michael Riech, and Thomas E. Weisskopf (eds.), *The Capitalist System: A Radical Analysis of American Society*, 2nd edition, (Englewood Cliffs, NJ: Prentice-Hall, 1978); also see Alvin W. Gouldner, *The Coming Crisis of Western Sociology* (New York: Avon, 1970); Charles A. McCoy and John Playford (eds.) *Apolitical Politics: A Critique of Behavioralism* (New York: Harper & Row, 1967); Marvin Surkin and Alan Wolfe (eds.), *An End to Political Science: The Causcus Papers* (New York: Basic Books, 1970); Philip Green and Sanford Levinson (eds.), *Power and Community: Dissenting Essays in Political Science* (New York: Vintage Books, 1970); and George J. Graham and George W. Carey (ed.), *The Post-Behavioral Era: Perspectives on Political Science* (New York: David McKay, 1972).
6. "The Study of Policy Content: A Framework for Choice," in Austin Ranney (ed.), *Political Science and Public Policy* (Chicago: Markham Publishing Co., 1968), pp. 3–21. In his categorization of reasons, Ranney is using Don K. Price's "four estates" classification originally presented in *The Scientific Estate* (Cambridge, MA: Belknap, 1965), pp. 122–135.
7. As will become evident as we consider each of these reasons, the categories applied here are far from exhaustive. In fact, there are several important reasons

not even mentioned. For example, some policy analysts are coerced into their tasks, as is the student who must complete an assignment involving policy analysis under threat of receiving a poor grade if it is not done or not done well. There are other analysts who do it "for financial" reward. Although these reasons are related to those briefly discussed under the category of "personal," they are quite different and, therefore, do not receive specific consideration.
8. "The Study of Policy Content," p. 13.
9. Martin Rein and Sheldon H. White, "Can Policy Research Help Policy?" *Public Interest*, 49 (Fall 1977), p. 135.
10. Thomas R. Dye, *Understanding Public Policy*, 3rd edition (Englewood Cliffs, NJ: Prentice-Hall, Inc., 1978), pp. 5–8. A related point is expressed by Elliot Feldman, "Analysis is the product of science, and science is not and cannot be prescriptive." See his "An Antidote for Apology, Service, and Witchcraft in Policy Analysis," in Phillip M. Gregg (ed.), *Problems of Theory in Policy Analysis* (Lexington, MA: Lexington Books, 1976), p. 19. Some scholars hold that even if policy analysis could have prescriptive value, it ought not to take on such a role. See Kenneth M. Dolbeare, "Public Policy Analysis and the Coming Struggle for the Soul of the Postbehavioral Revolution," in Green and Levinson (eds.), *Power and Community*, pp. 85–111; also Theodore J. Lowi, "The Politics of Higher Education: Political Science as a Case Study," in Graham and Carey (eds.), *The Post-Behavioral Era*, pp. 11–36.
11. The source for much of this discussion is Dye, *Policy Analysis: What Governments Do, Why They Do It, and What Difference It Makes* (University, AL: University of Alabama Press, 1976), pp. 15–19.
12. Although Feldman, Dolbeare, and Lowi (see n. 10) regard the scientific, nonprescriptive endeavor of policy analysts as primary, they would argue against an approach that did not involve critical analysis of current policies, proposed solutions to policy problems, or social conditions which are incorrectly approached by government. In this sense they are not quite so "objectively" scientific as Dye seems to advocate.
13. Jacob B. Ukeles, "Policy Analysis: Myth or Reality?" *Public Administration Review*, 37 (May/June 1977), p. 224.
14. Ranney, "The Study of Policy Content," p. 15.
15. Lasswell, "The Policy Orientation," pp. 8–10.
16. Lasswell continued to write on behalf of this idea; see *A Pre-View of Policy Sciences* (New York: American Elsevier, 1971). Also see the work of Yehezkel Dror, especially *Public Policymaking Reexamined* (Scranton, PA: Chandler, 1968) and *Design for Policy Sciences* (New York: American Elsevier, 1971).
17. *Systematic Thinking for Social Action* pp. 3–4. Since writing those words, analyst Rivlin was appointed to head the new Congressional Budget Office, where she played a major role in the decision process.
18. Cited in Rien and White, "Can Policy Research Help Policy?" p. 119.
19. See Selma J. Mushkin, "Policy Analysis in State and Community," *Public Administration Review*, 37 (May/June 1977), pp. 245–253.
20. Nor unstudied. See Arnold J. Meltsner, *Policy Analysts in the Bureaucracy* (Berkeley, CA: University of California Press, 1976).

21. See Rein and White, "Can Policy Research Help Policy?"; Feldman, "An Antidote for Apology, Service, and Witchcraft in Policy Analysis"; and Dolbeare, "Public Policy Analysis and the Coming Struggle for the Soul of the Post-Behavioral Revolution." Also interesting in this regad are comments in Ukeles, "Policy Analysis: Myth or Reality?" and Rivlin, *Systematic Thinking for Social Action.*
22. These suggestions for training objectives are drawn from Duncan MacRae, Jr., "Policy Analysis: An Applied Social Science Discipline." *Administration and Society,* 6 (1975), especially pp. 376–380.
23. This distinction is drawn from Dror, *Public Policymaking Reexamined,* p. 709.
24. Dror, *Design for Policy Sciences,* p. 102; details of the suggested curriculum are found in that work on pp. 103–111. Also see Lasswell, *A Pre-View of Policy Sciences,* Chapter 8.
25. See Ranney, "The Study of Policy Content," p. 18; and Dye, *Understanding Public Policy,* pp. 7–8.
26. "Liberalism and Knowledge," in Daniel P. Moynihan, *Coping: On the Practice of Government* (New York: Vintage Books, 1973), p. 263. Moynihan's views on policy analysis and the role of social science in policy arenas are discussed by Marvin Surkin in "Sense and Non-Sense in Politics," in Surkin and Wolfe (eds.), *An End to Political Science,* pp. 18–21.
27. See J. Peter Euben, "Politics, Piety, and Profession: The Ethics of Teaching Political Science," paper presented at annual meeting of American Political Science Association, Washington, DC, September 1977.
28. Herbert A. Simon, *Administrative Behavior: A Study of Decision-Making Processes in Administration Organization,* 2nd edition (New York: Free Press, 1975), pp.8, 61.
29. Aaron Wildavsky, "The Political Economy of Efficiency: Cost-Benefit Analysis, Systems Analysis, and Program Budgeting," in Ranney (ed.), *Political Science and Public Policy,* pp. 55–83.
30. For a discussion on this point, see Nicholas Henry, *Public Administration and Public Affairs* (Englewood Cliffs, NJ: Prentice-Hall, 1975), Chapter 6.

KEY TERMS
Administrative Policy Analysis
Application Problems
Contention Problems
Design Problems
Keynesian Revolution
Personal Policy Analysis
Policy Sciences
Political Policy Analysis
Professional Policy Analysis
Scientific Policy Analysis
Theoretical Problems
Value Maximization Problems

For Further Reading

Students interested in pursuing the study of public policy will not have any difficulty finding relevant material. In this short bibliographic essay we suggest some titles that might be useful in that regard. These books, however, are only a starting point where readers can begin their exploration of what governments do and say.

We relied quite heavily on Moshe F. Rubinstein's *Patterns of Problem Solving* (Englewood Cliffs, NJ: Prentice Hall, Inc., 1975) and it would be difficult to find a better introduction to problem solving in general. Two of the more challenging dimensions of problem solving are conceptualization and working with models. James L. Adams' *Conceptual Blockbusting: A Guide to Better Ideas,* 2nd edition (New York: W.W. Norton and Co., 1979), is a useful aid for those needing help in "prying loose" from everyday concepts and perspectives. On models and their use in studying social phenomena, Charles A. Lave and James G. March, *An Introduction to Models in the Social Sciences* (New York: Harper and Row, Publishers, 1975) provides an excellent foundation for the beginning student.

Those who wish to explore more sophisticated forms of policy analysis will find that there are a number of good books to help them on the road to understanding the field. An interesting starting point is a critique of social science research and how it can contribute to social problem solving. In *Usable Knowledge: Social Science and Social Problem Solving* (New Haven: Yale University Press, 1979), Charles E. Lindblom and David K.

Cohen argue that those involved in social science research—and this would include policy analysts—rely much too heavily on the information and methodologies of professional social inquiry and that they must take a broader approach if their work is to contribute to solving social problems. Aaron Wildavsky's *Speaking Truth to Power: The Art and Craft of Policy Analysis* (Boston: Little, Brown and Co., 1979) also explores the nature of policy analysis as problem solving. Both volumes provide students with skeptical yet more realistic views of the potential and limitations of applying knowledge to policy questions.

On general methodologies used in advanced policy analyses, students will find William N. Dunn, *Public Policy Analysis: An Introduction* (Englewood Cliffs, NJ: Prentice Hall, Inc., 1981) and E. S. Quade, *Analysis for Public Decisions*, 2nd edition (New York: North Holland/Elsevier Science Publishing Co., 1982) to be excellent introductions. Edith Stokey and Richard Zeckhauser, *A Primer for Policy Analysis* (New York: W. W. Norton and Co., 1978) is another basic textbook in the field which students will find useful as an introduction to policy analysis methods. On a more advanced (but still introductory) level is Stuart S. Nagel's *Policy Evaluation: Making Optimum Decisions* (New York: Praeger Publishers, 1982). The student should be aware of two biases in all these works. First, they are focused on the practical methods and tools of policy analysis and therefore promote and depend on the development of a reader's quantitative capabilities. Second and more significantly, they are highly prescriptive and strategic in their assumptions about policy analysis. For each volume, the primary and explicit purpose of policy analysis is to make better public decisions. To see how these methods and tools are applied at the administrative level, see Grover Starling, *The Politics and Economics of Public Policy: An Introductory Analysis with Cases* (Homewood, IL: The Dorsey Press, 1979), and Richard D. Bingham and Marcus E. Ethridge (eds.), *Reaching Decisions in Public Policy and Administration: Methods and Applications* (New York: Longman Inc., 1982).

There are also several useful introductions to evaluative methods applied in policy analysis that are far less prescriptive in nature. David Nachmias' *Public Policy Evaluation: Approaches and Methods* (New York: St. Martin's Press, Inc., 1979) is an easy-to-understand textbook and can be supplemented with his edited book of readings, *The Practice of Policy Evaluation* (New York: St. Martin's Press, Inc., 1980). The focus of Nachimas' textbook and reader are on policy *impacts*.

There are many other authors who concentrate on policy *processes*, particularly policy decisionmaking and program implementation. Fred M. Frohock's *Public Policy: Scope and Logic* (Englewood Cliffs, NJ: Prentice Hall, Inc., 1979) offers a unique survey of the various dimensions useful in examining public policymaking. Walter Williams and his colleagues initiate readers into the methods of assessing program implementation in *Studying Implementation: Methodological and Administrative Issues* (Chatham, NJ: Chatham House Publishers, Inc., 1982).

Obviously, most students of public policy will be ordinary citizens and therefore interested in knowing about and understanding substantive issues. For them there are several relevant books. To understand public policy, one must be knowledgeable of the policymaking processes that are involved. Two interesting books in this regard are James E. Anderson's *Public Policy-Making*, 2nd edition (New York: Holt, Rinehart and Winston, 1979) and Charles O. Jones, *An Introduction to the Study of Public Policy*, 2nd edition (North Scituate, MA: Duxbury Press, 1977). Among books that attempt to both describe and explain government activities in understandable, yet insightful ways, the following stand out:

- James E. Anderson, David W. Brady, and Charles Bullock III, *Public Policy and Politics in America* (North Scituate, MA: Duxbury Press, 1978).
- Clarke E. Cochran, et al., *American Public Policy: An Introduction* (New York: St. Martin's Press, Inc., 1982).
- Kenneth M. Dolbeare, *American Public Policy: A Citizen's Guide* (New York: McGraw-Hill Book Co., 1982).
- Thomas R. Dye, *Understanding Public Policy*, 4th edition (Englewood Cliffs, NJ: Prentice Hall, Inc., 1981).
- Robert L. Lineberry, *American Public Policy: What Government Does and What Difference It Makes* (New York: Harper and Row, Publishers, 1977).
- B. Guy Peters, *American Public Policy: Process and Performance* (New York: Franklin Watts, 1982).

Students interested in specific policy areas or issues will usually have no difficulty in finding relevant titles in the citations of these books and similar works. Another useful source of such information are the quarterly issues of the *Policy Studies Journal* and *Policy Studies Review* which contain bibliographies on a variety of topics.

There is no lack of material for the student wishing to pursue policy studies. In addition, as the value and practice of policy thinking becomes more important and commonplace, we can expect the list of information sources to expand both in volume and scope of coverage. The growth in policy studies material is an interesting phenomenon, for it reflects two relatively recent developments. First, it results from technological breakthroughs in information storage, retrieval, and communications that characterize modern American society. Second, it reflects the increasing attention

Americans are paying to public policies as they realize both its pervasiveness and problematic nature. Thus, while technology is more capable of supplying relevant information, the public is becoming more demanding in its need to know about government activities. As more Americans develop the capacity to think about public policies, that demand for information will increase still more. Given current trends, there will be no lack of information. The real problem might be for the analyst to keep up with it all.

INDEX

Adams, James L., 25n, 268
Afghanistan, 191, 193
Agenda, 7
Agriculture Department, 216, 247
Agricultural policies, 61, 81, 128, 190, 216, 245–246
Airline regulation policies, 127, 136
Air Quality Act (1965), 208
Alliance for Progress, 183, 185
Allison, Graham T., 25n, 164, 175n, 202n
Allocative policies, 64–65
Almond, Gabriel A., 86n, 200n, 201n
Analogies, *see* Models
Analytical decision-making model, 168–169
Anderson, James E., 10n, 270
Anti-ballistic missile system (ABM), 166
Antitrust Division, Department of Justice, 115
Antitrust policies, 115, 125–127
Appelbaum, Diana, 252n
Arms race, 200
Arrow, Kenneth J., 97
Assignment, and policy description, 60
Associational policy explanations, 151–152
Atomic Energy Commission (AEC), 22
Authoritative-command mechanisms, 92–93
Automatic stabilizers, 112, 150
Automobile emissions, 208, 211
Automobile industry, 121–122, 123, 143n, 208
Automobile safety impact studies, 212–213

Bailey, Kenneth, 85n
Balance of power models, 187–188
Bardach, Eugene, 167
Bardes, Barbara A., 265n
Bargaining model, 171-172
Barnet, Richard J., 201n
Bauer, Raymond A., 25n
Bay of Pigs, 197, 199
Beier, Helen, 201n
Bell, David V. J., 174n
Belth, Marc, 53n, 54n
Benefit-cost analysis, 260
Bentley, Arthur, 25n, 158
Berlin Airlift, 184
Bertalanffy, Ludwig von, 54n, 55n
Bingham, Richard D., 269
Black lung disease, 8
Blake, David, 201n
Blinder, Alan S., 25n
Bohr, Neils, 38
Bose, Arun, 176n
Boulding, Kenneth E., 54n, 55n, 85n, 142n, 241–242
Bounded rationality, 171
Bowles, Samuel, 9n
Brady, David W., 270
Braybrooke, David, 175n, 176n
Brown, Susan Love, 139n
Brown v. *Board of Education*, 69, 84

273

Browning, Edgar K., 242
Bruck, H. W., 163, 175n, 202n
Brzezinski, Zbigniew, 195
Budgets, as descriptive analysis, 78–80
Bullock, Charles III, 270
Bundy, McGeorge, 195
Bureaucratic decision-making, and foreign policy, 198
Burns, Arthur F., 141n
Burtt, E. A., 29, 30
Business Week editors, 137–138, 140n
Butler, Eamonn F., 143n

Calhoun, John C., 158
Canada-U.S. relations, 191
Capitalist policies, 99–101
  assumptions of, 100–101
Carey, George W., 265n, 266n
Carr, Edward Hallett, 184–185
Carter, Jimmy, 21, 113–114, 228
Caspary, William R., 201n
Central Intelligence Agency (CIA), 194, 198
Charlesworth, James C., 25n, 176n
Chase, Richard X., 140n
China-U.S. relations, 69, 75, 187, 190, 195
Chunking, 31
Churchman, C. West, 32–33
Civil Aeronautics Board (CAB), 127
Civil Rights Act (1964), 21, 84–85
Civil rights policy, 21
Classification, and policy description, 59–60
Clausen, Aage R., 86n
Clean Air Act Amendments (1970), 208, 211
Cloward, Richard A., 252n
Club of Rome, 44–48
Cobb, Roger W., 10n
Cochran, Clarke E., 270
Cohen, David K., 268–269
Cold War, 38, 185
Collender, Stanley E., 87n
Collins, James M., 143n
Computational Strategy model, 168–169
Constituent policies, 71
Consumer Products Safety Commission (CPSC), 135
Control policy, 65–66
  direct *vs.* indirect, 65
  use of sanctions, 65–66
Coplin, William D., 15–16
Copyright laws, as economic policies, 134
Correlations, and policy explanation, 151–152

Cost-benefit models, 214–215
Council of Economic Advisors, 119, 255
Council on Wage and Price Stability (COWPS), 119
Covering law explanations, 147–148, 152–153
  explanandum, 147-148
  explanans, 147-148
  policy variations, 148–153
  statistical, 148
  universal, 148
Crenson, Matthew A., 10n
Crick, Francis, 29, 30
Crisis policies, 72
Critical path method, 260
Cuba-U.S. relations, 23, 165–166, 187, 190
Cuban missile crisis, 22, 61, 165–166, 196–197, 200
Curry, R. L., Jr., 86n
Cybernetics, 39
Cyclical policy, 67–68

Dahl, Robert A., 86n, 90, 109, 138–139n, 157, 174n, 175n, 176n
Davis, Morton D., 176n
Decision-making models, in foreign policy, 197–199
Defense Department, 194–197, 256
Defense policies, 212, 220–221
Descartes, Rene, 29, 30
Destler, I. M., 201n
Dewey, John, 25n
Discontinuous policy, 69
Distributional effects scales, 220–221
Distributive policy, 69–70, 72
Dolbeare, Kenneth, 222n, 266n, 267n, 270
Downs, Anthony, 175n
Dror, Yehezkel, 175n, 176n, 266n, 267n
Drug regulation, impact studies of, 212
Dubnick, Melvin J., 265n
Dunn, William N., 269
Dye, Thomas R., 10n, 25n, 142n, 152, 158, 257, 259, 266n, 267n, 270

Easton, David, 10n, 25n, 40, 154
Economic growth rate, 105–106
Economic policies, 89–145, 150
  antitrust, 115, 125-127
  capitalist, 99–101
  Carter Administration, 21, 119, 142n
  copyright and patent laws, 134

INDEX

as cyclical policy, 67–68
degree of government involvement, 136–137
descriptive typologies, 98–99
  based on "purpose," 112–114
  levels of activity, 116–117
  specific activities, 120–137
  strategic, 98–111
  tools, 118–120
fine-tuning, 105, 141n
fiscal, 64–118
historical typologies, 137–138
incomes, 64, 119-120
Kennedy Administration, 119, 142n
Keynesian, 104–107, 255
licensing, 123, 126, 135–136
loans/loan guarantees, 109, 128, 133, 135
macroeconomic, 116–117
as market "treatments," 89–90, 138n
mercantilist, 103–104
microeconomic, 116–117
micro-microeconomic, 117
monetary, 64, 118–119
Nixon Administration, 119
policy relevant factors, 121–137
preventative, 114–115
promotional, 113–114
protective, 113
provision of infrastructure, 133
public enterprises, 126
Reagan Administration, 69, 112–113, 119–120
regulation, 126, 135–136, 143–144n
restorative, 115
socialist, 101–103
stabilization, 112–113
stimulative, 112
subsidies, 126, 127–128, 129–132
supply side, 106–107
Edelman, Murray, 20, 21, 25n
Education, 2-4, 9n, 66-67, 68
Edwards, George C., III, 167
Edwards, Richard C., 265n
Effectiveness models, 215–217
Efficiency models, 217–219
Einstein, Albert, 29, 30, 34
El Salvador, 180
Elder, Charles D., 10n
Emotive symbolic policy, 72
Encapsulation, 31
Energy Department, 206

Energy policies, 113–114, 155–156, 218
  Carter Administration, 113–114, 123, 172, 206
  Reagan Administration, 114, 206
  F. D. Roosevelt Administration 128
Environmental Protection Agency (EPA), 115
Equal Employment Opportunity Commission (EEOC), 117
Equity models, 219–221
Ethridge, Marcus E., 269
Euben, J. Peter, 267n
Exchange mechanisms, 91–92
Executive branch, and foreign policy, 194–197
Explanandum, 147–148
Explanans, 147–148
Explanation, *see* Policy explanation
Extractive policies, 65
Eyestone, Robert, 9n, 10n, 141n, 142n

Factors of production, 41
Federal Communications Commission (FCC), 70, 135–136
Federal Reserve System, 80–81, 118, 142n
Federal Trade Commission (FTC), 22, 115
Feldman, Elliot, 266n, 267n
Feldstein, Martin, 141n
Ferguson, C. E., 55n
Ferris, Wayne, 201n
Fineberg, Harvey B., 143n
Fiorina, Morris P., 161–162, 175n
Fiscal policy, 64, 118
Fiscal year, 87n
Food and Drug Administration (FDA), 77, 135
Foreign policy, 15–16, 60–62, 64, 149, 163–166, 178–202
  and agriculture, 190
  analytic perspectives, 181–185
  balance of power, models, 187-188
    bipolar, 187
    bipolycentric, 187
    tripolar, 187
  bureaucratic decision-making model, 198
  decision-making models, 197–199
  vs. domestic policy, 60–62, 178–181
  and economic strength, 191
  executive branch factors, 194–197
  external factor models, 182, 187–190
  and groupthink, 199
  ideological-historical models, 183–185
  internal factor models, 182, 190–197
  and international organizations, 181
  and military strength, 191–192

national capabilities model, 191–192
national character and belief model, 192–193
nationalist view, 183–185
"national personality" model, 190–191
and nuclear weapons, 191–192
and political culture, 192-193
political economy model, 188–190
process models, 197–200
psychological attributes of leaders, 194
and public opinion, 193
radical view, 183–185
realist view, 183–185, 187
role of the president, 179–181, 194–197, 198
scientific models, 183, 186–187
small group dynamics, 198–199
source models, 186–197
use of solar system model, 37–38, 51
Francis, Wayne L., 174n
Franck, Thomas, 200n
Franklin, Grace A., 72, 73
Friedan, Bernard J., 252n
Friedman, Barry, 176n, 252n
Friedman, Lawrence M., 174n
Friedman, Milton, 9n, 99–100, 119, 138n, 139n, 143n
Fritschler, A. Lee, 25n
Frohlich, Norman, 97
Frohock, Fred M., 269
Froman, Lewis A. Jr., 25n, 73, 74, 75, 76, 77, 78, 86n
Fulbright, William J., 197
Full employment, 105
Functional policy explanations, 150
Fusfeld, Daniel, R., 139n, 140n, 141n

Game theory models, 173
Garraty, John A., 141n
Garson, G. David, 9n, 158, 175n
Genetic/historicist policy explanation, 149
Gergen, Kenneth J., 25n
Gilder, George, 107, 139n, 252n
Gintis, Herbert, 9n
Glendening, Parris N., 175n
Goal achievement scales, 215–217
Gordon, William J. J., 30, 53n
Gouldner, Alvin W., 265n
Government reform and institutional/ constitutional model, 162–163
Graham, George J., 265n, 266n
Gramlich, Edward M., 223n

Grayson, C. Jackson, 142n
Green, Phillip, 265n, 266n
Greenstein, Fred I., 25n
Gregg, Phillip M., 266n
Group model, 158–159
Groupthink, 199

Haas, Ernest B., 201n
Hadley, Charles D., 175n
Halperin, Morton H., 165–166, 175n, 202n
Hamilton, Alexander, 123, 140n
Hamrin, Robert D., 143n
Harfmann, Eugenia, 201n
Haring, Douglas, 201n
Hausman, Leonard, 176n, 252n
Haveman, Robert H., 55n, 86n, 87n, 138n, 139n, 143n, 174n, 233, 252n, 265n
Hawkins, David, 36–37, 54n
Hayakawa, S. I., 59, 85n
Hayek, F. A., 139n
Health and Human Services Department (Health, Education and Welfare), 210, 247
Heclo, Hugh, 74, 75, 86n
Heffernan, W. Joseph, 233
Heilbroner, Robert L., 95, 139n
Heller, Walter W., 119, 141n, 265n
Henkin, Louis, 202n
Henry, Nicholas, 267n
Heuristics, 28
Hilsman, Roger, 201n
Hobbes, Thomas, 164
Hofferbert, Richard I., 10n, 152
Hoffman, Fred S., 265n
Hoffman, Paul J., 175n
Hollingsworth, Ellen Jane, 252n
Hoos, Ida R., 265n
Horowitz, Irving Louis, 252n, 265n
Housing and Urban Development Department (HUD), 248
Housing policy, 81, 127, 134, 142n, 232, 248, 250–251
Hughes, Barry, 200n

Illich, Ivan, 138n
Incomes policies, 64, 119–120
Incremental process model, 169–170
Individual decision maker models, 163–166
Individualism, 100, 102
 under capitalism, 100
 under socialism, 102
Inflation, 6–7, 80–81. *See also* Stagflation

INDEX

Infrastructure, as economic policies, 133
Inkeles, Alex, 201n
Institutional/constitutional model, 161–163
Institutional fragmentation, and policy explanations, 161
Interest satisfaction scale, 221
International system model, 199–200. *See also* Balance of power models
Interstate Commerce Commission (ICC), 136
Ippolito, Dennis S., 87n
Iran-U.S. relations, 193, 195, 198
"Iron law of oligarchy," 159
Isolationism, 182
Israel, 191–192, 199
Israeli-U.S. relations, 18, 179–180, 181, 199
Iteration, 212

Janis, Irving L., 202n
Jawboning, 119, 142n
Jensen, Lloyd, 194, 201n, 202n
Johnson, Lyndon Baines, and Kerner Commission, 67
Joint Chiefs of Staff, 194, 196
Jones, Charles O., 10n, 270
Jordan, Vernon, 21

Kaplan, Abraham, 9n
Kaplan, Morton, 188
Katz, James Everett, 265n
Kegley, Charles, 201n, 202n
Kennedy, John F., 22, 80, 197
Kerlinger, Fred N., 174n
Keynes, John Maynard, 104–105, 140n
Keynesian policies, 104–107
 objectives (standards), 105–106
Keynesian Revolution, 255
Khrushchev, Nikita, 197
Kissinger, Henry, 190, 195
Klingberg, Frank L., 201n
Kluger, Richard, 87n
Korea-U.S. relations, 82
Korean War, 184
Krasnow, Erwin G., 86n

Ladd, Everett Carl, Jr., 175n
Lasagna, Louis, 222n
Lasswell, Harold D., 9n, 255, 257–258, 265n, 266n, 267n
Lave, Charles A., 54n, 55n, 268
Leege, David C., 174n
Legitimacy, and authority, 93
Leibenstein, Harvey, 142n

Lekachman, Robert, 141n, 142n, 143n
Lerner, Daniel, 265n
Leviatan, Sar A., 174n
Levin, Henry, 252n
Levinson, Sanford, 265n, 266n
Libya-U.S. relations, 195
Licensing, 123, 126, 135–136
The Limits of Growth, 44–48
Lindblom, Charles E., 86n, 90, 91, 93, 97, 109, 138–139n, 139n, 175n, 176n, 268
Linear progress policy, 68
Lineberry, Robert L., 10n, 270
Loans/loan guarantees, as economic policies, 109, 128, 133, 135
Locke, John, 139n
Long, Senator Russell, 228
Longley, Lawrence D., 86n
Lowi, Theodore J., 25n, 69–73, 75, 77, 78, 86n, 138n, 139n, 140n, 143n, 266n
Lynn, Laurence E., Jr., 252n

McClosky, Herbert, 175n
McCoy, Charles A., 265n
McGaw, Dickinson, 24n, 148, 174n
McGowan, Patrick J., 15–16, 201n
McNamara, Robert, 256
MacRae, Duncan, Jr., 267n
Macroeconomic policies, 116–117
Madison, James, 158
Magdoff, Harry, 107
Mahan, Alfred T., 201n
Majak, R. Roger, 25n
Malthus, Thomas A., 105, 141n
March, James G., 54n, 55n, 176n, 268
Margolis, Julian, 265n
Market behavior and norms, and economic policies, 135–136
Market model, 40–43, 90, 92
 conditions for efficiency, 42–43
 factor market, 41–42
 product market, 42
 view of government, 90
 see also Supply and demand
Marketplace, 101
Market resources, and economic policies, 127–134
Market risks and liabilities, and economic policies, 134–135
Market size, and economic policies, 121–123
Market structure, and economic policies, 123–127

Marshall Plan, 184–185
Marx, Karl, 102
Marxist model, 51
Maurice, S. Charles, 55n
Mayaguez incident, 195
Mazmanian, Daniel, 222n
Meadows, Donella H., 55n
Meltsner, Arnold J., 266n
Mencher, Samuel, 252n
Mercantilist policies (neomercantilism), 103–104
Merewitz, Leonard, 265n
Metaphors, *see* models
Microeconomic policies, 116–117
Middle East, 18, 19, 20
Miller, George, 54n
Mills, C. Wright, 157, 174n
Mishan, E. J., 223n
Mitchell, Joyce M., 86n
Mitchell, William G., 86n
Model-building, 43–48
Model-selection, 49–53
  criteria, 50-53
Models, 35–53
  analogies, 37–38, 46
  criteria for evaluating, 38
  defined, 35–36
  deployability, 36, 37
  hard *vs.* soft, 36, 49
  metaphors, 29, 38, 46
Monetarists, 119
Monetary policies, 64, 118–119
Monopolies, 42, 124–125, 143n
  natural, 124–125, 143n
monopsony, 42
Monroe Doctrine, 20
Morgan, Dan, 201n
Morgenthau, Hans J., 184–185
Morris, William T., 55n
Moynihan, Daniel P., 221, 223n, 245, 259, 269n
Müller, Ronald E., 201n
Mushkin, Selma J., 266n

Nachmias, David, 222n, 252n, 269
Nagel, Stuart S., 265n, 269
National Advisory Commission on Civil Disorders (Kerner Commission), 67
National Aeronautics and Space Administration (NASA), 80, 169
National capabilities model, 191–192

National Highway Traffic Safety Commission (NHTSC), 135
National Security Advisor, 180, 194–197
National Security Council, 180, 194–197
Nationalist foreign policy perspective, 183–185
Neustadt, Richard E., 143n, 174n
"new economics," 141n
Newell, Allen, 28, 32, 53n, 54n
Nuclear power policies, 135

O'Connor, James, 139n, 140n
O'Hara, Rosemary, 175n
O'Leary, Michael K., 15–16, 200n
Occupational safety and health, 8
Occupational Safety and Health Administration (OSHA), 115, 117
Operations research (OR), 260
Oppenheimer, Joe, 97
Opportunity costs, 215, 234
Opportunity scales, 220–221
Organization of Petroleum Exporting Countries (OPEC), 64, 80, 113, 181, 187, 208
Outcome desirability scales, 217–219
Output costliness scales, 217–219

Pacific Doctrine, 20
Palestinians, 199
Panama Canal Treaties, 193
Party/electoral organization model, 159–161
Patent laws, as economic policies, 134, 143n
Patterning, 31–32
Peltzman, Sam, 222n
Peretti, Carol, 140n
Performance evaluation and review techniques (PERT), 260
Perkins, Dexter, 184–185
Persuasion mechanisms, 93–94
Peters, B. Guy, 270
Piven, Frances Fox, 252n
Playford, John, 265n
Plotnick, Robert, 86n, 233, 244, 252n
Plural elite model (pluralism), 157–158
Poland-U.S. relations, 191, 195
Policy actions, 22–24, 81–82
  as clusters, 22, 23
  as discrete events, 22, 23
  as undertakings, 22–23, 81–82
Policy assessment, 19. *See also* Policy evaluation
Policy attributes, 64–71

extrinsic, 64–69
intrinsic, 64
Policy consequences, 203–204, 206–213
  dimensions of, 206–213
    actual or perceived, 209
    direct or indirect, 210–211, 238
    intended or unintended, 209–211
    sequentially distinctive, 207–208, 237–238
    substantive impact, 212
    tangible *vs.* intangible, 212, 251
    temporally ordered effects, 211–212, 247
Policy description, 18, 57–85
  bias, 58–59
  economic policy typologies, 98–138
  nature of, 57-59
  types, 80–85, 138
    arena of activity, 85
    comparative, 83–84, 138, 151
    developmental, 81–82, 138, 149
    functional, 80–81, 138, 150
    institutional, 84–85
    intentional, 80, 138, 148
    population-focused, 81
    programmatic, 82–83
    temporal, 85
Policy evaluation, 203–224
  analytic purposes, 204–206
  vs. description and explanation, 203, 222n
  impact description *vs.* judgment, 204–206
  models:
    cost-benefit, 214–215, 234–235, 250–251
    effectiveness, 215–217, 234–235, 239–245
    efficiency, 217–219, 234–235
    equity, 219–221, 246–248
    social test, 221, 236–237
    see also Policy evaluation, scales of measurement
  scales of measurement, 213–222
    distributional effects (equity), 220–221, 246
    goal achievement (effectiveness), 215–217
    interest satisfaction (social test), 221
    opportunity (equity), 220–221, 246
    outcome desirability (efficiency), 217–219
    output costliness (efficiency), 217–219
    treatment (equity), 220–221
    valuation (cost-benefit), 214–215
Policy explanation, 18–19, 146–177
  bargaining model, 171–172
  causes *vs.* conditions, 153
  and correlation analysis, 151–152
  covering law types, 147–154

dynamic process models, 166–173, 186, 197–200
game theory models, 173
group model, 158–159
incremental process model, 169–170
individual decision-maker models, 163–166
institutional/constitutional model, 161–163
nature of, 146-154
party/electoral organization model, 159–161
policy implementation, 166–167
policy system model, 154–156
power elite models, 157–158
power structure model, 156–159
rational decision-making process, 168–169, 197–198
satisficing decision-making model, 170–171
source models, 154–166, 186–197
and theory, 147
types, 148–153
  associational, 151–152
  demographic, 153
  dispositional, 153
  functional, 150
  genetic/historicist, 149
  rational, 148–149
Policy feedback, 207–208
Policy impact studies, descriptive *vs.* judgmental, 204–206. *See also* Policy evaluation
Policy implementation, 166–167
Policy issue, 7
Policy outcomes, 207–208
Policy outputs, 207–208, 217
Policy performance, 207–208, 216–217
Policy sciences, 255, 257–258
Policy statements, 19–22
  indicative, 20
  symbolic, 20–21
Policy system model, 154–156
Political culture, 192–193
Political economy, 90, 91–98, 188–190
  international, 188–190
  mechanisms, 91–95
Political system model, 40, 154, 187–188
Polsby, Nelson W., 25n
Pomper, Gerald, 175n
Pork barrel policies, as distributive policy, 70
Poverty:
  relative *vs.* absolute, 240-241
  survival index, 241
Poverty lawyers, 239

Poverty policies, *see* Social welfare policies
Powell, G. Bingham, Jr., 86n
Power:
  defined, 156
  ingredients, 156–157
Power structure model, 156–159
Pressman, Jeffrey L., 166, 167, 175n
Presidential policies, 74–84
Presidential policymaking in U.S. foreign policy, 179–181, 194–197, 198
Preventative policies, 114–115
Price, Don K., 265n
Price stability, 106
Private property, 101
  redistribution under socialism, 102
Problems:
  analytic, 17
  application, 263–264
  contention, 263, 264
  design, 262–263, 264
  judgmental, 17, 19
  policy, 262–265
  private, 6–8
  production and distribution (economic), 94–98
  public, 5–8
  social, 6–8
  strategic, 17–18
  theoretical, 262–264
  value maximization, 263–264
Problem solving, 28–35
  behaviorist perspective, 28
  constraints, 32–33
  defined, 14, 30
  general precepts, 35
  information processing perspective, 28, 43–44
  ingredients, 30–35
  rational/scientific method, 28–29, 30
Program budgeting, 260
Programming-planning-budgeting (PPB), 255–256, 260
Progressive income tax, as redistributive policy, 70
Promotional policies, 113–114
Protectionism, 5, 61–62, 104
Protective policies, 113
Public enterprises, as economic policies, 126
Public goods, 43
Public health policy, as linear progress policy, 68
Public interest, as policy objectives, 206
Public opinion, and foreign policy, 193

Public policies:
  as application problems (administrative), 263, 264
  as design problems (professional), 262–263, 264
  pervasiveness of, 1
  problematic nature of, 5–7, 17–18, 262–265
  as problems of contention (personal), 263, 264
  as theoretical problems (scientific), 262, 264
  as value maximization problems (political), 263, 264
Public policy, defined, 5–8, 9–10n
Public policy analysis,
  as applied understanding, 12–14
  defined, 11
  defining characteristics, 11–12, 24
  development of, 255–256
  as ideology, 15–16
  as problem solving, 14–16, 262–265
  questions, 16–19
Public policy analysts, 9, 15–16, 256–265
  motivations, 256–262
    administrative, 259–262
    personal, 261–262
    political, 259, 261, 263
    professional, 257–258, 261, 262–263
    scientific, 256–257, 261, 262
Pure Food and Drugs Act (1906), 8
Pure rationality model, 168–169

Quade, E. S., 269

Radical foreign policy perspective, 183–185
RAND Corporation, 255
Ranney, Austin, 25n, 86n, 175n, 256, 257, 259, 265n, 266n, 267n
Rational decision-making process model, 168–169, 197–198
Rational policy explanation, 148–149, 164
Rational policymaking, under socialism, 102
Reagan, Michael D., 90, 139n
Reagan, Ronald, and fiscal policy, 69, 79
Reaganomics, 106–107
Realist foreign policy perspective, 183–185, 187
Redistributive policy, 70–71, 72
Redman, Eric, 176n
Reeves, Mavis Mann, 175n
Regulatory policy:
  competitive *vs.* protective, 72
  defined, 135, 143–144n

INDEX

as economic policies, 126, 135–136
as general policy type, 70, 72
and licensing, 135–136
prohibitions *vs.* mandates, 135
standards setting and enforcement, 136
Reich, Michael, 265n
Reilly, Thomas A., 176n
Rein, Martin, 266n, 267n
Restorative policies, 115
Ricardo, Davis, 141n
Riker, William H., 175n
Ripley, Randall B., 72–73, 200n
Rivlin, Alice M., 258, 265n, 266n, 267n
Robinson, James A., 25n, 200n, 201n
Robinson, Joan, 140n
Rodgers, Harrell R., Jr., 252n
Rose, Richard, 35, 54n, 67–69, 74, 75, 86n
Rosenau, James N., 22–23, 25n, 175n, 201n
Rosenbaum, Walter A., 156
Rostow, W. W., 195, 201n
Royce, Joseph R., 31, 54n
Rubinstein, Moshe F., 25n, 29, 30, 34, 35, 37, 53n, 54n, 55n, 268
Rule of law, 101
Rural electrification, 5, 128
Rural Electrification Administration (REA), 128

Sabatier, Paul, 222n
Sagan, Carl, 54n
Sapin, Burton, 163, 175n, 202n
Satisficing decision-making model, 170–171
Saudi Arabia-U.S. relations, 18, 181, 190
Say, Jean Baptiste, 104, 141n
Say's Law of Markets, 104–105, 106–107
Schelling, T. C., 176n
Schiesl, Martin J., 163
Schlesinger, Arthur, 201n
Schuettinger, Robert L., 143n
Schultz, Charles L., 143n
Schumpeter, Joseph A., 140n
Sectorally fragmented policy, 72
Securities and Exchange Commission (SEC), 77
Seidman, Harold, 175n
Self-sufficiency, 103–104
Sharkansky, Ira, 22, 25n, 142n, 174n, 222n
Shaw, J. C., 53n
Shepherd, William G., 124, 126, 127, 138n, 142n, 143
Shubik, Martin, 176n
Sigall, Michael W., 176n

Simon, Herbert A., 28, 32, 53n, 54n, 170–171, 176n, 260, 267n
Single elite model, 157–158
Skidmore, Felicity, 86n, 233, 244, 252n
Skinner, B. F., 28
Small group dynamics, and foreign policy, 198–199
Smith, Adam, 99–101, 104, 139n
Smith, T. Alexander, 71–72, 73
Smith, Thomas B., 222n
Sneath, Peter H. A., 85n
Snyder, Richard C., 163, 175n, 202n
Socialist policies, 101–103, 108–109
Social Security, 67, 204, 226, 230, 231, 239–240
Social test models, 221
Social welfare policies, 52, 70–71, 82, 149, 216, 225–253
   Aid to Families with Dependent Children (AFDC), 226, 232, 239
   alleviative, 226, 239, 241, 242
   Basic Education Opportunity Grants, 233
   defined, 225
   delivery mechanisms, 231–233
      cash transfers, 231–232
      community benefits, 233
      direct services, 232–233
      human capital/social investment, 233
      in-kind transfers, 232
   food stamp program, 216, 230, 232, 245–248
   general assistance, 226
   goals and objectives, 226–227
   guaranteed income programs, 240, 244–245
   Head Start, 213–214, 233
   Housing Allowance Experiment, 248, 250–251
   income maintenance programs, 231–232, 238–245
   Job Corps, 227
   Johnson Administration, 149
   Legal Services Corporation (LSC), 230, 235–239
   Medicare/Medicaid, 170, 232–233, 240
   negative income tax, 244–245
   Neighborhood Youth Corps (NYC), 227, 233–235
   nutritional program, 248
   policy perspectives, 227–230
      conservative *vs.* liberal, 227–228
      conservative-incrementalist, 229
      conservative-radicalist, 229

incremental vs. radical, 228
liberal-incrementalist, 228–229
liberal-radicalist, 229
preventative, 226–227, 233
public housing, 232, 243, 248, 250–251
punitive, 226, 232
Reagan Administration, 247–248
rehabilitative, 227
Supplemental Security Income (SSI), 240
unemployment insurance, 150, 231
War on Poverty, 82, 83, 227, 233, 240
see also Poverty; Social Security
Solar system models, 37–38
Somers, Gerald, 252n
Soral, Robert S., 85n
Sosnick, Stephen H., 265n
South Africa-U.S. relations, 190
Space exploration, 5, 80–81, 169
Spanier, John 201n
Spero, Joan, 201n
Spillover effects, 42–43, 207–208
Sports policy, 8
Stabilization policies, 112–113
automatic stabilizers, 113
Stagflation, 12, 51. *See also* Inflation
Starling, Grover, 222n, 269
State Department, 180, 182, 194–197, 198
Foreign Service, 196
Static policy, 67
Stein, Herbert, 141n
Steinbrunner, John D., 176n
Steiner, Gilbert T., 223n
Stevenson, Adlai, 197
Stimulative policies, 112
Stinchcombe, Arthur L., 174n
Stoessinger, John G., 16
Stogdill, Ralph M., 55n
Stokey, Edith, 222n, 269
Strategic policies, 72
Stromsdorfer, Ernest, 252n
Structural policies, 72
Subsidies, 126, 127–132
indirect (tax expenditures), 128, 129–132
Sunbelt vs. Snowbelt, 220–221
Sundquist, James, 21, 86n, 87n
Supply and demand:
curves, 41–42
law of, 42
Supply side policies, 106–107
Surkin, Marvin, 265n, 267n
Surplus value (profit), 41

Surrey, Stanley S., 128, 143n
Sweezy, Paul M., 107
Swine-flu vaccine affair, 135
Symbolic policies, 66–67
Synoptic policymaking model, 168–169
Systems analysis, 260
System models, 39–40, 187–188
dynamic, 39–40
feedback loop, 39
static, 39
use in foreign policy analysis, 187–188
Szanton, Peter, 163

Taxes, and economic policies, 126. *See also* Fiscal policy
Tax expenditures, 128, 129–132
Terry, Herbert A., 86n
"Think tanks," 255
Thompson, James D., 176n, 223n
Thompson, Victor A., 97
Thurow, Lester, 7, 242
Toulmin, Stephen, 36, 54n
Trade policy and mercantilism, 104
Trattner, Walter I., 252n
Treatment scales, 220–221
Truman, David, 158, 159
Typologies, 59–63, 73–78
constructing, 62–63
defined, 59–60
differentiation, 77
economic, 98–138
evaluating, 73–78
inclusiveness, 73
levels of measurement, 75–76
interval/ratio, 76
nominal, 75
ordinal, 75–76
mutual exclusivity, 73–74
operationalization, 76–77
reliability, 74–75
validity, 74

Ukeles, Jacob B., 266n, 267n
Union for Radical Political Economics, 265n
USSR-U.S. relations, 187, 190, 191, 192, 193, 200
United Nations, 181
U.S. Supreme Court, 69, 73–74, 84
Utils, 215

Valuation scales, 214–215
Van Meter, Donald, 174n

INDEX 283

Venezuela-U.S. relations, 190
Verba, Sidney, 201n
Vietnam War, 12, 153, 185
Vocke, William C., 201n
Voting Rights Act (1965), 21
Voucher system:
 education, 9n
 housing, 232

Wade, Larry L., 86n
Wage-price controls, 64, 119–120
Waldo, Dwight, 255
Walters, Robert, 201n
Wanniski, Jude, 107
Wardell, William M., 222n
Warwick, Donald P., 202n
Watson, George, 24n, 148, 174n
Watson, James D., 29, 30
Watson, John, 28
Watts, William, 44
Weisband, Edward, 200n
Weiss, Carol, 222n

Weisskopf, Thomas E., 265n
Welfare policies, *see* Social welfare policies
Western Europe-U.S. relations, 187, 190
White, Leonard D., 54n
White, Sheldon H., 266n, 267n
Wiener, Norbert, 55n
Wilcox, Clair, 124, 126, 127, 143n
Wildavsky, Aaron, 166, 167, 175n, 176n, 179, 223n, 260, 267n, 269
Wilensky, Harold L., 152
Williams, Walter, 167, 270
Williams, William Appleman, 185
Wittkopf, Michael, 202n
Wolfe, Alan, 265n, 267n
Woll, Peter, 25n, 161, 175n
Worthington, Mark D., 252n

Yarmolinsky, Adam, 202n

Zeckhauser, Richard, 222n, 269
Ziegler, Harmon, 158